...tum exortum est

& ðon · niopðo
# quoniam non habeba[t]

heanippo
altitudinem

˥ ða · an... · ...ðo
et qui exorto ex...

per · runna · 5° drug... · ˥ þ beþndo
est sol exaestuauit

˥ þ don · niopðo
eo quod non habere[t]

pyrt numa · 5°drugað
radicem exaruit

˥ rum · ðeoll · inðonnum
et aliud cecidit in spinis

˥ aprigon · ł upp eodun · ðonnap
et ascenderunt spinae

˥ under · ðulþon
et suffocauerunt

ł
illud

˥ pęrtm · neralde
et fructum non dedit

˥ oðer · ðeoll
et aliud cecidit

on eondu · 5°odu
in terram bonam

˥ ralde · pęrtm
et dabat fructum

prigende
ascendentem

˥ pęxende
et crescentem

˥ to brohte · onne tan
et adferebat unum

The Bible in Early English Literature

The Bible
in Early English
Literature

By DAVID C. FOWLER

UNIVERSITY OF WASHINGTON PRESS

Seattle & London

Endsheets: Mark 4:1–9, from the Lindisfarne Gospels, British Museum.

Library of Congress Cataloging in Publication Data

Fowler, David C   1921–
   The Bible in early English literature.

   Bibliography: p.
   Includes index.
      1. Bible—Influence—History.   2. Bible—Criticism,
   interpretation, etc.—History—Middle Ages, 600–1500.
   3. Bible. English—Versions.   4. Bible in literature.
   5. Cursor mundi.   6. Higden, Ranulph, d. 1364.
   Polychronicon.   I. Title.
   BS538.7.F68   220.6   76–7786
   ISBN 0–295–95438–8

TO MY MOTHER

Her children arise up, and call her blessed

Contents

Introduction

THIS book is the first part of a study of the influence of the Bible on early English literature from its beginning in Anglo-Saxon times to the end of the Middle Ages in the fifteenth century. During this important period of some ten centuries the impact of the Bible on vernacular writings was at its height, yet there has been no study which attempts to see medieval English literature as a whole in the light of biblical tradition. Of necessity, therefore, the present study is to some extent a survey, but an effort is made to avoid diffuseness by use of the "zoom" lens technique, that is, by looking closely at representative works rather than giving equal time to a more numerous array of texts, as might be expected in the standard type of literary history.

Because of the extensiveness of biblical influence in medieval culture, I thought it desirable to preface this study with an account of the importance of the Bible in the early Middle Ages. The first chapter attempts to depict the developing importance of scripture in the early Church. This includes the growing practice of regular scriptural readings, the crucial importance of holy writ in the development of liturgy, the interweaving of legendary (extrabiblical) materials, the growth of the legends of the saints, and the biblical art of the sanctuary.

Whereas the developments described in Chapter I focus primarily on influences at the grass roots level (the means whereby biblical teachings are imparted to largely illiterate congregations), Chapter II deals with the intellectual tradition: study of the Bible during the

Middle Ages, first in the monasteries and later in the universities. It includes a survey of the rise of biblical commentaries, the tradition of exegesis. By far the largest part of this chapter, however, is taken up with an account of Gregory the Great (whom the Venerable Bede called the Apostle to the English), and a close look at Gregory's *Morals on the Book of Job,* a commentary that serves as a noble illustration of the medieval exegetical tradition.

Separate chapters (III and IV) are devoted to a survey of Old and Middle English translations of the Bible, ranging from texts that are close and literal renderings, to poems that are very free paraphrases, of biblical materials. This section is climaxed by an account of the making of the Wyclif Bible, the first complete translation of scripture into English. The final two chapters of this volume deal, respectively, with the *Cursor Mundi,* a Middle English metrical Bible of about A.D. 1300, and Ranulph Higden's *Polychronicon,* a universal history in Latin that extends to the author's own time, to the year 1352, and that was translated into English a few decades later by the Oxford scholar John Trevisa. Both of these major works are described and discussed in Chapters V and VI for their intrinsic interest, but I also include them here because they are very important keys to understanding the late medieval vernacular literature to be discussed in a separate volume. This second volume will contain chapters on Arthurian romance, medieval drama, lyric poetry and ballads, Chaucer, the Pearl poet, and *Piers the Plowman.*

On a subject as large as the Bible and its influence, I am of necessity indebted to a host of friends and colleagues for both knowledge and insights, although the shortcomings of this study are entirely my own. I am glad to be able to thank my mother for seeing to it that I was introduced to the Bible at an early age; my undergraduate teachers for pressuring me to question my beliefs; and my graduate tutors for assuring me that it is entirely possible to respect the Bible and still maintain one's intellectual integrity. I also want to thank Robert B. Heilman for assigning me the "Bible as Literature" course at an early stage in my teaching career. Above all, I would like to express my indebtedness to D. W. Robertson, Jr., whose impact on current medieval studies needs no elaboration here. I trust that he will accept this testimonial, even though I am quite aware that he will by no means agree with everything contained in this study. Finally let me express, however inadequately, my gratitude to my wife and daughters, who have supported me, both at home and abroad, during the course of extensive research and writing.

The Bible in Early English Literature

CHAPTER ONE

The Bible in the Middle Ages

A GOOD way to begin our study of the role of the Bible in the medieval period is to take an imaginary journey to the ancient monastery of Saint Catherine on Mount Sinai. Its location, in the wilderness of the Sinai peninsula, is traditionally associated with the life of Moses and the receiving of the Ten Commandments by Israel; and at the same time its community of Eastern Orthodox monks serves as a reminder that here is an important survival in modern times of a rich monastic heritage, going back to the early years of Christianity. What was the origin of this monastery? Why is it dedicated to Saint Catherine? And what can it convey, through its history, to a modern reader interested in the Bible? These questions are worth considering, even if only briefly, in the hope that the answers may help provide that vital link between biblical and post-biblical times which is so important for a true appreciation of the position and influence of the Bible in the Middle Ages.

Even before Christianity came into being, of course, there were desert communities of men who rejected the commitments of Roman civilization and looked for the coming of the Kingdom of God. Dramatic discoveries near the Dead Sea over the last twenty-five years have revealed to us such a community, complete with its monastery and library of biblical scrolls, hidden for over two thousand years in nearby cliff caves. As a result of these discoveries, it is likely that future historians will increasingly emphasize the influence

[3]

of Palestinian monasticism, particularly the Qumran community by the shores of the Dead Sea, on the desert asceticism of the early Christian saints. Thus John the Baptist may be seen as an ancestor of Saint Antony and the desert fathers of the early church.

Under the influence of Saint Antony the cells of solitary ascetics, or anchorites, spread inland from the great cultural centers, such as Alexandria, until, in the late fourth century, the pilgrim Etheria (or Egeria) noted in her diary that numerous cells of hermits were scattered over the landscape in the vicinity of Mount Sinai, and that there was even a chapel built beside the bush which had burned for Moses, a bush which she reported to be flourishing still on the slope of the holy mountain. Within a century of Etheria's visit, however, the hermits of Sinai were being slaughtered mercilessly by desert raiders, and the very existence of the ascetic community was threatened. Fortunately, when news of this danger reached Constantinople, the Emperor Justinian, for the protection of the holy men, ordered the erection of the great, fortresslike monastery which still stands to this day.

The dedication of Justinian's monastery, completed about A.D. 550, to Saint Catherine of Alexandria, may reflect a local attachment to her memory, although reliable information about her is not easy to find. If she is indeed to be identified with the anonymous heroine of Alexandria mentioned by the historian Eusebius, then she may be placed in the period of the persecutions by the eastern Emperor Maximin in the early fourth century, some two hundred and fifty years before the completion of the monastery. According to her legend, disseminated and popularized in the west by the returning crusaders in the twelfth century, Saint Catherine was a highly intelligent and attractive woman of Alexandria, who, under the influence of the desert fathers, in particular one named Adrian, undertook to live a life of chastity as a bride of Christ. Later, when she defied the Emperor Maximin, she was first tortured on a wheel of spikes and then beheaded. It is thus possible, at least, that she visited one of the lonely cells noticed by the pilgrim Etheria, for it was near such a hermitage, according to her legend, that she saw the vision of a beautiful monastery in the desert on the occasion of her marriage to Christ. For when Christ departed from her and returned to heaven, according to the life of Saint Catherine, "then for sorrow of his departing she fell in a swoon so that she lay still a large hour without any life, and then was Adrian a sorry man, and cried upon her so long that at the last she came to herself and revived and lift up her eyes and saw nothing about her save an old cell, and the old man Adrian by her weeping."

Centuries later, according to the legend, the monks of Saint Catherine's monastery discovered her body not far from the famous burning bush, and, with the guidance of an angel holding a palm branch, carried it to the top of Mount Katherîna, the highest peak on the Sinai peninsula, where they built a chapel which survives to the present time. Even now, on the feast of Saint Catherine (November 25), the monks of Sinai carry in procession two magnificent jeweled reliquaries, said to contain the skull and a hand of St. Catherine. It is indeed a marvel that these reliquaries, and indeed the whole treasury of icons and manuscripts in the monastery, have survived over fourteen hundred years of human history.

Apart from its sheer antiquity, the monastery of Saint Catherine is distinguished by an unparalleled storehouse of early Christian art and a library of some three thousand manuscript books. The full extent of this treasure was not generally known until modern times, when scholars have been allowed to photograph and catalogue its contents. Moreover, the recent skillful restoration of the biblical mosaics and other adornments of the sanctuary now enable visitors to appreciate the art of Justinian's day in its full Byzantine splendor. Before the altar of the main sanctuary stands the marble tomb of Saint Catherine, and above, filling the half dome behind the altar, is the powerful Transfiguration, showing a heroic Christ with Moses and Elijah, and below them the disciples Peter, James, and John. The greatest discovery at Sinai, however, for our present purposes, was made over one hundred years ago by the biblical scholar Konstantin von Tischendorf.

In 1844 Tischendorf was traveling the Near East in search of Bible manuscripts, and came finally to Mount Sinai. In the course of searching through the ancient library of the monastery he discovered 129 leaves of what must once have been a very early Bible in Greek uncial script (all capital letters). "I perceived in the middle of the great hall," he says, "a large and wide basket full of old parchments; and the librarian, who was a man of information, told me that two heaps of paper like these, mouldered by time, had been already committed to the flames." Tischendorf convinced the monks that these pages were much too valuable to be destroyed, and he was permitted to take forty-three of these sheets with him on his return to Leipzig. The text thus rescued turned out to be a portion of the Septuagint, or Greek translation of the Old Testament, which Tischendorf proceeded to transcribe and publish for the use of scholars, without, however, revealing where he had found it, for he hoped someday to return to Sinai in the expectation that more of this precious text had survived.

Tischendorf did return to the monastery nine years later, without success, but finally in 1859 a third visit led to another discovery. Even this trip at first seemed fruitless. But then, shortly before his scheduled departure, the steward invited him to his cell for some refreshments. When they came to the cell, Tischendorf recalls, "he took down from the corner of the room a bulky kind of volume wrapped in red cloth, and laid it before me. I unrolled the cover, and discovered, to my great surprise, not only [some of] those very fragments which, fifteen years before, I had taken out of the basket, but also other parts." Indeed, taken all together, Tischendorf's discoveries formed the greater portion of an early Christian Bible, entirely in Greek, which scholars now agree was written about the year A.D. 350. Thus the Codex Sinaiticus, as it is called, became an indispensable witness for modern textual study of the Bible. Tischendorf, after some delay, took the manuscript to St. Petersburg, where he officially presented it to the Tsar, titular head of the order of the Sinai community.

Before looking more closely at the form and content of Tischendorf's manuscript, I would like to mention one further incident in its romantic history. After the Communists came to power in Russia, the new regime of course had little regard for the Codex Sinaiticus, and let it be known that this famous treasure was up for sale. Eventually, after considerable bargaining, it was sold in 1933 for one hundred thousand pounds to the British Museum in London. There it can be seen to this day, many miles from its home in the Monastery of Saint Catherine.

Ancient Versions, Canon, and Text of the Bible

Although much of the earlier portion of the Old Testament is missing from Sinaiticus, enough fragments were recovered to suggest that it originally contained all the usual books, beginning with Genesis. Thus identifiable bits of Genesis, Numbers, I Chronicles, and Ezra have survived, after which the following are complete: Nehemiah (entitled II Esdras), Esther, Job, Psalms, Proverbs, Ecclesiastes, Song of Solomon (entitled Canticle of Canticles), Isaiah, and Jeremiah. Then Lamentations breaks off at chapter 2, verse 20, and Ezekiel and Daniel are missing. There follow the twelve minor

[6]

prophets, of which three are lacking: Hosea, Amos, and Micah. Fortunately the New Testament is present in its entirety.

But this does not tell the whole story. A close examination of the book of Esther (which is included in the forty-three leaves that Tischendorf deposited at Leipzig) reveals that this text is considerably longer than the ten chapters found in the average Bible today. Moreover, there are whole books in the Old Testament of Sinaiticus that are not likely to be familiar to the modern reader, namely, the Wisdom of Solomon, Ecclesiasticus, Tobit, Judith, I Maccabees, and (even rarer) IV Maccabees. Most surprising, perhaps, is the fact that while the New Testament is complete, our codex has two additional books not now a part of the New Testament canon: the Epistle of Barnabas and the Shepherd of Hermas (a fragment). The conclusion to draw from this, of course, is that at the time of the copying of Sinaiticus (A.D. 350), the contents of the Bible had not been sharply defined, and we must therefore review the development of the biblical canon during these early centuries in order to see what kind of Bible the western church inherited and used in the medieval period.

Anyone who has seen or read of the Dead Sea discoveries will remember that the original Hebrew Bible existed for the most part as individual books copied in separate scrolls. Thus one of the most famous of the original discoveries in 1947 was a complete scroll of the Book of Isaiah, miraculously preserved from the period of its transcription nearly one hundred years *before* the birth of Christ. Yet although the scroll by its nature did not allow the copying of the Bible as a single unit, a strong sense of canon, or list of received or inspired books, existed in the pre-Christian Jewish community. The oldest part of the Bible, the Pentateuch or Five Books of Moses (Genesis, Exodus, Leviticus, Numbers, Deuteronomy), had been fixed and established after the return of Ezra and his followers from Exile in the fifth century B.C., as can be seen in the account in Nehemiah (8:1–8). The historical books or Former Prophets (Joshua, Judges, Samuel, Kings), together with the Latter Prophets (Isaiah, Jeremiah, Ezekiel, and the twelve minor prophets) were probably recognized as part of the sacred canon near 200 B.C. These were the two main portions of scripture known to Jesus, who often, in his references to the Bible, speaks of "the Law and the Prophets" (e.g. Matt. 7:12).

There was, however, a third cluster of books known as the Writings, or Hagiographa, which had not been clearly defined at the time

[7]

of the birth of Christianity. Hence when Christianity and Judaism diverged in the course of the first century, their respective judgments regarding the Old Testament canon quite naturally differed. It is unlikely, for example, that early Christians were aware of the deliberations of the rabbinical Council of Jamnia (ca. A.D. 90), which were apparently decisive (though there is some disagreement about this) in establishing the Writings, namely Psalms, Proverbs, Job, Song of Solomon, Ruth, Lamentations, Ecclesiastes, Esther, Daniel, Ezra, Nehemiah, and the two books of Chronicles.

To understand how the Christian Old Testament diverged from this we need first to recall that already among the Jews of the first century there were two major versions of the Bible, the Hebrew and the Septuagint or Greek translation. The former was in reality *the* Bible, of course, but the Septuagint became very popular, particularly among Greek-speaking Jews scattered throughout the territorial empires established by Alexander the Great. According to a traditional story, the Greek translation was made in Alexandria at the request of Ptolemy II Philadelphus (285–47 B.C.), and consisted of the Pentateuch, or first five books of the Bible, the only part generally recognized at that time as belonging to the canon of sacred writings. Seventy-two elders from Palestine were sent to do the work (six from each of the twelve tribes of Israel) and, if we may believe later embellishers of the story such as Philo, Irenaeus, and Clement of Alexandria, each man worked on the translation in a separate cell provided for the purpose. Finally, after seventy-two days, the elders emerged simultaneously from their cells, each holding a complete Greek translation of the Pentateuch. And lo, when they were compared, they were found to be identical!

Whether we choose to believe this story in every detail, it highlights the fact that by the middle of the third century B.C., Greek-speaking Jews had a Bible which they could understand, and as the years passed and the canon grew, the books of the Prophets and the Writings were added. This is not all. Other books, not destined to be accepted by the rabbinical councils, were also incorporated, so that the Septuagint that circulated among the synagogues of the Jewish dispersion included a varying number of these additional writings, later called the Old Testament Apocrypha, which merged with and were indistinguishable from the canonical books. A few, like the Wisdom of Solomon, which Paul utilizes in his letter to the Romans, were not even translations from the Hebrew, but were original compositions in Greek. Besides the additions to the canonical

[8]

books of Esther and Daniel, the Septuagint included the apocryphal books of Esdras, Tobias, Judith, Wisdom of Solomon, Ecclesiasticus, Baruch, and four books of Maccabees.

This, then, is the Bible that was inherited by Christians of the first century, and to it they eventually added the Greek New Testament as we know it today. But during the first four centuries, and indeed later as we shall see, the line between canonical and extracanonical writings was not always easy to draw. Barnabas and the Shepherd of Hermas, as noted, found their way into Sinaiticus, and parts of the two epistles of Clement are to be seen in the New Testament text of Codex Vaticanus, a manuscript of about the same date as Tischendorf's discovery. These and other writings of the Apostolic Fathers, such as the epistles of Ignatius of Antioch and the Didache, or Teaching of the Twelve Apostles, were highly regarded but finally not included in the canon which took shape around A.D. 400. During this very period, moreover, there occurred a revolution in bookmaking, perhaps indeed of Christian origin, that made possible the production of complete Bibles: this was the replacement of the scroll by the codex, that is, a book consisting of leaves bound together. From this technological development came the early Christian Bible that we see exemplified in Codex Sinaiticus.

In addition to the Hebrew and Greek Bibles there were other ancient versions such as the Samaritan Pentateuch, the Syriac Peshitta, and the Targums, or Aramaic paraphrases of the Old Testament. The one that must concern us here, however, is the Latin Vulgate, for this is the version that became the Bible of western Christendom in the Middle Ages, and indeed has remained the official Bible of the Roman Catholic Church, in the Clementine revision of the late sixteenth century.

The earliest texts for Latin-speaking Christians appear to have been translations of the Septuagint and the Greek New Testament, forming eventually a complete Bible known as the Old Latin version. It was this that Saint Jerome began to revise in A.D. 383 at the suggestion of Pope Damasus, on the basis of authoritative Greek texts. The controversies that beset Jerome after the death of the pope, however, forced him to leave Rome at a time when he had done little more than revise the New Testament and perhaps the Psalter along very conservative lines. Yet this interruption was of the utmost importance, for when Jerome returned to the east and settled in Bethlehem, the presence of men qualified to help him with his Hebrew made it possible for him to translate the entire Old Testament directly from the original text, rather than from the Septuagint. At considerable expense he obtained tutors from the Jewish community, and one of these, named Baranina, came to Jerome at night, apparently to keep from his neighbors the knowledge that he was teaching the sacred language to an outsider. From about the year 390, Jerome's reliance on "the Hebrew Truth," as he calls it, became a firm commitment, and the resulting new translation of the Old Testament was eventually recognized as an outstanding achievement of biblical scholarship.

As is so often the case, acceptance of Jerome's achievement was slow in coming. Custom and tradition have always been powerful forces, particularly when holy writ is involved, and controversy arose over some of the new readings that he introduced. His translation of Psalms, in fact, never did displace the Gallican Psalter. Of particular interest is Jerome's attitude toward the canon of Scriptures. His veneration for the Hebrew Text is perhaps the reason that he came to regard the deuterocanonical books (Tobias, Judith, etc.) as apocryphal writings: They were not, as he discovered, in the Hebrew canon, even though some of them had Hebrew or Aramaic originals. Certain of these books, namely Wisdom, Ecclesiasticus, I and II Maccabees, and Baruch, were not translated by Jerome at all, and survive in the Vulgate from the Old Latin version. But the opinion of the Church in this matter went against Jerome, and the argument over the Old Testament canon was not seriously renewed until the Reformation of the sixteenth century. Nevertheless the Latin Bible which was copied and recopied in medieval monasteries, and which became the standard text of western Christendom, was in essence the work of Saint Jerome.

Before taking leave of the Latin Bible, it is well to note its relationship to the growing body of New Testament apocrypha. These works, which had begun to appear in Greek as early as the second century, soon spread in all directions and have survived in various languages including Syriac, Coptic, Armenian, and Latin. All categories of New Testament literature are represented: there are gospels, acts, epistles, and apocalyptic visions. Those most influential in the Latin tradition are the Gospel of Pseudo-Matthew, containing stories of the childhood of Jesus, the Gospel of Nicodemus (also called the Acts of Pilate), with its famous account of Christ's descent into Hell after the Crucifixion, numerous books of Acts, a few epistles, and apocalypses attributed to Peter and to Paul. Although these apocryphal works were associated with biblical tradition during the medieval period, and were very influential in religious art and literature, they were never regarded as serious contenders for admission to the sacred canon. Perhaps the attitude toward these matters then was more relaxed than it is now. A few years ago, while examining some of the Latin manuscript Bibles in the British Museum, I was struck by the fact that one of them contained five gospels: Matthew, Mark, Luke, John, and Nicodemus. This was probably not very common, but it is indicative of the freedom with which apocryphal narrative was often interwoven with the sacred story, a freedom which we will have occasion to observe more than once when we consider the influence of the Bible upon vernacular literature.

The Bible in the Church

Because of the Reformation controversy, the medieval church has often been represented as busily engaged in the suppression of the Bible, and the entire Middle Ages has been regarded as a period of darkness before the dawn of the biblical age in the sixteenth century. Thus when Thomas Fuller writes in his *Church History of Britain* (1655) about the pre-Reformation translators of the Bible, he adds, "Whereby we may observe, that midnight being past, some early risers even then began to strike fire and enlighten themselves from the Scriptures."

To some extent it is true that the Church reacted against the making of vernacular translations, particularly because of their association with the heresies of John Wyclif (d. 1384). It was the Wycliffite Bible that prompted the interdict of 1409, and led to such extravagances as likening the translation of the Bible to casting pearls before swine. But the gap that developed between Protestants and Catholics on this issue should not be allowed to obscure the fact that the whole history of the medieval church is essentially the history of an effort to disseminate and extend knowledge of the Bible throughout Christendom. If the effort was not wholly successful, the explanation is to be found, not in some conspiratorial suppression, but in the enormous problems of educating large, illiterate congregations of believers in an era of frequent social disruption and anarchy. The remarkable thing, indeed, is the extent of the Church's success in this endeavor against considerable odds. Before we can deal with the influence of the Bible on early English literature, therefore, we need to consider the role of the Bible in the Church, and the ways in which knowledge of it was imparted to the average citizen.

[11]

The fundamental means of communicating the Bible to the congregation was of course the liturgy, by which is meant all formal worship services of the Church. Apart from the administration of various sacraments such as marriage and baptism, and such rituals as consecration and blessing, the liturgy consisted of two main parts: the Mass, or eucharistic service, and the service of the canonical hours, known as the Office. Both the Mass and the Office included scriptural readings organized with an eye to the Church calendar, but the two systems were largely independent of each other, and should perhaps be considered separately and from a historical point of view.

The Mass is undoubtedly the oldest feature of Christian worship, based as it is upon the New Testament account of the Last Supper, and there is good evidence that from a very early date it included the singing of hymns and reading from the Scriptures. Both of these practices were doubtless inherited from the synagogue, and both became a fundamental part of Christian liturgy. Thus there developed the characteristic biblical features, some of which can still be seen in the Mass: after the *introit* and *collect,* with accompanying psalm and biblical responses, comes the reading of the *epistle;* and after the chanted prayers of the *gradual* occurs the reading of the *gospel* of the day; this then is followed by the main part of the eucharistic service, including *offertory, secret, communion,* and *post-communion.* Normally on Sunday the first reading would be from one of the Pauline epistles (hence the term *epistle*), and the second from a gospel, but on the other days of the week the first reading, although called the *epistle,* might be taken from the Old Testament, chosen often for its relevance to the *gospel.*

The liturgy of the canonical hours, known as the Office, is of ancient origin, but it did not become systematized until it was incorporated into the monastic rule established by Saint Benedict in the sixth century. The pattern of worship developed by the monks was a series of services, or "hours," based upon intervals derived from the Roman watches, but varying according to the length of days or seasons of the year. Originally there were seven hours, until the addition of compline made eight, and they are as follows (the clock times are only approximate, and vary according to season):

matins (midnight)	sext (to midday)
lauds (daybreak)	none (to 3:00 P.M.)

prime (to 6:00 A.M.) vespers (to 6:00 P.M.)
terce (to 9:00 A.M.) compline (the hour of retiring)

Moreover, at a very early date (fifth century) matins was prolonged, and biblical reading thereby extended. Thus matins included eventually three nocturns, spaced out through the night, usually at 9:00 P.M., midnight, and 3:00 A.M. In this dedicated fashion prayer and praise were lifted to God in the monasteries, along with extensive readings designed to cover the entire Bible in the course of a year. Eventually this rigorous program adopted by the regulars had an influence on the secular clergy, but it is doubtful that the busy parish priest of medieval times was able to add much more than a morning and an evening service to his daily Mass. It was in effect the monasteries, therefore, that assumed the responsibility for these numerous daily services on behalf of the Christian community.

To aid in visualizing the liturgy of the early church there is fortunately preserved for us an eyewitness account of services in Jerusalem written down toward the end of the fourth century (ca. 390). This is an account of the pilgrimage of Etheria, whose journey from Spain to the holy land took place a few decades after the copying of Codex Sinaiticus, and a century and a half prior to the building of the Monastery of Saint Catherine. Etheria was, as she confesses, a very inquisitive woman, so that as she toured the biblical countryside she asked about and was directed to practically every sacred site then in existence, and from her description we may suppose that such sites were almost as numerous then as they are now. She visited both Mount Sinai and Mount Nebo, including all the points in between made notable by incidents that occurred during the wanderings of Israel, and all the churches and shrines of Jerusalem and its environs, together with lesser-known sites such as the burial place of Job in the city of Carneas.

Etheria tells us that in each of these holy places it was her custom first to offer prayer, next to read the biblical passages relating to the particular site, then to sing an appropriate song, and finally to offer a concluding prayer. If the place was associated with one of the saints or martyrs, then the reading would be from the life of that saint. Indeed, on one occasion, the whole of the (apocryphal) Acts of Saint Thecla was read.

For our present purpose Etheria's account of Christian services in Jerusalem is most important. Even the reception of new members

[13]

in the congregation and the preparation for baptism is described: "Beginning from Genesis," she says, "he [the Bishop] goes through all the Scriptures during those forty days [of Lent], explaining them, first literally, and then unfolding them spiritually. They are also taught about the Resurrection, and likewise all things concerning the Faith during those days. And this is called the catechising." She goes on to explain that these lessons in the Bible and the Faith are taught for three hours a day over a period of seven weeks, and then adds an interesting aside: "And God knows, reverend sisters, that the voices of the faithful who come in to hear the catechising are louder (in approval) of the things spoken and explained by the bishop than they are when he sits and preaches in church."

Fortunately Etheria was in Jerusalem for Easter and hence we have her account of the services for Holy Week. The description of the climax of Palm Sunday is especially impressive:

> And as the eleventh hour approaches, the passage from the Gospel is read, where the children, carrying branches and palms, met the Lord, saying, *Blessed is he that cometh in the name of the Lord* [Matt. 21:9], and the bishop immediately rises, and all the people with him, and they all go on foot from the top of the Mount of Olives, all the people going before him with hymns and antiphons, answering one to another: *Blessed is he that cometh in the name of the Lord.* And all the children in the neighborhood, even those who are too young to walk, are carried by their parents on their shoulders, all of them bearing branches, some of palms and some of olives, and thus the bishop is escorted in the same manner as the Lord was of old.

The services for Good Friday are especially revealing of the importance attached to biblical readings:

> The chair is placed for the bishop before the Cross, and from the sixth to the ninth hour [noon to 3:00 P.M.] nothing else is done, but the reading of lessons, which are read thus: first from the psalms wherever the Passion is spoken of, then from the Apostle, either from the epistles of the Apostles or from their Acts, wherever they have spoken of the Lord's Passion; then the passages from the Gospels, where He suffered, are read. Then the readings from the prophets where they foretold that the Lord should suffer, then from the Gospels where He mentions His Passion. Thus from the sixth to the ninth hours the lessons are so read and the hymns said, that it may be shown to all the people that whatsoever the prophets foretold of the Lord's Passion is proved from the Gospels and from the writings of the Apostles to have been fulfilled.

From this remarkable fourth-century description we can easily perceive the central role of the Bible in the services of the early church.

It is evident from the tone of her account that Etheria was greatly impressed by the church services, and indeed at one point in the narrative she exclaims: "But what is above all things very pleasant and admirable here [in Jerusalem], is that the hymns, the antiphons, and the lessons, as well as the prayers which the bishop says, always have suitable and fitting references, both to the day that is being celebrated and also to the place where the celebration is taking place." This observation may well indicate, as some students of the liturgy have concluded, that in Spain Etheria had been accustomed only to canonical reading of the Scriptures, that is, an annual schedule of readings designed to cover the Bible book by book, and that in Jerusalem she heard for the first time sets or clusters of readings associated with the season of Easter.

Whatever may be the truth of our deduction regarding Etheria's liturgical experience, the fact is that early in the history of the Church the tradition of reading the Bible through in a year was interrupted by the growing importance of anniversaries related to Easter and Christmas, which combined to form a calendar of symbolic seasons known as the *temporale*. The principal commemorations of the *temporale* were Advent, the Nativity, Circumcision, and Epiphany, all associated with Christmas; and these were followed by the Lenten season, especially the Passion, Palm Sunday, and the entire Holy Week climaxed by Easter Sunday, after which came the Ascension, Pentecost, Trinity Sunday, and (a later addition) Corpus Christi. As these feasts and commemorations grew in importance, so too did the program of biblical lessons associated with these dates in the liturgy. While this development was taking place, moreover, the independent recital of the psalms had already become established in the west, both by the use of psalms in the Mass and by the recital of the entire psalter each week in the canonical hours of the Office.

As early as the sixth century the program I have just described constituted a very full schedule of biblical readings of increasing complexity. And yet we must realize that there were, in addition, numerous readings from the New Testament Apocrypha and lives of the saints and martyrs, added to the biblical texts on certain commemorative days. Our pilgrim Etheria illustrates this in her devotional reading of the lives of Saints Thecla and Euphemia during her Palestinian travels. The development of the Mass as we know it discouraged the use of these extrabiblical materials, with the result that they were gradually shifted over and added to the canonical hours. In the Office, therefore, this resulted in the development of a separate calendar of saints, known as the *sanctorale*, which to some extent came into competition with the earlier *temporale*, or calendar of traditional church festivals and commemoratives. Eventually the number of saints who found a place of honor in the *sanctorale* became so great that it was necessary to rank liturgical commemorations as a means of resolving the problem of conflicting memorials. These rankings are often indicated in medieval calendars by colors (usually red, blue, and gold), so that one could tell at a glance, for example, which were the "red letter days." In the Mass, the saints were commemorated by the reading of appropriate texts from the Bible; in the Office, readings were from the lives of the saints themselves.

It may seem strange that the *sanctorale* achieved such liturgical importance in the Church. But if we set aside the rather exact modern distinction between canonical and noncanonical writings — a distinction sharpened, incidentally, by controversy — it should not be difficult to see that the continuous line of martyrs and confessors of the Name that extended from New Testament times helped to enhance the eternal relevance of the Scriptures in the minds and hearts of later worshippers. It is true, of course, that hagiography experienced a period of decadence in the later Middle Ages, but it is still remarkable that the writing of saints' lives enjoyed such an extended vitality, and was indeed a very influential force in the rise of vernacular literature in the twelfth and thirteenth centuries.

The pressure to add to the lessons of the *sanctorale* is well illustrated in a story told in connection with the recovery of the bones of Saint Nicholas in the time of the Crusades. The brothers of a certain Church of the Holy Cross, hearing of a newly composed history of Saint Nicholas, urgently asked their prior for permission to sing this new history in their divine service, but the prior, evidently a conservative in liturgical matters, firmly refused, commenting that "they ought not change their old for no new." And when they pleaded with him a second time, he responded even more emphatically, saying: "Go your way, for in no manner shall ye never have license of me that this new song shall be sung." The story continues:

And when the feast of S. Nicholas came, the brethren said their matins all in heaviness, and their vigils. And when they were all in their beds, S. Nicholas appeared visibly and much fearfully to the prior, and drew him out by the hair, and smote him down on the pavement of the dortour, and began to sing the history: *O pastor eterne;* and at every note

[16]

he smote him with a rod that he held in his hand right grievously on his back, and sang melodiously this anthem unto the end, and then the prior cried so loud that he awoke all his brethren, and was borne to his bed as half dead, and when he came to himself, he said: Go ye and sing the new history of S. Nicholas from henceforth.

The Golden Legend

This story of Saint Nicholas was included in a famous thirteenth-century collection of lives of saints by Jacobus de Voragine, known as the *Legenda Aurea,* and first printed in English by William Caxton in the fifteenth century with the title *The Golden Legend.* The organization of this collection reflects the liturgical developments just considered, and hence provides a good illustration of the evolution of the church calendar, combining, as we shall see, both the *temporale* and the *sanctorale.* Of equal importance for our purpose, I believe, is the fact that this collection embodies that mixture of biblical and apocryphal materials which is characteristic of the use of the Bible in the Middle Ages. The saints and martyrs of the legendary are simply the latest segment in a continuous line of the Elect extending back through the Old Testament. Abraham and Antony are both a part of this tradition.

The first section of *The Golden Legend* contains stories and commentary on the principal commemorations of the *temporale,* that is, it begins with Advent and ends with the feast of Corpus Christi. The text for Advent is essentially a sermon on the two "comings" of the Lord: first, when He came in the flesh; and second, when He shall come to judge the quick and the dead. The relationship between these two comings, however, is expressed in the liturgy for Advent, which is interpreted in detail. The seven anthems sung before the Nativity, for example, are explained as the voice of mankind, crying out for a Savior. Here is the comment on the third anthem: "And what availeth unto prisoners to be bought again and delivered, if they were not unbounden and free to go where they would? Little should it profit, and therefore we demand that we may be unbound and loosed from all bond of sin when we cry in the fourth anthem: *O clavis David, etc.,* O key of David, that closeth that no man may open, and openest that no man may shut, come to us and cast the prisoner out of the prison that sitteth in darkness and shadow of death." All of the anthems contain biblical echoes—note the phrases from Isaiah in the fourth anthem just quoted—and all are explained in relation to the coming of the Savior. The other part of the sermon,

[17]

considerably longer than the first, is taken up with the second coming of Christ, including the fifteen signs of approaching Doom, and the Last Judgment itself. Thus Advent is made the occasion for emphasizing the biblical view of human history, from beginning to end, and the central importance of the Incarnation.

Although the various texts for the *temporale* have their foundations in the Bible, there are some surprises in the differing degrees of emphasis given to the individual commemorations. The Nativity, for example, is much briefer than Advent, consisting mainly of a summary of the account in Luke's Gospel, with the addition of signs and wonders reported at the time of Christ's birth taken from apocryphal sources. Much fuller treatment is given the Octave of the Circumcision, with its extended sermon on the three names of Christ, and the Feast of the Epiphany, with its commentary on the story of the Three Kings, whose bodies, we are told, now rest in Saint Peter's Church in Cologne.

The weeks leading into the lenten season are placed in their biblical context, while at the same time they are given a personal meaning for each penitent in the congregation: "At Septuagesima beginneth the time of deviation or going out of the way, of the whole world, which began at Adam and dured unto Moses. And in this time is read the Book of Genesis. The time of Septuagesima representeth the time of deviation, that is of transgression. The Sexagesima signifieth the time of revocation. The Quinguagesima signifieth the time of remission. The Quadragesima [the first Sunday of Lent] signifieth of penance and satisfaction." Thus each penitent is led to meditate on the history of the fall of man in relation to himself, as he hears the story read in the services of the church, beginning three Sundays before Lent, and continuing through into Holy Week. In this highly biblical fashion is he conducted, with fasting and prayer, through the purifying stages of contrition, confession, and satisfaction required by the penitential procedures of the medieval church.

After a brief explanation of Ember Days (the four seasons of fasting), the *Legend* continues with texts on the Passion and the Resurrection of the Lord. The first part of the Passion is essentially a sermon on the Crucifixion using clusters of quotations from the Fathers of the Church and expanding on ideas and motifs from the New Testament. One of the favorites, of course, is Paul's antithesis (I Corinthians 15:22): *For as in Adam all die, even so in Christ shall all be made alive.* The *Legend* provides us with an elaboration of this from the Fathers which can only be described as baroque: "For thus as saith S. Austin in the book, *De doctrina christiana:* By a woman he was deceived, and by a woman he was born a man, and the man delivered the men. One mortal delivered the mortal, and the death by his death. And S. Ambrose saith: Adam was of the earth a virgin; Jesu Christ was born of the virgin; Adam was made to the image of God; Jesus was the image of God; by a woman folly was showed; by a woman wisdom was born. Adam was naked; Jesu Christ was naked. The death came by the tree, the life by the cross." This fondness for antithetical elaboration is very popular, not only in the homilies of the *Legend,* but also in biblical art and literature. One sees this particularly in the medieval absorption in trees of various kinds—the Tree of Jesse, for instance, and the elaborate trees of vices and virtues.

An appendix to the Passion relates the birth, life, and death of Pilate, taken, as the narrator informs us, from an "apocryphum." This popular story tells how the Roman Emperor Tiberius, who had fallen ill, ordered Pilate to send him Jesus, whose reputation as a healer had reached as far as Rome. The messenger discovers, however, that Christ had been crucified on orders from Pilate, but fortunately he brings back with him Veronica, whose precious cloth, impressed with the image of Jesus, effects a miraculous cure and the emperor is restored to health. Tiberius then angrily summons Pilate to Rome to answer for his unwarranted sentencing of Christ. At length Pilate, wearing the seamless robe which he had taken from Jesus, is brought before Tiberius: "And as soon as the Emperor saw him all his wrath was gone, and the ire out of his heart; he could not say an evil word to him. And in his absence he was sore cruel towards him, and in his presence he was always sweet, and debonair to him, and gave him licence and departed." Then the emperor angrily calls him back again and the farce is repeated before he discovers that Pilate's seamless coat is miraculously melting his anger each time he sees it. When the coat is removed, therefore, Pilate is quickly sentenced to death for his crime, but manages to frustrate the decision by committing suicide.

The vindictive narrator then pursues Pilate to the grave and beyond, relating abortive efforts to sink his body in the Tiber and the Rhone, and so forth. The spirit in which this story was received is probably best illustrated by the Death of Pilate episode in the Cornish drama of the Resurrection, where the incident is given a comic treatment. The author of the *Golden Legend* does not give the story any particular twist of his own, but he does add an editorial comment at the end: "And hitherto is this story called apocryphum read. They that have read this, let them say and believe as it shall please them."

The Resurrection text is similar to that of the Passion just considered, in that it consists of a sermon, followed by an apocryphal narrative, in this case the famous account of the Harrowing of Hell from the gospel of Nicodemus. According to the story, two men, Carinus and Leucius, were transported to the underworld, where they were privileged to witness Christ's descent into Hell after the Crucifixion. The first thing they saw was a great light, shining in the darkness of Hell and illuminating the famous patriarchs and prophets of old, who had been confined there, awaiting their deliverance. As Christ approaches, they realize that their hour of freedom is at hand, and each prisoner in turn rejoices, beginning with Adam and continuing with other Old Testament figures. Isaiah, for example, exclaims: "This is the light of God the Father, like as I said living in the earth: The people that were in darkness saw a great light." When the prophets have spoken, the devils are thrown into confusion, each accusing the other of failure in their effort to thwart God's plan for the Redemption of mankind. At last, at the very gates of Hell a voice of thunder speaks in the words of Psalm 24:7, "*Attollite, etc.:* Take away your gates, ye princes, and lift ye up the gates perdurable, and the King of Glory shall enter in." Whereupon the devils bar the gates, and, when the Voice repeats its challenge, Hell responds with the next verse of the Psalm: "Who is this King of Glory? To whom David answered: This is our Lord, strong and mighty in battle, which is King of Glory." Then the Lord enters the gates, and takes Adam by the hand, saying, "Peace to thee and to all thy sons that be just. And then our Lord departed from hell, and all the saints followed him." Adam and his companions are next led to the gates of Paradise by the Archangel Michael. On their way there, however, they are amazed to see three men coming to meet them; for they had thought that before Christ came, no man had escaped imprisonment in Hell. But the puzzle is resolved when the three identify themselves: one is Enoch, whom God took (Genesis 5:24); the second is Elijah, who ascended in the fiery chariot (II Kings 2:11); and the third is the penitent thief, to whom Jesus said: *Today shalt thou be with me in Paradise* (Luke 23:43). Thus concludes a story which, though apocryphal, was nearly as well known in the medieval period as the canonical gospels themselves. It is perhaps significant that the ending contains no disclaimer by the author such as was given after the death of Pilate episode.

Next in order the *Legend* explains the origin and purpose of the greater and lesser litanies which occur in this period, the former on St. Mark's day, and the latter on the Rogation days preceding the Ascension. The *temporale* is then completed with sections on the Ascension (thirty-nine days after Easter); Pentecost, or Whit Sunday (seven weeks after Easter); Corpus Christi, or the Holy Sacrament (eleven days after Pentecost); and the Dedication of the Temple (date varies). The texts for the Ascension, Pentecost, and Corpus Christi are essentially sermons that need not concern us now. The most interesting of the three is undoubtedly the Ascension sermon, because so little is said directly about the event in the Bible that a highly imaginative reconstruction of it has been made from a symphony of biblical passages, notably Isaiah 63:1ff.: *Who is this that cometh from Edom, with dyed garments from Bozrah?* The result is an impressive, liturgical exchange between Christ and the Angels similar to the questions and answers in the Harrowing of Hell.

The Dedication of the Temple is placed at the end of the list of feasts because it is celebrated on the date of the original consecration of each individual church. The sermon on this subject is therefore generalized, but nevertheless quite interesting in its biblical explanations for the services of the church, and the symbolism of the ceremony of consecration. After all aspects of the ceremony are covered, the sermon concludes with an exhortation on rededication of the spiritual temple, that is, the individual members of the congregation. We thus come to the end of the feasts of the *temporale*.

The next main division of the *Legend* brings us directly back to the Bible, for it consists of the "histories" of Adam, Noah, Abraham, Isaac, Esau, Jacob, Joseph, Moses, Joshua, Saul, David, Solomon, Rehoboam, Job, Tobit, and Judith. The reason for the inclusion of these histories is given by Caxton in the heading to the section on Adam: "The Sunday of Septuagesima beginneth the story of the Bible, in which is read the legend and story of Adam which followeth." As we noted earlier, Genesis is read in the churches beginning with Septuagesima, three weeks before Lent, and continues into the lenten season. The list of books is obviously not complete, however, for only a limited portion of the Old Testament could be read during this period. The actual schedule of Bible readings, established at Rome in the first half of the eighth century, was as follows:

[21]

Septuagesima to Passion Sunday: Genesis through Judges
Passion Sunday to Easter: Jeremiah and Lamentations
Easter to Trinity Sunday: Acts, Catholic Epistles, and Apocalypse
June and July: Samuel, Kings, and Proverbs
August: Wisdom literature
September: Job, Tobit, Judith, Esther, and Esdras
October: Maccabees
November: Ezekiel, Daniel and Minor Prophets
December (Advent): Isaiah
January (to Septuagesima): Letters of St. Paul

This list of course does not include Psalms or the four Gospels, since all of these were read throughout the year both in the Mass and in the canonical hours. Moreover it is evident that the histories included in the *Legend* do not cover the entire year, since Caxton seems to have used only those books of the Bible that have a strong narrative interest. Nevertheless it is clear, from a passage in the history of Joshua, that these texts are supposed to be read according to the schedule of the *temporale:*

> Joshua was a noble man and governed well Israel, and divided the land unto the twelve tribes by lot. And when he was an hundred and ten years old he died. And divers dukes after him judged and deemed Israel, of whom be noble histories, as of Jephthah, Gideon, and Sampson, which I pass over unto the histories of the kings, which is read in holy church from the first Sunday after Trinity Sunday unto the first Sunday of August. And in the month of August is read the Book of Sapience, and in the month of September be read the histories of Job, of Tobit, and of Judith, and in October the history of the Maccabees, and in November the book of Ezechiel and his visions. And in December the history of Advent, and the book of Isaiah unto Christmas and after the feast of Epiphany unto Septuagesima be read the Epistles of Paul. And this is the rule of the temporal through the year.

Thus we see that in little more than three centuries after Etheria visited Jerusalem, the western Church had developed an annual scheme of biblical readings adjusted to the calendar of the *temporale.* And it is an impressive fact that we find this same scheme reflected, albeit incompletely, toward the end of the medieval period in the pages of Caxton's *Golden Legend.*

The Old Testament histories included in the *Legend* are for the most part mere summaries of the biblical narrative, but here and there may be found additions taken from apocryphal sources. Some of these are very brief, as in the case of Adam's trance, when God caused a deep sleep to fall upon him (Genesis 2:21), in which he was shown the celestial court: "Wherefore when he awoke he prophesied of the conjunction of Christ to his church, and of the flood that was to come, and of the doom and destruction of the world by fire he knew, which afterward he told to his children." Later we are informed that Jubal, father of music (Genesis 4:21), hearing of Adam's prophecy, and wishing to preserve knowledge of his craft from destruction, "did do write it in two pillars or columns, one of marble, another of clay of the earth, to the end that one should endure against the water, and that other against the fire." The source for this detail was undoubtedly Josephus, the Jewish historian, who is quoted by our author as saying that the marble pillar still stands in the land of Syria. Perhaps the most famous apocryphal story associated with Adam describes the journey of his son, Seth, to Paradise in quest of the oil of mercy. This incident, however, is disposed of in the *Legend* in a few sentences.

Before we leave the Old Testament histories, it will be well to remember that in the medieval period oral tradition was still an important means of transmitting knowledge, including information about the Bible. The author of the *Legend* gives us a good example of this in his history of David:

> For as I once was beyond the sea riding in the company of a noble knight named Sir John Capons, arsd was also doctor in both laws, and was born in Malyorke, and had been viceroy and governor of Arragon and Catalonia, and that time counsellor unto the Duke of Burgundy, Charles, it happed that we communed of the history of David; and this said nobleman told me that he had read that David did this penance following for these said sins. That he dolved him in the ground standing naked unto the head, so long that the worms began to creep in his flesh, and made a verse of this psalm *Miserere* [Psalm 51], and then came out, and when he was whole thereof he went in again and stood so again as long as afore is said and made the second verse, and so as many times he was dolven in the earth as be verses in the said psalm of *Miserere mei deus*, and every time was abiding therein till he felt the worms creep in his flesh. This was a great penance and a token of a great repentance, for there be in the psalm twenty-one verses, and twenty-one times he was dolven. Thus this nobleman told me, riding between the town of Ghent in Flanders and the town of Brussels in Brabant.

A brief but colorful addition to the history of Solomon may likewise have reached our author via oral tradition: "It is said, but I find it not in the Bible, that Solomon repented him much of this sin of idolatry and did much penance therefor, for he let him be drawn through Jerusalem and beat himself with rods and scourges, that the blood flowed in the sight of all the people." It is not difficult to see in this spectacular but anachronistic penance of David and Solomon the influence of the Desert Fathers, particularly ascetics of the later (decadent) period, like St. Simeon the Stylite.

The *temporale* of the *Legend,* which we have just surveyed, is about one fifth of the entire collection. Nearly all of the rest, with the exception of a history of the Mass placed at the end with a commentary on the Apostles' Creed, is taken up with the *sanctorale,* or lives of the saints, occurring usually in the order of the calendar of their feasts. The *sanctorale,* as we have seen, found a place in the liturgy of the canonical hours. Thus it begins at Advent with Saint Andrew (December 2), and completes the annual cycle with Saint Saturnine (November 29). Thereafter is added a group of about thirty "divers feasts," as the author calls them. Even so, of course, by no means is the whole multitude of saints represented here, for no legendary of this kind can be expected to include them all.

Even though the feasts are normally placed in chronological order, it may help to envision the whole collection if we first take note of the various categories of saints and feasts that it contains. Of the biblical saints, by far the most popular is the Blessed Virgin Mary, in whose honor no less than five feasts are included: the Conception (December 8), Purification (February 2), Annunciation (April 7), Assumption (August 15), and Nativity (September 8). Four New Testament saints are honored with one feast in addition to that which commemorates their respective martyrdoms: thus we have the Nativity of Saint John the Baptist, the Chairing of Saint Peter, the Conversion of Saint Paul, and the Invention (discovery of the tomb) of Saint Stephen.

All of the Apostles, of course, are represented by feasts, as well as the Evangelists Mark and Luke, and Paul's companions, Barnabas and Timothy. The list of New Testament commemorations is completed with a day for the Holy Innocents, the children slain by Herod (Matthew 2:16), and, finally, a day for Saint Longinus, the name given in the apocrypha to the soldier who pierced the side of Christ at the Crucifixion (John 19:34). The Old Testament could be said, perhaps, to be represented by the feast of Saint Michael, and the feast of the Seven Maccabees. Difficult to categorize, but highly regarded, are the Invention (discovery) of the Cross and Exaltation of the Cross, and the feasts of All Saints and All Souls, which occur at the beginning of November.

The remainder of the saints—and they are certainly the majority—belong in the postbiblical period, from the second century to the thirteenth, when *The Golden Legend* was compiled. They include martyrs of the Roman persecutions, early missionaries, the Fathers of the Church (Saints Gregory, Ambrose, Augustine, and Jerome), and numerous others. One of these, Saint Thomas à Becket, has in addition to the commemoration of his martyrdom a feast of the Translation of his body to its present resting place in Canterbury Cathedral. This extra attention to the English Saint Thomas may well represent a local emphasis (the feast of his Translation is not in the French version), and can serve to remind us that the *sanctorale* varied from region to region, in order to accommodate the popularity of local saints. Even within Britain, for example, the calendar of saints in Cornwall was quite different from that found in the English speaking areas. One looks in vain in the present collection for such saints as Petroc, Neot, Piran, and Meriazek.

The saints of *The Golden Legend*, however, number in the hundreds. A good representative legend is the life of Saint Maurice, soldier and martyr in the Roman persecutions of the third century, a story which shows how the force that impels men to battle was turned by Christianity to the service of God and renunciation of self.

Maurice was a Christian of Thebes and the officer in charge of a highly disciplined and proud unit of the Roman army that was ordered to active duty by the Emperors Diocletian and Maximian to suppress the growing number of Christian "rebels." The Theban legion responded to this call, but its members took up arms with the understanding among themselves that they would help in just and lawful battles, "and not to bear arms against christian men, but rather to defend them." When they reached Rome, they were put under the command of Maximian, who was planning to march north into France. Before they departed, however, Saint Maurice and his knights were exhorted by Marcel, the Pope, "that they should rather suffer death than to corrupt the faith of Jesu Christ." The story continues as they join in the march with other units of the Roman army:

> And when this great host without number had passed the mountains and came beneath, the emperor commanded that all they that were with him should sacrifice to the idols, and on them that would not, they should swear to run upon them as rebels, to be destroyed, and specially on christian men. And when the holy knights heard that, they departed from the host eight miles farther, and took there a certain place delec-

table, by the river of Rhone, which was named Aganum. And when Maximian knew it, he sent knights to them, and commanded that they should come hastily unto the sacrifices of the gods with the other; and they answered that they might not do so because they held the faith of Jesu Christ.

The enraged emperor then had the legion surrounded and, when they continued to refuse the pagan rites, he ordered every tenth man to be slain. When this had no effect on the survivors, he took a second "tithe" (as Saint Ambrose terms it), again without effect. In the midst of all this slaughter, Maurice encourages the executioners: "Enjoy ye with us, and I thank you, for we be all ready for to die for the faith of Jesu Christ." And then to his own soldiers: "We have suffered our fellow knights to be slain, and I have suffered your fellows to suffer death for Jesu Christ, and I have kept the commandment of God which said to Peter: Put thy sword into the sheath. But now, because that we be enclosed with the bodies of the knights our fellows, and have our clothes red of their blood, let us then follow them by martyrdom." The grim episode concludes with the emperor's command to exterminate the legion.

It is difficult to convey the spirit of this narrative in a brief summary. There is something paradoxical in the tone of it that eludes analysis. On the one hand, we see brave, disciplined soldiers submitting to execution as meekly as if they were orthodox Jews in the path of a Syrian battalion, on the Sabbath, in the days of the Maccabees. Little wonder that frustrated Roman officials looked upon Christianity as some mysterious disease. On the other hand, the joy of the martyrs in running to meet the sword could almost be described as berserk, and, although this is a story of nonresistance to violence, its atmosphere is that of a battle, with eternal life as the reward for victory. Maurice and his soldiers seem to be engaged in an all-out assault on mortality.

Among the miracles attributed to Saint Maurice is one that seems to catch, in muted form, the spirit that radiates from the story of his life, the conviction that death is swallowed up in victory:

There was a woman which delivered her son, to learn, unto the abbot of the church in which the holy saints lie in. And the son died in short time after, wherefore the mother wept without remedy. Then St. Maurice appeared to her and inquired why she wept so for her son. And she answered that as long as she should live she should weep for him. And he said to her: Weep no more for him as he were dead, for know thou for certain he is with us, and if thou wilt prove it, arise to-morn and every day of thy life, and come to matins, and thou shalt

[26]

hear his voice among the monks singing. And ever after, during her life, she came every day, and heard the voice of her son singing among the monks.

The Biblical Message of the Sanctuary

The preceding review of the ecclesiastical calendar, both *temporale* and *sanctorale*, is sufficient to emphasize the importance of the liturgy in communicating the Bible and the subsequent history of the early Church to each member of the worshiping congregation. But no study of this matter is complete that does not take into account the brilliant use of biblical art in the medieval sanctuary. The great cathedrals of western Europe are of course famous for this, but more often than not even the parish churches could boast an impressive display of Christian art for the edification of the local membership. Ornamental carvings were frequently sermons in stone, and wall paintings were probably much more widespread than the few surviving examples would suggest. Above all, the biblical message was expressed through the medium of stained glass in the magnificent gothic windows of the later Middle Ages. This ecclesiastical art must be seen in order to be appreciated. Even then, the passage of time and a good deal of reformation iconoclasm have combined to turn most of the churches into grey stone shadows of what they formerly were. But in England one can find an occasional church which has to some extent miraculously preserved its colorful medieval interior. To round out our picture of the Bible in the Middle Ages, therefore I would like to describe one such church, situated in the little town of Fairford, in Gloucestershire, a short drive west from Oxford on the road to Cirencester.

Fairford Church was almost completely rebuilt in the late fifteenth century by John Tame, a wealthy woolstapler of Cirencester, who died in 1500. The chief glory of this church is its stained glass, which has somehow survived the hazards of storm, war, and iconoclasm for over four and a half centuries. On the occasion of the latest threat, at the outbreak of World War II, every piece of the glass was removed and stored underground by Mr. Oscar G. Farmer, whose scholarly guide to the church windows, incidentally, is a masterpiece. After the war, Mr. Farmer, working steadily for two years, replaced the glass single-handedly.

Although it is somewhat larger than the average sanctuary for a parish of that size, Fairford looks very much like other churches of its kind. You enter by the south door, and as you look to the right after entering, your eye catches the chancel and main altar at the east end. A rather unusual feature, which makes Fairford resemble a small cathedral, is the tower rising almost in the center of the church, between the nave (west end) and the choir and chancel (east end). The presence also of north and south aisles adds width to the general appearance of the interior. At the east end, in addition to the chancel with its main altar, there are chapels on either side which are really extensions of the aisles. On the north is the Lady Chapel, and on the south the Corpus Christi Chapel. Carved wooden screens in the arches formally separate these chapels from the chancel and from the aisles. Finally it should be mentioned that the roof of the nave, from the tower to the west end of the church, is higher than that of the aisles, thus creating a lofty clerestory above the congregation, and at the same time making possible the construction of a magnificent west window, by far the largest in the church.

Even with this architectural knowledge, however, it comes as a surprise to discover that Fairford has no less than twenty-eight windows: three each in the two chapels, two in the chancel, five in the north aisle and four in the south aisle (one less because of the door), three at the west end, and eight up in the clerestory (four north and four south). Moreover the subjects are chosen in accordance with a carefully designed symmetrical scheme for the church as a whole. The twelve prophets in the north aisle, for example, are carefully placed so as to correspond with the twelve Apostles of the south aisle; while overhead, in the north clerestory, twelve evil persecutors with devils flying above them in the tracery lights glare fixedly at the windows of the south clerestory, in which are twelve martyrs, attended by angels in the tracery.

At the west end of the church the large central window sets forth the Last Judgment, while windows on either side of it show two Old Testament judgments, on the left (south) David's condemnation of the Amalekite (II Samuel 1:15), and on the right (north) Solomon's decision in the case of two mothers claiming the one living child (1 Kings 3:16–28). Adjoining these, at the west end of the aisles, are, on the north, the four evangelists (Matthew, Mark, Luke, John), and facing them, on the south, the four Fathers of the Church (Jerome, Gregory, Ambrose, and Augustine). The absence of a door on the north side permits an extra window at its eastern end, which contains scenes from the Old Testament that were interpreted as types of the coming Redemption. This completes our survey of the windows of the main part of the church, from the west end to the

[28]

Rood Screen which separates it from the inner sanctuary at the eastern end.

As we look toward the front or east end of the church, we find that the windows are meant to be viewed from left to right. This is accomplished by entering first the Lady Chapel on the north side, with its three windows, thence into the main sanctuary with its two windows, and so finally into Corpus Christi Chapel on the south side for the last three windows. Taken in that order, these eight windows cover the subjects of all the principal commemorations of the *temporale*, from Advent to Corpus Christi. The main topics in the windows of each area, moreover, fit the purpose of that particular place of worship. Those of the Lady Chapel emphasize events in the life of the Blessed Virgin Mary; the main window of the chancel depicts the Passion of Christ, while the other shows the Harrowing of Hell; and finally the windows of Corpus Christi Chapel contain scenes beginning with the Resurrection so as to emphasize the meaning of the Blessed Sacrament (Corpus Christi). Thus it can be seen that the arrangement of topics in the windows of Fairford Church is highly complex, symmetrical, and meaningful. But in order to appreciate their biblical message, we must take a closer look, beginning with the Old Testament window just outside the Lady Chapel in the north aisle.

Like most of the windows, this one has four "lights," or panels, and the first one shows Eve receiving fruit offered to her by the serpent, who is twined around the Tree of Knowledge. Interestingly, this serpent has the head of a woman, an idea perhaps taken from a comment in the history of Adam, in *The Golden Legend:* "Bede saith that he chose a serpent having a maiden's cheer [countenance], for like oft apply to like." The choice of Eve here, rather than Adam, is undoubtedly deliberate, since the temptation of Eve was regarded as the Old Testament counterpart of the Annunciation, which awaits us in the Lady Chapel. As Saint Augustine says, "By a woman he was deceived, and by a woman he was born a man."

In the second light is the Burning Bush, an object which, in medieval commentaries (and in the Prologue to Chaucer's *Prioress' Tale*), was understood to be a type of the Blessed Virgin, in whose unblemished body burned the divine Presence. Incidentally, it will be noticed that Moses, kneeling below and to the left of the bush, has a pair of unmistakable horns on his head. These served as a convenient means of identifying Moses in medieval art but they also have an interesting origin in a text from the Vulgate Bible. When

[29]

Moses came down from Sinai after receiving the Law from God, he did not know, according to the Authorized Version, "that the skin of his face shone" (Exodus 34:29). Jerome, however, translated this, "Moses did not know that his face was horned (*cornuta*)," because of a confusion between the Hebrew words *qaran* ("to shine") and *qeren* ("horn"), which in fact appear identical in an unpointed Hebrew text.

The other two lights of this first window contain subjects also chosen for their significance as prefigurations of New Testament events. Gideon is shown kneeling beside the dew-covered fleece (Judges 6:36–38) which, with a supporting verse from Isaiah (45:8), is understood to foreshadow the Holy Ghost descending upon the Blessed Virgin, thereby bringing salvation to mankind. The fourth light depicts King Solomon receiving gifts from the Queen of Sheba (I Kings 10:10), anticipating the gifts of the Magi to the Christ child.

In the Lady Chapel the four lights of its first window contain incidents from the life of the Blessed Virgin. First, her parents, Saint Joachim and Saint Anne, are shown embracing near the golden gate of the Temple. To understand the meaning of this moment, we must turn to the account provided in *The Golden Legend* for the commemoration of the Nativity of Our Lady. Here we read that when Joachim went to make his offering at the Temple, he was shamed by the priest because he had no children. The story thus makes use of a venerable device from the Old Testament, the child-less couple who later are miraculously provided with a child that is destined for greatness. In this case Joachim, crushed by the priest's harsh words and reluctant to return home, is visited by an angel who comforts him and reminds him of the examples of Isaac, Joseph, Samson, and Samuel, whose mothers were thought to be barren. He then promises Joachim that his wife Anne shall have a daughter to be named Mary, who shall be filled with the Holy Ghost. "And I give to thee the sign," said the angel, "that when thou shalt come to the golden gate at Jerusalem, thou shalt meet there Anne thy wife, which is much amoved of thy long tarrying, and shall have joy of thy coming." The meeting depicted in this light, therefore, signifies more than the joy of reunion; it is the confirmation of the angel's promise of a child named Mary.

The three remaining lights of the first window depict the Birth of the Virgin, her Dedication at the Temple, and her Marriage to Saint Joseph. The most intriguing of these is the Dedication. Mary is shown as a child of three, gracefully ascending a flight of stairs leading into the Temple. She is wearing a blue robe over a red dress. The stairs she is climbing, as explained in *The Golden Legend,* have fifteen steps, representing the fifteen psalms of Ascents (Psalms 120–34). "And then our Lady was set on the lowest step, and mounted up without any help as she had been of perfect age." It is a delightful story, told with affection and reverence. Like the parents of Samuel, Joachim and Anne leave their child to be brought up in the Temple. The story concludes: "And the Virgin Mary profited every day in all holiness, and was visited daily of angels, and had every day divine visions."

The four lights of the next window contain famous moments associated with the birth of Christ, taken from the canonical gospels: the Annunciation (Luke 1:28–38), the Nativity (Luke 2:1–20), the Adoration of the Magi (Matthew 2:1–12), and the Presentation of the Savior in the Temple (Luke 2:22–40). In the Nativity the traditional ox and ass can be seen obediently peering at the Christ child in accordance with the words of Isaiah (1:3): *The ox knoweth his owner and the ass his master's crib.* In the rich, blue distance beyond the stable, moreover, stands the tower of Micah's prophecy (Micah 4:8): *And thou, O tower of the flock, the stronghold of the daughter of Zion, unto thee shall it come, even the first dominion.* The biblical art thus stresses the connection between prophecy and fulfillment by placing the two together in the same picture.

The east window of the Lady Chapel is a bit larger than the average, containing five lights. The first two show the Flight into Egypt, the third has the Assumption of the Blessed Virgin, and the last two portray Jesus in the Temple with the Doctors (Luke 2:42–50). The Temple scene is conventional enough, but the other two require a closer look. The first shows us a pause in the Flight. The ass is grazing in the foreground. Mary is seated beside the road with the Child in her lap and is feeding him some fruit. Behind her is a tree, from which Joseph is plucking bunches of fruit, assisted by an angel hovering overhead and bending down the branches. In the distance can be seen the slaughter of the Innocents ordered by Herod, from which the Holy Family has just escaped. This event, of course, has a biblical basis (Matthew 2:13–18), but the scene involving the fruit tree and the angel comes from the infancy gospel of Pseudo-Matthew in the New Testament Apocrypha. This story was very popular throughout the Middle Ages, and eventually found its way into vernacular works like the Middle English stanzaic poem, "The Childhood of Jesus." Even after the Reformation, when apoc-

[31]

ryphal material of this kind was repressed, the infancy stories found a second life in oral tradition, as can be seen in the folk song known as "The Cherry Tree Carol." Here the setting has been changed from the Flight into Egypt to the courtship of Joseph and Mary, and the palm tree of Pseudo-Matthew has become a cherry tree. In the carol, moreover, Mary's hunger comes not from the rigors of travel, but from the expectant mother's arbitrary desire for some particular thing to eat:

> Mary spoke to Joseph,
> So meek and so mild,
> "Joseph gather me some cherries
> For I am with child."

Joseph, normally depicted as understanding and obliging, is given a sharper, more human character in the song:

> Joseph flew in anger
> In anger he flew,
> Saying, "Let the father of your baby
> Gather cherries for you."

Joseph's intransigence leads naturally to the miracle:

> The Lord looked down from heaven,
> These words He did say:
> "Bow you low down you cherry tree
> While Mary gathers some."
>
> The cherry tree bowed down
> It was low on the ground
> And Mary gathered cherries
> While Joseph stood around.

One can only wish that more pre-Reformation songs of this type had survived. The particular version I have quoted was found some years ago in the Blue Ridge mountains of North Carolina, in a solidly Protestant community.

Turning back to our window, we see that the center light depicts the Assumption of the Virgin, an event not found in the Bible, but one which has an important place, it will be recalled, among the commemorations of the Virgin in the *sanctorale*. The account of her assumption in *The Golden Legend* is based on an apocryphal book attributed to John the Evangelist, to which has been added a series of sermons and miracles associated with the event. But no attempt has been made by the artist to introduce any of these materials. We have simply a radiant Virgin in blue against the golden rays of the sun, ascending to heaven accompanied by angels. Above her, expectantly, sits God the Father in Paradise, holding the orb and cross. The splendor of this light, and its central position in the main window, remind us forcefully that we are standing in the Lady Chapel, before the altar.

As we move past the tomb of John Tame, builder of Fairford Church, into the chancel, we find ourselves facing the main east window, containing the events of Holy Week leading up to the Passion. These are set forth in an upper and lower series of five lights each. The lower lights have five episodes, which are, from left to right, Christ entering Jerusalem, the Agony in the Garden, Christ before Pilate, the Scourging, and Christ bearing the cross. Above these, occupying the entire series of five lights, is a traditional Crucifixion. The two thieves are readily distinguished: over the head of the penitent thief hovers a blue angel, while a red devil hovers near the impenitent thief, ready to seize his soul. A skull at the foot of the Savior's cross reminds us that the locale is *Golgotha, that is to say, a place of a skull* (Matt. 27:33). One detail of the Crucifixion may owe something to the New Testament Apocrypha. According to the canonical Gospel of John (19:34), a soldier pierced Christ's side with a spear. In the Gospel of Nicodemus, however, a much fuller story is told. The soldier's name is Longinus, and we are informed that he was blind, so that his hand had to be guided to strike the blow. When the blood of the Lord flowed down the shaft of the spear to his hand, Longinus instinctively put his hand to his eyes, so that suddenly he was healed of his blindness, and thus became a follower of Christ. According to *The Golden Legend,* he was eventually martyred in Cappadocia, and hence found a place in the calendar of the *sanctorale* (March 15). The only hint of this story in the Fairford Crucifixion, however, is the fact that the soldier who is in the act of piercing Christ's side is being assisted by another figure on horseback, apparently a priest, who also has his hands on the spear.

The smaller window of the chancel, in the south wall, shows the Deposition from the Cross, the Entombment, and the Harrowing of Hell. The last, as we noted earlier, is found in the Gospel of Nicodemus, and was very popular during the medieval period. This view catches Christ at the moment He is releasing the patriarchs and prophets from Hell. The damned are summed up in a figure pleading in agony behind glowing red bars, while overhead angels drive back a band of purplish devils, one with green, bat-like wings. The whole scene is pierced with rays of light emanating from heaven, in ac-

[33]

cordance with the prophecy of Isaiah (9:2): *The people that walked in darkness have seen a great light.*

With one exception, all of the scenes depicted in the three windows of Corpus Christi Chapel, south of the main sanctuary, are appearances of Jesus after his death on the cross. The first appearance, to his mother Mary, is not recorded in the New Testament, but is mentioned with approval in *The Golden Legend;* the other cases are all canonical: the Women at the Sepulchre (Luke 24:1–10), on the road to Emmaus (Luke 24:13–32), to doubting Thomas (John 20:26–29), and, finally, at the Sea of Tiberias (John 21:1–23). The last two lights of the third window contain the Ascension of Christ and the Descent of the Holy Spirit at Pentecost (Acts 2), thus completing the cycle of commemorations of the *temporale*. It might at first seem strange that the one exception to this series on the Resurrection is the Transfiguration (Mark 9:2–8), which takes place during Jesus' lifetime. But a closer look at the picture makes it clear that the Transfiguration is portrayed so as to emphasize the importance of the Blessed Sacrament. The Lord appears glorified amidst blue clouds and hovering angels, with Moses and Elijah at His feet; the center of attention is a wafer of the Sacramental Bread on the Lord's breast, from which three rays of light shine down toward the three surprised Disciples below. In this fashion is the Divine nature of Christ dramatically made known to them. This further dimension of meaning in the Transfiguration may perhaps have been suggested by the revelation at Emmaus (Luke 24:30–31): *And it came to pass, as he sat at meat with them, he took bread, and blessed it, and brake, and gave to them. And their eyes were opened, and they knew him; and he vanished out of their sight.*

We have now passed in review the Old Testament prefigurations of the Incarnation, the life of the Blessed Virgin, and the Nativity, Passion, and Resurrection of Christ as set forth in the windows of the Lady Chapel, the Chancel, and the Corpus Christi Chapel. And in so doing we have moved visually through the calendar of the *temporale*, from Advent to Corpus Christi. There is an admirable symmetry and balance in this arrangement, and furthermore the two chapels provide strong support to the main sanctuary, symbolized by the matching central lights of the Assumption in the Lady Chapel, and the Transfiguration in the Chapel of the Sacrament.

Along the aisles of the church, as we walk toward the west end, are the prophets on the north and the Apostles on the south. Encircling the heads of the former are certain Old Testament prophecies, and similarly placed over the apostles are phrases from the Apostles' Creed. Although the correspondences are imperfect, it is evident that the ambitious plan of the designer was to match a prophecy with each phrase or clause of the Creed. Indeed tradition assigned each article of the Creed to one of the twelve apostles, as can be seen in the commentary on the "Twelve Articles of the Faith" at the end of *The Golden Legend*, although the attributions there do not agree entirely with those of the Apostles at Fairford, nor does the *Legend* have the corresponding prophecies from the Old Testament. Here are three samples of the correspondences between prophet and Apostle. Jeremiah (3:19, 32:17): "Thou shalt call me, My father. . . . [who] hast made the heaven and the earth"; Peter: "I believe in God the Father Almighty, maker of heaven and earth." Isaiah (7:14): "Behold, a virgin shall conceive and bear a son"; James the Great: "Who was conceived by the Holy Ghost, born of the Virgin Mary." Hosea (13:14): "O death, I will be thy plagues; O grave, I will be thy destruction"; Thomas: "He descended into hell; the third day he rose again from the dead."

The four Evangelists and the four Doctors of the Church, facing each other at the ends of the aisles, can serve to remind us of the interesting devices used for identification of portraits in medieval art. The Apostles and other saints, for example, were identified by the instruments of their martyrdom. The four Evangelists, however, take their emblems from a verse in the Book of Revelation (4:7): *And the first beast was like a lion, and the second beast like a calf, and the third beast had a face as a man, and the fourth beast was like a flying eagle.* In medieval portraiture Matthew was assigned the face of a man (usually, as at Fairford, depicted as an angel), Mark had the lion, Luke the calf (or rather an ox), and John the eagle. Since few people could then read, this was an effective way to identify the portraits. Emblems of the four Doctors were perhaps less well known, but no one would be likely to miss Jerome, shown accompanied by a lion holding up its paw toward the saint. Worshipers familiar with the lessons of the *sanctorale* would remember the story told of this in *The Golden Legend*:

On a day towards even Jerome sat with his brethren for to hear the holy lesson, and a lion came halting suddenly in to the monastery, and when the brethren saw him, anon they fled, and Jerome came against him as he should come against his guest, and then the lion showed to him his foot being hurt. Then he called his brethren, and commanded them to wash his feet and diligently to seek and search for the wound. And

[35]

that done, the plant of the foot of the lion was sore hurt and pricked with a thorn. Then this holy man put thereto diligent cure, and healed him, and he abode ever after as a tame beast with them.

Among the other Doctors, Gregory is unique in the Papal vestments he wears, and the book he holds may be intended to indicate his importance as a biblical commentator. The position of Ambrose beside his famous convert, Augustine, is of course very appropriate, and the identification of the latter is aided by the fact that Augustine holds his heart in his hand, an emblem of contrition for the sins of his youth. Perhaps also the proximity of these two saints is intended to remind the onlooker of a story in the *Legend* regarding their improvisation of the beautiful hymn, the *Te Deum*, on the occasion of Augustine's baptism by Ambrose: "And then, as it is read, St. Ambrose said: *Te deum laudamus*, and St. Austin answered *Te dominum confitemur*, and so they two together ordained and made this hymn and sung it unto the end."

But we must not become so absorbed in the prophets, Apostles, Evangelists, and Doctors that we neglect the confrontation of persecutors and saints taking place in the clerestory. Among the twelve villains in the four north windows we can identify Annas, Judas, Caiaphas, and the two Herods. Annas is handing pieces of silver to Judas, who holds out his money-bag to receive them, while Caiaphas appears to be counting with his fingers to assist in the transaction. Herod the Great stands with a sword in his right hand, while in his left he holds one of the innocents slaughtered by his command after the Nativity. Herod Antipas is crowned, and holds a scimitar. The remaining figures are not identified, but carry various weapons associated with the persecutions.

In the south clerestory only four of the martyrs are identified: Dorothea, Sebastian, Agnes, and Margaret; a fifth saint is in fragments, impossible to recognize. The remaining figures are generalized according to rank: archbishop, kings, emperor, cardinals, and pope. Perhaps originally certain correspondences were intended: evil king opposite good king, and, in the case of the saints, a figure bearing arms facing a martyr who died by that particular weapon — for example, the persecutor armed with bow and arrow may have stood originally opposite Saint Sebastian, who is shown bound to a tree and wounded with eight arrows. For "the archers shot at him," according to his legend, "till he was as full of arrows as an urchin is full of pricks." Saint Dorothea holds her basket of fruit and flowers, reminding us of the story of her martyrdom. As she was being led to execution, a youth scoffingly asked her to send him some fruit and flowers from the garden where she was going. After her death a strange messenger appeared to the youth, bringing him three roses and three apples.

Next in order stands Saint Agnes with her lamb. She was first tortured, then martyred, for refusing to worship the gods or to marry the son of an important official because she had pledged herself to Christ: "I will have none other spouse but him, I will seek none other, in no manner may I leave him, with him am I firm and fastened in love, which is more noble, more puissant and fairer than any other, whose love is much sweet and gracious, of whom the chamber is now for to receive me where the virgins sing merrily." After her death, according to the *Legend:*

> It happened that when the friends of St. Agnes watched at her sepulchre on a night, they saw a great multitude of virgins clad in vestiments of gold and silver, and a great light shone tofore them, and on the right side was a lamb more white than snow, and saw also St. Agnes among the virgins which said to her parents: Take heed and see that ye bewail me no more as dead, but be ye joyful with me, for with all these virgins Jesu Christ hath given me most brightest habitation and dwelling, and am with him joined in heaven whom in earth I loved with my thought.

The other identifiable martyr is Saint Margaret, shown here with a dragon curled and resting at her feet. According to her legend, Margaret was imprisoned for refusing to worship pagan gods. "And whilst she was in prison, she prayed our Lord that the fiend that had fought with her, he would visibly show him unto her. And then appeared a horrible dragon and assailed her, and would have devoured her, but she made the sign of the cross, and anon he vanished away." This monster is doubtless the great dragon of the Apocalypse, *that old serpent, called the Devil, and Satan,* who pursued the woman into the wilderness (Revelation 12:17): *And the dragon was wroth with the woman, and went to make war with the remnant of her seed, which keep the commandments of God, and have the testimony of Jesus.*

On either side of the main west window are two Old Testament scenes, the judgment of David on the south, and Solomon on the north. Both of these windows, unfortunately, suffered heavy damage from a great storm in 1703, so that we cannot fully appreciate the artist's conception. The better preserved of the two is the judgment of Solomon, where the contrasting expression of the two women is dramatic and effective: the pretended mother staring grimly at

Solomon, and the real mother appealing pathetically for the life of her child. One other curious and interesting figure in this window is worthy of comment. Above, looking down from a balcony, is a fool or jester dressed in yellowish-brown clothes and carrying a wooden spoon. It is tempting to suppose that this fool is Marcolf, that wise and witty prankster who plays such a mischievous role in the medieval legend of "Solomon and Marcolf."

Our final subject, of course, is the Last Judgment in the great west window, by far the largest in the church. In the seven upper lights, Christ on the throne of judgment is surrounded by saints and angels; in the lower half Saint Michael, holding his scales, weighs the souls of mankind. Both scenes are filled with vivid detail, yet manage to retain a sense of pattern and order. The upper half in particular, showing Christ in majesty, is tranquil and momentous, appealing to the eye just as the memorable words of the Apocalypse appeal to the ear: *Behold, he cometh with clouds, and every eye shall see him, and they also which pierced him: and all kindreds of the earth shall wail because of him. . . . His head and his hairs were white like wool, as white as snow; and his eyes were as a flame of fire; and his feet like unto fine brass, as if they burned in a furnace; and his voice as the sound of many waters . . . and his countenance was as the sun shineth in his strength* (1:7, 14–15, 16).

Great circles of color radiate outward from the central figure of Christ enthroned. Around him extend the rays of the sun; then a circle of brilliant red made up of the Cherubim; next a variegated circle of apostles, saints, and martyrs, many with identifying emblems; these in turn encompassed by a brilliant blue circle of Seraphim; and finally a last variegated circle of angels holding symbols of the Passion. Into this apocalyptic scene are woven details taken from other parts of the Bible. Thus Christ is shown with His feet placed on a globe representing the earth, with its cities crumbling in flames, for, as it is written, *The Lord said to my Lord, Sit thou on my right hand, till I make thine enemies thy footstool* (Psalm 110:1; Mark 12:36). And scrolls on either side of the Lord's head read "Justice" and "Mercy," echoing the famous verse from Psalm 85: *Mercy and truth are met together; righteousness and peace have kissed each other.* To His right is the lily of the Resurrection; to His left, the two-edged sword of Revelation (1:16). Kneeling below and to the left is the Blessed Virgin, while opposite her kneels Saint John the Baptist. Between them, and extending around the throne on which the Savior is seated, is a rainbow, recalling another detail of Saint

John's vision (Revelation 4:3): *And there was a rainbow round about the throne, in sight like unto an emerald.*

In contrast to the order and tranquility of heaven, the scene below is one of turmoil swirling around the stable center of Saint Michael with his scales (Daniel 12:1): *And at that time shall Michael stand up, the great prince which standeth for the children of thy people: and there shall be a time of trouble, such as never was since there was a nation even to that same time: and at that time thy people shall be delivered, every one that shall be found written in the book.* Below the Archangel the graves open and give up their dead, who stand in their grave clothes, ready for Judgment, thus enacting the prophecy of Daniel (12:2): *And many of them that sleep in the dust of the earth shall awake, some to everlasting life, and some to shame and everlasting contempt.* On the left, the Blessed are being led by angels to Saint Peter, who stands on the golden stairway to Paradise; while on the right the damned are being dragged, carried, or hauled in wheelbarrows to the fiery furnaces of Hell. In between, around the figure of Michael, a fierce contention is taking place between the angels and the devils for the souls of men. On the right, opposite Saint Peter, Satan sits enthroned, his huge dragon's tail extending to the bottom of the light. Once more the scene recalls the words of the Apocalypse (Revelation 12:7–8): *And there was war in heaven: Michael and his angels fought against the dragon; and the dragon fought and his angels, and prevailed not; neither was their place found any more in heaven.*

This completes our review of the biblical message of the sanctuary expressed in the stained glass windows of Fairford Church. As we turn now to consider other manifestations of the Bible in medieval thought and literature, it will be well to keep this message in mind, for it expresses clearly the medieval view of man and the universe, the world-picture which is the heritage of western civilization.

CHAPTER TWO

Medieval Exegesis:
Gregory's Morals on Job

B EHIND the liturgy and the art of the sanctuary was a system of biblical exegesis or commentary which provided the lens through which the Bible was viewed in the Middle Ages. This system represents an approach to the text quite different from that of modern biblical scholarship.

My own experience as a teacher has impressed on me how great this difference is. On the one hand, I have presented the Bible as literature to a college class, with the aid of a modern translation and modern commentaries based on the higher criticism; on the other hand, in studying medieval literature with graduate students, I have often made use of medieval commentaries. As a result I am greatly indebted both to medieval and to modern exegetes, but, at the same time, I am quite conscious of differences in the method-ology or hermeneutics of the two systems.

A few years ago I engaged in a friendly argument with a colleague whose special interest, like mine, was medieval literature. He was (and is) a militant advocate of medieval exegesis, and I found myself beginning to defend modern higher criticism out of a conviction based on my experience in teaching the Bible as literature. "Could I use the allegorical method as a means of interpreting the Bible to students in this day and age?" I demanded. After a moment's pause he replied, "No, I guess you couldn't." At first I thought he was conceding my point—something he was not in the habit of doing—

but gradually it dawned on me that what he really meant was, "No, I guess they just wouldn't be up to it."

Fortunately there is no need to explore in depth the question of the compatibility of medieval and modern methods of exegesis. My purpose here is to describe briefly the development of biblical studies in the Middle Ages, and then to review in detail one very famous medieval commentary: the *Morals on the Book of Job* by Saint Gregory the Great. In this way I believe we can best understand the medieval approach to the Bible, and perhaps also appreciate the sense in which this approach was a valid and even a powerful means of bringing the light to the nations.

Study of the Bible in the Middle Ages

Although the interpretation of the Bible was developed and refined over the course of many centuries, the basis for it already existed in the New Testament. Different terms have been used to describe it — figurative, typological, allegorical — but the foundation of the method is the establishment of connections between the Old and New Testament. We have seen this illustrated in the juxtaposition of prophets and Apostles in the windows of Fairford Church, and it is also evident in the opening chapters of the Gospel of Matthew, where again and again occurs the formula: *Now all this was done, that it might be fulfilled which was spoken of the Lord by the prophet . . .* (Matt. 1:22).

In addition to explicit predictions, however, actual events recorded in the Old Testament are themselves seen as having a significant relationship to New Testament events. Thus Paul exhorts the Corinthians by reminding them of the circumstances of the Exodus: *Moreover, brethren, I would not that ye should be ignorant, how that all our fathers were under the cloud, and all passed through the sea; and were all baptized unto Moses in the cloud and in the sea; and did all eat the same spiritual meat; and did all drink the same spiritual drink: for they drank of that spiritual Rock that followed them: and that Rock was Christ* (1 Cor. 10:1–4). Paul then goes on to list the sins of Israel during the Exodus and the punishment inflicted on them, and urges the Corinthians not to repeat these faults and thereby be in danger of a similar judgment. Then he concludes: *Now all these things happened unto them for examples: and they are written for our admonition, upon whom the ends of the world are come* (1 Cor. 10:11). Thus not only does the Exodus serve as an example and a warning, its very

[41]

meaning was prophetic: the Rock that brought forth water for Moses was Christ. Other examples could be given (e.g., Gal. 4:21–31), but this is perhaps sufficient to indicate that the fundamental method of interpretation of the Scriptures adopted in the Middle Ages was already present in the Bible itself. The Old Testament was seen as a foreshadowing of what was actually fulfilled in the New Testament.

This method of seeing historical correspondences between the two Testaments has often been called typology, to distinguish it from later developments, and its validity has been skillfully defended by Erich Auerbach in his essay called "Figura." Even in historical terms such as we use today it is possible, I think, to see the typological connection between the offering of Isaac (Gen. 22) and the sacrifice of Christ in the Gospels, a connection often made in patristic commentaries. In this sense, therefore, it is possible for a modernist to acknowledge that medieval exegesis rests on solid foundations.

Early in the history of the Church, however, the picture was complicated by the growth of the New Testament canon and the consequent doctrine of uniformity of revelation. When this happened the temptation to use allegory became irresistible. The New Testament itself was now seen as containing mysteries and enigmas that could be illuminated or resolved by recourse to the allegorical method. The development of biblical exegesis during the patristic period, therefore, was inevitably characterized by a certain amount of controversy over methods of interpretation. While it is difficult to generalize, nevertheless the Palestinian school of exegetes tended to be more conservative, while the Alexandrian school, in particular the very influential scholar and commentator Origen, developed the allegorical method to a very great extent. On the one hand typology, which was essentially Hebraic, emphasized the importance of historical connections between the Testaments, while on the other hand allegory, which was of Hellenistic origin, could, if uncontrolled, undermine the historical significance of biblical events. Saint Gregory was conscious of this danger, as we shall see, when he insisted on the historical record of Job's virtues, "lest," he says, "we make void the verity of the deed." Neither side in the controversy won a clear victory, but the hazards of free-wheeling allegory were guarded against in the future by an insistence on the importance of the historical meaning of the text. This can be clearly seen, for example, in Saint Augustine's important treatise, "On Christian Doctrine," even though at times the great Doctor outdoes Origen in the extravagance of his allegorizing.

[42]

It was Gregory the Great, however, who adopted the best of Ambrose, Jerome, Augustine, and especially Origen, and from these produced a synthesis that governed the subsequent development of biblical exegesis in the Middle Ages. His method, as we shall see, was to deal with the text on three levels: the literal, the allegorical, and the moral. The literal level represented historical meaning in accordance with the sacred author's intention. The allegorical level was for Gregory an extension of New Testament typology, not only including fulfillment of Old Testament foreshadowings in the history of the early Church, but also extending the frame of allegorical reference to the future, including the Day of Judgment and life after death. The moral level, where Gregory is at his best, involves the application of the text to the life of the individual. Later commentators sometimes added a fourth level, the anagogical, to which are assigned all references to the hereafter, thus creating a subdivision of the allegorical level. Nevertheless, Gregory's three main categories, literal, allegorical, and moral, provided the pattern which most commentators followed down to the close of the Middle Ages.

From the time of Gregory (d. 604) until the beginning of the twelfth century biblical exegesis developed in a monastic setting. As we have seen, this encouraged a close relationship between the Bible and the liturgy, both in the Mass and in the services of the Canonical hours. During these centuries some important tools for study were produced, for instance the *Etymologies* of Isidore of Seville (a kind of biblical encyclopedia), and commentaries by the Venerable Bede, Alcuin, and Rabanus Maurus. Further efforts, notably by Alcuin, were made to stabilize and disseminate a standard, reliable text of Jerome's Vulgate, although variant forms of the Latin Bible persisted to the very end of the Middle Ages. But the real importance of this period lay in its establishment of a central role for the Bible in religious life, a development that reached its climax in the early twelfth century with the energetic biblical revival of the Cistercians, led by Saint Bernard of Clairvaux. Bernard did not write commentaries, but his *Sermons on the Song of Songs* is a remarkable example of the wide-ranging use of the Bible as a treasury of texts designed to illuminate doctrine. As might be expected, therefore, the Cistercian influence was less important in biblical studies, and more significant in providing a model of biblical style at a time when vernacular literature was just beginning to emerge.

The rise of the universities in the twelfth century marked the shift of the center of gravity of biblical studies from the monasteries to the secular faculties of Paris, and later Oxford and Cambridge. This led to a restructuring of knowledge, and the rise of theology as an independent discipline, with the result that the Bible was no longer the only text in the educational curriculum. By the middle of the twelfth century Peter Lombard's *Sentences* was available for study as a set theological text consisting of a collection of sentences, or as we would say "opinions," on theological issues. At the same time, new biblical aids began to appear, the most important of which were the *Ordinary Gloss,* a commentary arranged in canonical order, book by book, and the *Historia Scholastica* of Peter Comestor, a retelling of the biblical narrative for use in the schools. Both of these compilations were widely used; the *Historia* in particular is frequently cited as a source in the *Golden Legend,* and it often provided the materials for vernacular Bible narratives such as may be found in the English *Cursor Mundi* and the cycle plays.

In the thirteenth and early fourteenth centuries the greatest contributions to biblical and theological studies came from the orders of friars, especially the Dominicans and Franciscans. Bypassing the slower arts curriculum of the secular faculty the friars covered only what they considered essential, and then went straight into theology and biblical studies at an early stage of their education. Saint Thomas Aquinas, who represents the pinnacle of the achievement of scholasticism in theology, was also a skilled Bible commentator. His emphasis on the human element in divine revelation, which can be seen in his exposition of the book of Job, led him to stress the importance of the literal level as against the allegorical. The turning point in biblical studies, however, can perhaps be seen in the commentary of the Franciscan Nicholas of Lyra (d. 1349), whose "postills" on the whole Bible included allegorical interpretation but were revolutionary in their emphasis on the literal level. Hence it is not surprising that Lyra was the favorite exegete of the Wycliffite translators, as we shall see, in the latter half of the fourteenth century. In this connection it is interesting to observe that Lyra himself is considerably indebted to the earlier work of the man he calls Rabbi Solomon, a famous Jewish exegete named Rashi of Troyes (d. 1096), and recent studies seem to indicate that communication between Jewish and Christian exegetes was more extensive than has been generally assumed. At any rate, Lyra's commentary represents the climactic achievement of scholastic exegesis in the later Middle Ages, for despite the achievement of Wyclif (or perhaps because of it), biblical studies in the fifteenth century declined sharply, and it was not until the Reformation that Nicholas of Lyra's devotion to the literal level became the norm for biblical scholarship.

Gregory the Great

To see concretely what the long and rich tradition of biblical exegesis was like, we turn back now to Gregory the Great and his *Morals on the Book of Job*. Gregory was born of a patrician family about A.D. 540, some fifteen years after the execution of Boethius, that last of the Romans, whose *Consolation of Philosophy* became one of the great books of the Middle Ages, and a major influence on Geoffrey Chaucer. Perhaps it is no coincidence that Boethius' *Consolation* is the classical equivalent of the Hebraic book of Job (why do the righteous suffer?), and that Gregory made Job the occasion for his most intensive and searching exegesis. This age was indeed peculiarly characterized by suffering and unrest. The light of Rome had been extinguished in the death of Boethius, and a man could no longer afford emotional or intellectual attachment to the imperial tradition. In this time of cultural crisis, therefore, Gregory's devotion to the monastic ideal, which appears in all of his writings, provided the basis for a new way of life. According to this view, promulgated by the Desert Fathers, the world is but a passing show, and man's real home is in the world beyond, for which the present life is merely a preparation. And yet—an admirable paradox—Gregory spent the most active years of his youth in the imperial service as an administrator, including a tour of duty as Prefect of Rome.

Eventually, however, Gregory abandoned the secular life, founded his own Monastery of Saint Andrew in Rome, and became himself a member of the brotherhood. "I had fled from the world," he says, "I had come to a monastery, as to a port, and I had saved myself, naked, from shipwreck." He was a great admirer of Saint Benedict, and would no doubt have liked nothing better than to spend the rest of his life under the discipline of his rule, in contemplation and chanting of psalms, and practicing poverty, obedience, and humility. But the world would not let him alone. Before he reached the age of forty, he was made deacon by Pope Pelagius II (579–90), and sent as papal envoy to Constantinople. "It was when I was obliged to abandon it," he observes, "that I appreciated the peace of the cloister."

Gregory dutifully assumed his post in Constantinople, taking with him some of his brothers from the Monastery of Saint Andrew. On his arrival he met Leander, Bishop of Seville, at whose request he undertook the composition of his commentary on Job, although this work was not completed until after Leander's death in 585, and after Gregory had returned to Rome. While in the east Gregory became involved in controversy with Eutychius, Patriarch of Constantinople, over the doctrine of the Resurrection. Even then he must have been well launched into his commentary, for he tells us about the dispute in the midst of his exegesis on Job 19:26–27: . . . *yet in my flesh shall I see God: whom I shall see for myself, and mine eyes shall behold, and not another.* . . . The Patriarch Eutychius believed that the resurrected body would be "impalpable" and cited Saint Paul's famous dictum (I Cor. 15:36–37): . . . *that which thou sowest is not quickened, except it die: and that which thou sowest, thou sowest not that body that shall be, but bare grain.* . . . The argument is involved, but the essence of Gregory's reply was that Paul, "in heightening the glory of the resurrection, did not say that *what it was* is wanting to it, but that *what it was not* is present; but this man [Eutychius], whereas he denies the real body to rise again, does not say that *what was wanting* is there, but that *what it was* is wanting."

The interesting outcome of this argument is related by Gregory:

> Upon this, then, we being led on in long disputing on this point, we began to recoil from one another with the greatest animosity, when the Emperor Tiberius Constantine, of religious memory, bringing myself and him to a private audience, learnt what dispute was being carried on between us, and weighing the statement of both sides, and by his own allegations as well disproving that same book which he had written concerning the resurrection, determined that it ought to be consumed in the flames. Upon our leaving whom, I was seized with a grievous sickness, while to that same Eutychius sickness and death shortly followed. And when he was dead, because there was wellnigh no one who followed his statements, I held back from prosecuting what I had commenced, lest I should seem to be darting words at his ashes. But while he was still alive and I sick of violent fever, if any of my acquaintance went to him for the sake of greeting him, as I learnt from their relation, he used to take hold on the skin of his hand before their eyes, saying, "I confess that we shall all rise again in this flesh"; which as they themselves avowed he was before wont altogether to deny.

When Gregory was called back to Rome, he resumed residence in his monastery, continuing the work on Job, and perhaps also commenting to the brothers on other books of the Bible. Within four years after his return from Constantinople, a great plague struck Rome, and Pope Pelagius died of it. In spite of his own urgent desire to escape the responsibility, Gregory was chosen as his successor, and was consecrated Pope on September 3, 590. It is not hard to understand Gregory's reluctance to assume the high office. "We have no longer a Senate, no longer a people," he remarks in his *Homilies on Ezekiel;* "or, for those who still exist, sorrows and groanings are multiplied daily. Deserted Rome is in flames. . . ." The city was also thoroughly demoralized by a plague. Gregory recalls the ghastly scene in his *Dialogues:* "One saw with one's own eyes arrows shoot from heaven and strike the people one by one." Indeed, the arrows of the Almighty were falling upon Rome, and their poison was drinking up its spirit. The secular arm was no longer effective, and the people looked to the Pontiff for leadership. For Gregory, this was the final irony: having escaped from his appointment as Prefect, he was now thrust back into public life as Pope, at precisely the time when the Papacy had to take on responsibility for the salvation of Rome.

To meet the crisis of the plague, Gregory himself led a penitential procession through the streets of Rome, with the clergy chanting the *Kyrie eleison.* This solemn procession, as we are told in the *Golden Legend,* became the occasion for the establishment of the Greater Litany of the *temporale,* the liturgical prayers offered on the three days before Ascension. For the Romans of Gregory's time, it brought an end to hysteria, and the beginning of recovery from the devastation of the plague.

Having accepted his responsibility, the new Pope proceeded to act decisively both in the political and in the religious spheres. It is not possible here to review his numerous problems as a secular leader, nor to do justice to his many achievements in ecclesiastical administration during his fourteen hard-working years in office. One of his earlier reforms, however, may serve to illustrate the decisiveness of his leadership, and it is of particular interest for our present purpose in revealing his attitude toward the liturgy. The case is best described by quoting the decree written by Gregory himself:

Into the holy Roman Church, at the head of which the divine dispensation has wished me to be placed, a very reprehensible custom has, for a long time, made its way. Certain persons are called to the ministry of the holy altar with the title of singers, and thus it is seen that nothing is thought of in the order of the diaconate but the training of the voices of the deacons, who should be attending to the business of preaching and the giving of alms. It very often happens that for this sacred ministry beautiful voices are sought for, but that no attention is paid to the candidate's worthy life, and that the singer offends God by his morals, while he pleases the public by his voice. Therefore, by the present decree, I order that, in this see, the ministers of the sacred altar are not to sing,

[47]

and that they shall have for their only duty to read the gospel lesson in the solemnities of the Mass. The psalms and other lessons I reserve for the sub-deacons, or, if necessary, to the minor orders. If anyone seeks to neglect this command, let him be anathema.

In view of the demanding nature of Gregory's responsibilities, it is all the more remarkable that he was able to continue his writing, even after assuming office in September of 590. His sermons on the Gospels, no doubt, were a part of his regular duties as a preacher. Out of his experience as Pontiff came the famous treatise on *Pastoral Care*, which was so greatly admired by King Alfred three hundred years later. In this work, addressed to the bishop of Ravenna, one can occasionally glimpse Gregory's shrewd observation of human nature, as when, in speaking of certain bishops of his acquaintance, he remarks: "They actually find pleasure in being overwhelmed by business affairs, and while they congratulate themselves on being driven along by the tumult of the world, they become strangers to the spiritual things which they ought to be teaching to others." His other great achievement in the realm of biblical exegesis was the commentary on Ezekiel. There, in his discussion of the opening vision, with its *wheel in the middle of a wheel* (Ezekiel 1:16), we can see how Gregory avoids the fanciful allegorizing of the Alexandrian tradition, and clearly aligns himself with the typology of the apostolic age: "The wheel is within another wheel," he explains, "because the New Testament is in the Old Testament. And, as we have already often said, what the Old Testament promised the New Testament has revealed to us; and what the former announced in obscure terms, the latter proclaims in clear terms. The Old Testament is the prophecy of the New, and the New is the fulfilment of the Old."

In the midst of all his duties, Gregory managed to carry on a voluminous correspondence with many friends and colleagues, both men and women, throughout the Mediterranean area. From his letters to Rusticiana we learn that this dedicated Christian woman had visited the Monastery of Saint Catherine on Mount Sinai, and, in commenting on this, Gregory professes not to understand how, having visited there, she could ever persuade herself to leave. His letters contain numerous such passages, showing that the desire to return to the cloister never left him. Yet he continued to be an effective leader through crisis after crisis. Not the least of his accomplishments was the treaty of peace with the Lombards, which ended a terrible period of suffering and bloodshed. This was, indeed, an act of conscience, toward which Gregory worked long and hard, a pacifist effort which he justified by saying: "Because I fear God, I did not wish to participate in the destruction of anyone whomsoever."

Partly because of his genius, and partly because of the time in which he lived, Gregory was scarcely able to put pen to paper without writing something of importance for the history of the Church. Such is his collection of saints' lives known as the *Dialogues*. The idea for this work came indirectly from his long-time friend, the deacon Peter, who, in a moment of discouragement, remarked that it seemed the age of miracles was past. Gregory responded immediately with instances of miracles that he had heard about, and in the course of conversation it occurred to him that Italy as yet had no collection of biographies of her saints. The result of this discussion was the *Dialogues*, which turned out to be one of the most important source books for the *Golden Legend*. In it he wanted to show that the Kingdom of the Lord was at hand, and was daily being proclaimed in the actual lives and miraculous deeds of the saints and martyrs. This purpose is admirably summed up by Gregory's biographer, Monseigneur Pierre Batiffol: "The *Dialogues* were *The City of God* rewritten for the simple."

One of Gregory's most famous achievements, of course, is his conversion of the Angles and Saxons to Christianity. Familiar as the story is, its revolutionary import is not always appreciated. The monastic tradition, which Gregory inherited from Saint Benedict, and which he so much admired, was nevertheless inherently static; it had no program beyond the carrying out of its cultivation of the ascetic life in prayer and praise of God. A few individuals, notably Saint Columbanus (with whom Gregory corresponded), had moved out to the borders of Christendom as witnesses to the richness of the spiritual life. But Gregory, as a matter of conscious policy, added another dimension to the role of the monasteries by turning monks into missionaries. When Augustine and his companions landed in Kent at Easter of 597, an important new phase in the expansion of Christianity had begun. Seven years later, still in his early sixties, the great pope died, not old, but full of days.

Morals on the Book of Job

In setting forth his exegesis on the book of Job, Gregory deals successively, as we have noted, with the literal, allegorical and moral levels of meaning. Of necessity, therefore, our survey of the commentary will to some extent follow these structural divisions. But before reviewing the work as a whole, I would like first to offer some examples of Gregory's general style and technique, and, second, to discuss briefly how his approach resembles and differs from the methods of modern higher criticism of the Bible.

Though Gregory's commentary is concerned only with one book, the references in it to other parts of the Bible make it clear that his knowledge of both Testaments was very extensive. No doubt he had or devised some kind of index to help him locate the differing usages of words which he so often refers to, but at times his cross references spring spontaneously from the imagination, showing at once an intimacy of knowledge, and a profound admiration for holy scripture. In the preface to the first book, for example, Gregory speaks eloquently and with emotion of the relationship of the two Testaments: "But amongst these marvelous works of Divine Providence it yields us satisfaction to mark, how, for enlightening the night of this present life, each star in its turn appears in the face of Heaven, until that towards the end of the night the Redeemer of mankind ariseth like the true Morning Star." Among the stars in this sky Gregory identifies Abel, who stands for innocence, Enoch for purity of practice, Noah for endurance, Abraham for obedience, and so forth through the roll call of Old Testament heroes, all of whom lighted the way of erring man "till the true Morning Star should rise, Who, being the herald to us of the eternal morning, should outshine the other stars by the radiance of His Divinity."

Extended images of this kind in Gregory's exegesis often seem to grow out of his study of the sacred page. Here we are reminded of the graphic quality of the Lord's promise to Abraham (Genesis 15:5): *And he brought him forth abroad, and said, Look now toward heaven, and tell the stars, if thou be able to number them: and he said unto him, so shall thy seed be.* And to this is perhaps added a line from St. Paul (Romans 13:12): *The night is far spent, the day is at hand.*

In spite of his severity with singing deacons, Gregory seems to have been fond of music. In one passage, for example, he likens the Scriptures to a harp: "They that attune the harmony of stringed instruments arrange it with such exceeding skill, that frequently, when one chord is touched, a very different one, placed with many lying between, is made to vibrate, and when this last is sounded, the former, which is attempered to the same tune, rings without the other being struck. According to which Holy Scripture very often so deals with the several virtues, and vices too, that while by express mention it conveys one thing, it does by its silence bring before

[50]

us another. . . ." Elsewhere, in a passage on the art of teaching, Gregory maintains that teachers should fashion what they say to suit each type of learner: "For what are the attentive minds of hearers, but certain strings which are strained tight in a harp? Which the skilful performer touches in different ways, that they may not produce a discordant sound. And the strings give back an harmonious sound, because they are struck with one plectrum, but with different force. Whence also every teacher in order to build up all in one virtue of charity, ought not to touch the hearts of his hearers with one and the same exhortation."

Sometimes Gregory's thought leaps with lightninglike rapidity from one book to another, and indeed from Old Testament to New, as he pursues an idea or a definition to its conclusion. The torrent of waters in Job 28:4, for example, represents the sermons of holy preachers, who swoop like ravens from the torrents to pick out the eyes of heretics that despise Mother Church (Prov. 30:17) from whom they have become alienated (1 John 2:19). The preacher is called a raven because of his humility, in that he says, through the voice of the Church, *I am black, but comely* (SS 1:5). Thus the flight of the ravens from the torrents takes us from the text of Job to Proverbs, John, the Song of Solomon, and finally back to Job, where the meaning, thus enriched, is recapitulated.

Though there are limits, as we have observed, to Gregory's employment of allegory, he nevertheless makes liberal use of the method, and shows an awareness of the traditional figure whereby the literal level is likened to the crust of bark which, if peeled away, exposes the inner sweetness of the spiritual meaning. The pejorative view of the literal sense suggested by this comparison was often reinforced, by some commentators, with the words of Saint Paul (2 Cor. 3:6): *For the letter killeth, but the spirit giveth life.* Gregory, however, in practice backs away from this extreme, arguing for a variation in emphasis determined by common sense and the meaning of the text. One of his arguments for restraint in the use of allegory, amusingly, is cast in the form of an allegorical interpretation of the story of Jacob's peeling of the rods (Genesis 30:37–39). Gregory turns to this story to explain why in chapter 31 of Job he intends to restrict himself almost completely to the literal level. "Now the words of grief," he says, alluding to Job's monologue in chapter 30, "we have run through by an historical and allegorical explanation; but the deeds of virtuous qualities [in chapter 31] we in great measure hold according to the text of the history alone, lest if we draw these to the

[51]

exploring of mysteries, we should perchance appear to be making void the verity of the deed."

Gregory then goes on to observe that the senses of Scripture must be nicely balanced between the extremes of excessive allegorizing on the one hand and "the deadness of unconcern" on the other. It is at this point that he cites the story of Jacob's rods. The row of rods planted before the cattle, he explains, are sentences of Holy Scripture designed for our instruction. The peeled portions lay bare the inner sense, while that which still retains the bark shows forth the literal meaning. Jacob rightly set these rods by the watering troughs, to indicate the teaching of Scripture by which we are inwardly watered. Likewise the rams mingled with the sheep while looking at the mottled rods, and thus brought forth spotted offspring, even as our reasoning spirits, on contemplating the sentences of Holy Writ, bring forth the progeny of good works, which are variegated in color insofar as the precepts are viewed both from a literal and a figurative point of view. The diplomacy of this stricture against excessive allegorizing is admirable. I suspect the technique is akin to that of Saint Paul, who, in the course of his critique on speaking with tongues, remarks (1 Cor. 14:18): *I thank my God, I speak with tongues more than ye all.*

Later on in the same passage Gregory adds another support to his argument against excessive allegory, this time taking as his text Proverbs 30:33: *He that strongly presseth the udder for drawing forth milk squeezeth out butter, and he that wringeth violently draweth out blood.* "For we 'press the udder strongly,' " he says, "when we weigh with minute understanding the word of sacred revelation, by which way of 'pressing' whilst we seek 'milk,' we find 'butter,' because whilst we seek to be fed with but a little insight, we are anointed with the abundance of interior richness. Which, nevertheless, we ought not to do too much nor at all times, lest while milk is sought for from the udder there should follow blood."

One of the problems that constantly besets the allegorizer is what might be called the question of the propriety of types. How can we know when the mystical strings of Scripture are being skillfully and harmoniously sounded? Saint Augustine, in commenting on the verse of the Song of Solomon that begins, *Thy teeth are as a flock of sheep* (5:6), was reminded of the way in which holy men ingest heretics, chewing them and softening them so as to absorb them back into the body of the Church. Ingenious as this is, I cannot avoid the feeling that the great Doctor has struck a discordant note, important as the corrective function of the bishops undoubtedly was. Even when the interpretation rings true—for example, the mysterious Person who appears with the three young men in the fiery furnace of Babylon (Daniel 3:24–25) is in medieval exegesis regularly interpreted as Christ—somehow the basis for such a judgment never really comes up for discussion in medieval commentaries.

Gregory does not really solve the problem of propriety, but he clearly realizes its existence, as can be observed in his comments on the verse of Job which begins, *Who hath sent out the wild ass free?* (39:5). He first identifies the ass as a type of the Desert Father, *Whose house I have made the wilderness,* says the Lord, *and the barren land his dwellings* (39:6). "But all these things which have been said of the wild ass," Gregory adds, "can be understood in another way also. Which we explain . . . in order to leave to the judgment of the reader what he believes is to be preferred." Following this modest disclaimer, he goes on to identify the ass with Christ, and then adds: "Nor let any consider it unbecoming that the Incarnate Lord can be typified by such an animal; whilst it is admitted by all that He is spoken of in Holy Scripture, as, in a certain sense, both a worm and a beetle. As it is written: *But I am a worm, and no man* [Psalm 22:6]. And as it is said by the Prophet in the Septuagint, *A beetle cried out from the wood* [Habakkuk 2:11]. Since then he is typified by the mention of such vile and abject things, what is said offensively of Him, of whom it is admitted that nothing is said appropriately?" This last is a most important qualification, as Gregory brings out in his conclusion: "For he is called a lamb, but it is for His innocence. He is called a lion, but it is for His might. He is also sometimes compared to a serpent, but it is for His death, or for His wisdom. And He can therefore be spoken of figuratively by all these, because none of all these can be essentially believed of Him."

Gregory's style as an exegete is clear and straightforward, so much so that we may sometimes fail to appreciate its judiciousness and its highly functional quality. Introducing the speeches of Elihu, for example, he warns us that this young man speaks many things that are true, but that he utters them in a spirit of pride, which the reader must notice and avoid. "For when we hear these persons speaking powerful words, and yet observe them proud of their powerful words, we enter, as it were, the garden of learning, and pluck roses from thorns. We need, therefore, careful discrimination, to cull that which is sweetly scented, and to avoid that which pricks us: lest the incautious hand of the gatherer should be wounded with the thorn of their habits, if the flower of their words happens to be carelessly gathered."

Sometimes a verse becomes the occasion for satire, though this is not as common as one might expect. The ostrich, for example, is identified as a type of hypocrite, concerning whom it is said (Job 39:16), *She is hardened against her young ones, as though they were not hers.* Gregory comments: "For thou mayest often behold them [hypocrites], having put aside the care of their children, prepare themselves for dangers of immense labour, cross seas, approach tribunals, assail princes, burst into palaces, frequent the wrangling assemblies of the people, and defend with laborious watchfulness their earthly patrimony. And if it is perchance said to them, Why do ye, who have left the world, act thus? they immediately reply, that they fear God, and that therefore they labour with such zeal in defending their patrimony." There can be little doubt that Gregory is here reflecting on the numerous visitors from all parts of Christendom who regularly and noisily besought the Pope's blessing on their various enterprises. Yet he rarely allows his impatience to get the better of him. A little later on in the discussion of hypocrites just quoted he adds thoughtfully: "When therefore we behold any persons of no mean conversation defending worldly interests passionately or immoderately, we ought to reprove this fault of theirs charitably, and yet not despair of them, while reproving them. Because there frequently exist in one and the same person certain censurable points which are apparent, and great qualities which lie concealed."

During his exposition of one of the verses in the speech of Elihu (36:30), Gregory takes the liberty of referring to one of his major interests as Pope—namely, the conversion of the gentile nations to Christianity: "For, lo! He has now penetrated the hearts of almost all nations; lo! He has joined together in one faith the boundaries of the East and of the West; lo! the tongue of Britain, which knew only how to grate barbarian sounds, has begun long since to resound in the Divine praises the Hebrew Alleluia." This allusion to his plans for the conversion of Britain, one of his most notable achievements, seems to have stirred Gregory deeply, for he inserts it in a passage charged with emotion:

> And when these clouds rain down with words, and when they disclose, by miracles, the power of their glittering light, they convert to divine love even the farthest boundaries of the world. Whence it is rightly subjoined, *He will cover also the ends of the sea.* A thing which we heard by

the voice of Elihu was to take place, but which we at this time see performed by the power of God. For the Almighty Lord has covered, with His lightening clouds, the ends of the sea; because, by the brilliant miracles of preachers, He has brought even the ends of the world to the faith. . . . Behold the ocean, which before was swelling, is now calmed beneath, and subject to, the feet of the saints; and its barbarous motions, which the princes of the earth had been unable to control with the sword, do the mouths of priests bind with simple words through fear of God: and he who, when unbelieving, had not dreaded the bands of combatants, now fears, when faithful, the tongues of the humble.

The grandness of the conception here, and the reality behind it, is matched by a brilliant fusion of biblical texts in the expression of it. A sense of wonder pervades the passage, echoing the wonder of the prophet, who said that *the kings shall shut their mouths at him* (Isaiah 52:15) and the disciples who exclaimed, *What manner of man is this, that even the wind and the sea obey him?* (Mark 4:41).

For a final example of Gregory's style as an exegete let us turn to Job's famous lines on the good fortune of the ungodly, beginning with the verse (21:7): *Wherefore do the wicked live, become old, yea, are mighty in power?* Following each of these statements, Gregory pretends to acknowledge the prosperity of the wicked as described in the verse, but then goes on to dispose of it by postulating some other respect in which the wicked man may *not* be happy, only to disclose, by quoting the next verse, that this supposition is overthrown. For example, after quoting the verse beginning *Wherefore do the wicked live . . . ?* he responds: "What good then if everything be forthcoming, but children be wanting who may become their heirs? It proceeds: *Their seed is established in their sight with them. . . .* But what if children are vouchsafed, yet the children themselves stricken with barrenness? . . . *And a crowd of kinsfolk and grandchildren before their eyes.*" Thus the exegesis continues through the entire passage, till at the end Gregory addresses Job directly: "But, O blessed man, wherefore dost thou tell us all those many things of the delights of the wicked? It is now a long time that thou runnest on in the description of them; after much said, in one word point out what thou thinkest. It goes on: *They spend their days in wealth, and in a point of time go down to the lowest parts.*" Then Gregory triumphantly announces the conclusion: "Yes, O blessed man, thou hadst for long dilated on their joys, how does thou now declare that 'in a point of time they go down to the lowest parts,' saving that all length of time of the present life is then known to be but a 'point,' when it is cut short by the end?" Thus the entire speech is seen as an

[55]

expression of ascetic contempt of the world. For Gregory, Job's dung-hill (2:8, A.V. ashes) is a thinly disguised hermitage on the slopes of Mount Sinai.

The Morals *and Modern Exegesis*

The modern reader may find the ascetic interpretation of Job attractive—indeed the popularity of the Desert Fathers appears to be growing these days—and yet it is difficult not to be conscious of the way in which it conflicts with modern interpretations of the book. An example of this is the verse just considered, on the prosperity of the wicked (Job 21:13), which in the new Revised Standard Version reads: *They spend their days in prosperity, and in peace they go down to Sheol.* Reading "peace" instead of "a point of time" naturally robs the statement of ite ascetic meaning. The modern *Interpreter's Bible* has the following comment on this verse: "He [Job] does not lower himself to formulate his envy, his resentment, or his bitterness; but he forcefully clinches his argument by concluding that the wicked 'live out their days in happiness and peace' . . . ; or [referring to the A.V. reading, "instant"] 'in an instant (i.e., without the crippling infirmities of old age and the slow disintegration of an incurable disease) they descend into the grave.' " The translation "peace" represents an unusual meaning for the Hebrew word in question, but it is confirmed by the reading of the Septuagint in this verse, and by a similar usage of the same Hebrew word in Jeremiah 6:16 ("find *rest* for your souls"). In any case, modern exegesis seems committed to this general meaning, even if the word be translated "instant" or "point of time." Before examining the *Morals on Job* directly, therefore, we need to assess the extent to which a medieval-modern conflict threatens to interfere with the modern reader's appreciation of Gregory's exegesis.

Although it would be absurd to expect Gregory to concern himself with precisely those matters that have become the business of biblical scholarship in modern times, it is only reasonable to hope that he realized the need for an accurate text—and in this respect he does not disappoint us. Near the beginning of the work he explains that he is using two translations, the "old" and the "new," referring presumably to the Old Latin version and to Jerome's Vulgate, respectively. Elsewhere he refers to the Septuagint, or Greek translation, but this may have been a way of referring to the Old Latin (which was essentially a translation of the Greek). Gregory may have picked up some Greek in Constantinople, but it is doubtful that he was able to use it with ease in biblical studies. Normally, in discussing a textual problem, he gives the variant readings, discusses them, and then concludes that either reading, or both, may be correct. This is, of course, a far cry from modern textual criticism. Here are a few examples.

Job, in answering Eliphaz, observes that *the life of man upon earth is a warfare* (7:1). Gregory comments: "In this passage in the old translation the life of man is not called 'a warfare' at all, but 'a trial,' yet if the meaning of either word be regarded, the sound that meets the ear outwardly is different, yet they make one and the same concordant meaning." This is the simplest kind of case, where no larger issues of interpretation are involved. Another instance of textual divergence occurs in the poem in praise of wisdom, where the underground path of miners is being described (28:8): *The children of the dealers have not trodden it, nor hath the lioness passed through it.* Here the crux is the word translated "dealers," as Gregory explains: "In all the Latin copies we find the word 'instructors' (*institutores*) put down, but in the Greek we find 'traders' (*negotiatores*), whereby it may be inferred that in this passage the several copyists from being ignorant put 'instructors' (*institutores*) instead of 'dealers' (*institores*)." The modern solution here, going back to the Hebrew, is very different, but given the resources he had, Gregory's resolution of the problem is quite sound, involving only what A. E. Housman ironically calls "the application of *thought* to textual criticism." Having dealt with the matter so skillfully, however, Gregory goes on to make assurance doubly sure by resolving the crux allegorically: "But both the one phrase and the other, though they disagree in utterance, yet are not at variance in meaning, because all those who instruct the practice of the faithful, carry on a spiritual dealing, that while they supply preaching to their hearers, they should receive back from them faith and right works; as where it is written touching Holy Church, *She maketh fine linen, and selleth it* [Proverbs 31:24]."

A final example of textual difficulties, and an important one, shows Gregory dealing decisively with a problem that involves larger issues of interpretation. The verse occurs in Job's monologue on his present suffering (30:21) and, as quoted, the text is similar to modern versions: *Thou art changed to cruel unto me; and in the hardness of Thy hand Thou opposest Thyself against me.* Here is Gregory's comment: "The old translation is widely at variance with this sense, because what is spoken in this concerning God, is related in that of adversaries and persecutors. Yet because this new translation is said to have transferred everything from the Hebrew and Aramaic more truly, we should believe whatever is delivered in it, and the right way is that into the word of it our interpretation should search with exactness." Thus he refuses the pious evasion of the old version, and accepts, with Jerome, Job's statement that God is cruel. This then leads him into an extended discussion of anthropomorphisms in the Bible, where the Lord is described as jealous (Exodus 34:14), repentant (Genesis 6:7), compassionate (Psalm 86:15), and foreknowing (Romans 8:29). These are explained as Holy Writ's accommodation to our infirmity, translating into human terms, as it were, the ineffable qualities of the divine. We should therefore understand that the unfavorable connotations of these words when applied to God are set aside, and Gregory concludes that "in this passage 'cruel' should be taken for one striking with severity, and not sparing the avenging of sin." We are cautioned to notice, moreover, that Job's exact words are "cruel *unto me*," thus emphasizing the subjective and emotional quality of the statement. Gregory, in other words, meets textual problems head-on, and seeks no easy escape when these in turn raise larger issues of interpretation.

When we turn from textual problems to Gregory's handling of ideas and concepts, the divergence between medieval and modern exegesis becomes more evident. In the modern view, for example, the original audience postulated for the book of Job had no generally received belief in life after death, and against this background Job's urgent quest for some such belief is seen as conducted in opposition to the prevailing orthodoxy. Hence when Eliphaz refers to death, he obviously regards it, in accordance with the general opinion, as the mellow, golden conclusion of the life of the individual (5:26): *Thou shalt come to thy grave in fulness, like as a shock of grain cometh in in his season.* Because his view of death is so completely different, Gregory turns to allegory in his exegesis of this verse: "For what is denoted by the name of the grave, saving a life of contemplation? Which as it were buries us, dead to this world, in that it hides us in the interior world away from all earthly desires." Thus at times the modern reader may feel, understandably, that Gregory is moving in one direction while the clash of ideas between Job and his friends is moving in another.

Another instance of divergence of interpretation involving death occurs in one of those dramatic passages where Job expresses his longing for some assurance of life after death, but ends in despair as he concludes that no such assurance is possible (14:1–22). *For there is hope of a tree,* he says, *if it be cut down, that it will sprout again, and that the tender branch thereof will not cease. . . . But man dieth, and wasteth away.* The thought of this becomes intolerable to Job: *O that thou wouldst hide me in the grave, that thou wouldst keep me secret, until thy wrath be past, that thou wouldst appoint me a set time, and remember me! If a man die, shall he live again? all the days of my appointed time will I wait, till my change come. Thou shalt call, and I will answer thee: thou wilt have a desire to the work of thy hands.* But after evoking this warm and intimate glimpse of life after death, at one with the Lord, Job falls back in despair, concluding that when man dares to look for something beyond the grave, he cannot sustain his faith without some assurance, and thus his hope is eventually eroded away: *The waters wear the stones; thou washest away the things which grow out of the dust of the earth; and thou destroyest the hope of man.*

As might be expected, Gregory does not give his attention to this alternating hope and despair, which means, of course, that some of Job's statements are not easy to interpret: "But herein," says the commentator, "that seems to be exceedingly hard which is added [14:12], *So man lieth down, and riseth not.* Wherefore do we so toil and labour, if we are not straining after the recompence of the Resurrection? . . . But the sentence subjoined points out what distinction there is concealed in the sentence preceding. For it is added: *Till the heavens be no more, they shall not awake, nor be raised out of their sleep.* For it is plain that they shall not rise again, that is, till the heavens be no more, in that except the end of the world come, the race of mankind shall not wake to life from the sleep of death."

The verse in which Job cries, *O that thou wouldst hide me in the grave* (Hebrew "sheol," 14:13), is in Gregory's translation rendered, *O that thou wouldst defend me in hell!* This of course invites the application, allegorically, of Christ's Harrowing of Hell to Job's words. Gregory therefore explains that the patriarchs and prophets of the Old Testament were imprisoned in Hell before the time of Christ, and then he adds:

Nor yet do we maintain that the souls of the righteous did so go down into hell, that they were imprisoned in places of punishment; but it is to be believed that there are higher regions in hell, and that there are lower regions apart, so that both the righteous might be at rest in the upper regions, and the unrighteous be tormented in the lower ones. Hence the Psalmist, by reason of the grace of God preventing him, says, *Thou hast delivered my soul from the lowest hell* [Psalm 86:13].

[59]

These divisions within the boundaries of Hell were remembered and invoked by theologians in the later Middle Ages, when theories about the salvation of the righteous heathen posed a threat to belief in the finality of damnation.

Aside from the doctrinal issues raised in this passage, however, Gregory's view of life after death sometimes affects his handling of poetic images and figures of speech. Job's metaphor of the erosion of man's hope, for example, is interpreted morally, and is taken to refer to various kinds of temptations which, unchecked, will erode man's salvation: "Again, because there is another sort of temptation, which infuses itself gently into the heart of man, and wears and wastes all the hardness of its resolution, let it be said [14:19] *The waters wear the stones;* in this way, viz. that the unremitted and soft flatteries of lust suck away the hardness of the soul, and the slow and penetrating evil habit corrodes the hard and forcible purpose of the mind." This is moral Gregory at his best, and we are grateful for it, even as we are conscious of its divergence from the drama of Job's quest for assurance of life after death.

In the next verse, near the end of this passage, Job elaborates the description of God's destruction of man's hope (14:20): *Thou prevailest for ever against him, and he passeth: thou changest his countenance, and sendest him away.* In the modern view, this verse depicts God as a stern Judge, and man as the defendant, coming before Him and wearing a hopeful expression to hear the verdict. When the Judge says, Guilty! the man's face falls, and the Judge sends him away to his doom. Gregory takes a different view: " 'The face of man is changed,' " he says, "when his form is wasted by death; but 'he is sent away,' in that from those things which he kept willingly [in his life] he is necessitated to pass away to the eternal world against his will." Here again, while we sense a digression from the central drama, we must surely be impressed by the striking ascetic reading of man's changed countance as the face of death.

Another foundation stone of modern interpreters is the assertion that Job charges God with failure to act in accordance with a system of rewards and punishments. At times, because of his own monastic outlook, Gregory reaches a curious accommodation with Job on this question, arguing that holy men are reluctant to submit to the caresses of worldly fortune, because they see prosperity as an impediment to their spiritual progress. This is of course precisely the counsel of Lady Philosophy in Boethius' *Consolation*. Worldly rewards are, for the ascetic, virtually a form of punishment, retarding him on the pilgrimage to his true home. It is his belief in the after-life, therefore, that enables Gregory to accommodate Job's idea that God permits the innocent to perish: "It often happens," he remarks, "that in this life both 'the innocent perish' and 'the righteous are utterly cut off,' yet in perishing they are reserved to eternal glory."

Gregory is quick to perceive that Job's friends do in fact believe in the doctrine of rewards and punishments, and he criticises them explicitly for this: "This is used to be the special conclusion of those going weakly, that in such proportion they esteem a man righteous as they see him obtain all that he desires; whereas in truth we know that earthly goods are sometimes withheld from the righteous, while they are bestowed with liberal bounty upon the unrighteous; see-ing that to sick persons also when they are despaired of, physicians order whatever they call for to be supplied, but those whom they foresee may be brought back to health, the things which they long for they refuse to have given to them."

Difficulties occasionally arise when Job's words are especially severe, as in his first reply to Bildad (chapter 9). Here he is goaded into arguing that God actually enjoys the suffering of the innocent (9:23): *If the scourge slay suddenly, he will laugh at the trial of the innocent.* Gregory observes: "Who would not suppose that this was uttered in pride, unless he heard the sentence of the Judge, who pronounces (42:7), *for ye have not spoken of me the thing that is right, as my servant Job hath.* He then concludes with a paraphrase of Job 9:23, interpret-ing it as an expression of longing for the coming of a Savior who will take upon himself the suffering of mankind. But he must have felt some doubt about this, for he goes on to offer an alternative: "Or indeed if he uses the expression of God's 'laughing' for His joy, the Lord is said to 'laugh at the pains of the innocent,' in that the more ardently He is sought of us, the more graciously He rejoices over us. For we as it were cause a kind of joy to Him by our pain, when by holy desires, we chasten ourselves for the love of Him."

One of Job's most explicit accusations against God, very difficult to rationalize, comes later on in another reply to Bildad (19:6): *Know now at least that God hath afflicted me with no just judgment.* The sharp-ness of the charge is a little blunted in the Authorized Version, *Know now that God hath overthrown me,* and perhaps also in the modern Revised Standard Version, *Know then that God has put me in the wrong;* but the modern understanding of this verse is made clear by the comment in the *Interpreter's Bible:* "Job is plainly and bluntly stating that God, the author of his plight, has willfully distorted the truth concerning him."

Gregory responds to this verse:

> O how hard does the voice of the righteous man sound, suffering under the infliction of the rod! which same, however, not pride, but grief gave vent to! Now he is not righteous, who gives up righteousness under sorrow; and blessed Job, because he had a meek spirit, did not sin even by a hard word. For if we say that he did err by this voice, we make out that the devil accomplished what he purposed, when he said [2:5, A.V.], *Touch his bone and his flesh, and he will curse thee to thy face.* Therefore a serious question arises; for if he did not sin in that he says, *Know now at least that God has not afflicted me with a just judgment,* we agree to God's having done something unjustly, which is profane to say; but if he did sin, then the devil made appear concerning him the thing that he promised.

Faced with this apparent dilemma of exegesis, Gregory proceeds to introduce, not one, but a series of brilliant solutions. Here is the first:

> Thus blessed Job had turned his eyes to his own life, and he estimated the strokes which he was undergoing, and saw that it was not just that upon such a life such strokes should be dealt. And when he says that he was not afflicted by a just judgment, he spoke that, with unreserved voice, which God in his own secrecy had said concerning him to his adversary [2:3], *thou movedst me against him, to afflict him without cause.* For what God expresses, that He "had afflicted blessed Job without cause," this blessed Job asserts again in the words that he was not "afflicted of the Lord by a just judgment." Wherein then did he sin, who was in nothing at odds with the sentence of his Maker?

Not satisfied with this, Gregory continues: "But perhaps some one will say, that for us to speak that good concerning ourselves, which the Judge may have said in secret concerning us, cannot be done without sin." And he goes on to dispose of this objection by saying that no sin is incurred if the truth is not spoken in pride. He then raises a more difficult question, namely, since God does nothing without a reason, why does He say that He has afflicted Job "without cause"? The solution to this problem is found in the doctrine of the chastising of the righteous: "For our just Creator by those many strokes inflicted upon blessed Job did not aim to do away with evil qualities in him, but to increase his merits; and so that was just, which he did in the heightening of his good deserts; but it did not seem equitable, because it was thought to be the punishing of instances of sin." Once more, Gregory's monastic viewpoint brings him safely through a perilous passage in the text of Job.

These examples of the divergence of medieval and modern exegesis should not be allowed to obscure the fact that Gregory clearly apprehended the central thesis of the book of Job, with its emphasis on the protagonist's acceptance of God's will under all circumstances of this life. This is the heroic state of mind recommended to Boethius by Lady Philosophy; it is what Shakespeare, in *Antony and Cleopatra*, calls the shackling of accidents. Gregory makes his point decisively when he says, in speaking of the state of Job's mind, that "no bad fortune throws down the man, whom no good fortune corrupts. For he who is attached to the truth is in no degree brought under to vanity, because, whereas he has planted with a firm foot the bent of the thought within, all that is brought to pass in change without, reaches not in the least degree to the citadel of the interior."

A true appraisal of Gregory's exegesis must include an acknowledgement that his approach to Job is static, in that he sees no dramatic progression from ignorance to spiritual knowledge, whereas this progression is the essence of the modern interpretation. In this respect Gregory's view corresponds to the flatness of medieval art, as opposed to the three dimensional quality of art in the Renaissance. But since this observation is merely flattering to our modern inclinations, perhaps we should pay more attention to those features of Gregory's exposition which underline the superiority of his approach, namely the ways in which his intense faith and conviction illuminate the text, and render irrelevant the groping, despairing Job of modern exegesis.

The Three Levels of Meaning

"There are some parts," says Gregory in his introduction, "which we go through in a historical exposition, some we trace out in allegory upon an investigation of the typical meaning, some we open in the lessons of moral teaching alone, allegorically conveyed, while there are some few which, with more particular care, we search out in all these ways together, exploring them in a threefold method." For a true impression of the commentary as a whole, therefore, we will follow its organization by considering our examples in the order of historical, allegorical, and moral exegesis.

Although we are frequently admonished to maintain "reverence for the history" of Job, there are times when this literal level seems to make non-sense, and requires careful analysis. Such is the case with the opening speech of Job in chapter 3, when he curses the day of his birth. "He who looks to the text," observes Gregory,

> and does not acquaint himself with the sense of the holy word, is not so much furnishing himself with instruction as bewildering himself in uncertainty, in that the literal words sometimes contradict themselves; but whilst by their oppositeness they stand at variance with themselves, they direct the reader to a truth that is to be understood. . . . For as we see the face of strange persons, and know nothing of their hearts, but if we are joined to them in familiar communication, by frequency of conversation we even trace their very thoughts; so when in holy writ the historical narration alone is regarded, nothing more than the face is seen.

The commentator goes on to pile example upon example of the difficulty of the literal level, and then he adds: "Therefore because these words are, on the surface, at variance with reason, the letter itself thereby points out, that in those words the Saint delivers nothing after the letter." Other examples in the Old Testament are David cursing the mountains of Gilboa (2 Samuel 1:21), and Jeremiah who, like Job, curses the day of his birth (20:15). Since these also do not "make sense," they are interpreted according to the spirit—David's curse allegorically and Jeremiah's morally. Speaking in general of this type of text, Gregory concludes, "Doubtless this is so much the more full of deeper mystery within, as it lacks human reason without."

In spite of this traditional precaution about the literal level, which could easily become a license for reckless allegorizing, Gregory rarely invokes it, though the book of Job offers many opportunities. Instead he often takes great pains to justify the historical reading by elaboration of its context. Thus we are told that Job's friends speak in a spirit of pride, which God rebukes at the end of the book when He praises Job, and rejects the words of his friends. Yet some of these words are quoted with approval in the New Testament, for example, Paul, when addressing the Corinthians, quotes Eliphaz (Job 5:13), saying (1 Cor. 3:19), *For it is written, He taketh the wise in their own craftiness.* Gregory conscientiously points out the problem: "How then do we reject as evil what Paul establishes by authority? or how shall we account that to be right by the testimony of Paul, which the Lord by His own lips determined not to be right?" He then points out that the sentiments of the friends were often true and good, but they were wrong in applying them to Job, the good man. Thus Gregory does not take the easy way out by invoking the doctrine of uniform revela-

[64]

tion, but often goes to great lengths to justify his reading with common sense and discrimination.

One of the criticisms leveled by Eliphaz is that Job despises the chastening of the Almighty (5:17), or, as it is in the Vulgate, he "reproves the correction of the Lord." This of course raises the issue whether Job, in questioning God about his suffering, is guilty of impatience. Gregory meets this issue by distinguishing between suffering which is inflicted because of sin, and suffering which is a testing or trial of the virtues of a good man: "But they that are stricken, not for the cleansing of guilt, but for the testing of their fortitude, when they inquire into the causes of the stroke, must by no means be said to 'reprove the correction of the Lord'; for their aim is to discover in themselves what they are ignorant of. And hence blessed Job, breaking out into a voice of liberty, amidst the visitings of the scourge, the more rightly questions the judgments of the smiter concerning him, the more he is really ignorant of causes for his suffering in himself." Thus Eliphaz is in the wrong for assuming that Job's suffering was a form of punishment for sin.

A more difficult case occurs in Job's reply to Eliphaz (7:16): *I have given over hope, I will not live any longer.* "Far be it from us," Gregory exclaims, "to think that the holy man should despair of the bountifulness of God's mercy. . . . But lest we seem violently to wrest his sayings according to the caprice of our own view, we ought to form our own estimate of what is promised by that which follows after. For in what sense he said this, he does himself immediately point out, in that he adds, *Spare me, O Lord, for my days are nothing.*" Notice that here Gregory resolves a contradiction without resorting to allegory; he does this by reading Job's words dramatically, seeing them as expressions of emotion, rather than statements of fact.

In some cases, however, after providing sound dramatic motivation for Job's words, Gregory will go on to give an allegorical interpretation as well. This happens, for example, when he is introducing Job's recitation of his own good deeds in the monologue of chapter 29: "For amidst so many pains of wounding and words of despair, when he tells the things which he did, his mind as it were sunk down by words and wounds, he sets anew to hope. So let him say the good things he has done, that he may not be forced, in the midst of so many evil things that he hears, to despair of himself [29:15]: *I was eyes to the blind, feet was I to the lame.*" This is then further supported by the example of Paul (2 Cor. 11:22ff.) in his "boasting" to the Corinthians. Thus Gregory supplies realistic psychological motivation, above and beyond the good intended to the friends by the example of Job's virtues. Yet he continues: "Which same words, if we refer to the utterance of Holy Church by a typical mode of interpretation, the same is 'eyes to the blind,' because she gives light by the word, and the same 'feet to the lame,' because she stays them up by support. . . . Thus then Holy Church, being seized by tribulation at the end, calls to mind the old times when she was accustomed both to enlighten by teaching and to establish by helping, and speak with the lips of her foregoing member, saying, *I was an eye to the blind, and a foot was I to the lame.*"

Occasionally Gregory will provide a historical note to the text in the fashion of modern exegesis, as when he comments on a legal reference in Job's oath of clearing (31:21): *If I have lifted up my hand against the fatherless, when I saw my help in the gate.* "It was the custom with those of old," he explains, "that the elders should sit at the gate to make out by judicial trial the quarrels of persons at strife, in order that the city, in which it was befitting that they should dwell in concord, they should never enter at variance. And hence the Lord saith by the Prophet [Amos 5:15]: *Establish judgment in the gate.*" Similarly, a little further on in the same chapter he explains Job's reference to sun and moon worship by citing the worship of the hosts of heaven (2 Kings 17:16) during the reign of King Ahaz. But these notes are few and far between, perhaps partly because they were not considered so important a part of exegesis, and partly because references requiring this kind of historical explanation are comparatively rare in the book of Job.

The climax of the entire book, of course, and a crux in its interpretation, is the speech of God from the whirlwind. It is certainly difficult for the modern reader not to regard this speech as an arbitrary display of divine power, crushing Job's questions rather than answering them. College students, I have noticed, almost without fail take exception to it. "I think," said one ironically, "we could do without that lesson in meteorology at the end." I have also noticed, in a few students, a positive reaction, more difficult to cope with than the negative one. Such was the response of a student who came to see me after class one day, obviously impressed by the magnificent lines of God's cross-examination (38:33), *Knowest thou the ordinances of heaven? canst thou set the dominion thereof in the earth?* and his devastating question (40:9), *Hast thou an arm like God? or canst thou thunder with a voice like him?* To which my student responded with great enthusiasm: "The answer is—yes! We are doing it!"

Such a reading, of course, is worlds away from the medieval view. Gregory does not, however, regard God's speech as having the purpose or the effect of crushing Job. After all, he says, God is about to announce his decision in favor of Job, and to restore his possessions double fold. Hence "Almighty God is obliged," he explains, "to reprove with strict justice him whom He preserves alive, lest his very victory should lay him low with the sword of pride." And he continues: "But O how mightily is he exalted, who is so sublimely humbled! O how great is the victory of the man, to have been foiled on comparison with God! O how much greater is he than men, who is proved by testimony to be less than God!" Thus by placing the speech in the context of the book as a whole, Gregory effectively supports the justness of God's response. To this, furthermore, he adds a remarkable bit of dramatic realism by suggesting, among various alternatives, that God's words did not come to Job as an external voice, but from within Job himself: "For commotions of the air could have been made by an angel, and these words, which are subjoined [that is, the speech of God], could have been delivered by him. And again, both an angel could agitate the air in a whirlwind without, and the Lord could sound into his heart, without words, the force of His sentence by Himself within; in order that it may be believed that he who, when filled with God, heard these things without words, himself uttered in words the sayings of the Lord." This comes very close to the traditional conception of divine inspiration, and strikes a nice balance between the extremes, on the one hand, of submerging the divine initiative in the human agency, and, on the other hand, of allowing God, as it were, to override the personality of Job. In exegesis like this, Gregory is unsurpassed in his penetrating psychological insight.

Turning now to the allegorical level, we may begin by briefly describing how the allegory works in Gregory's commentary. Job is seen, first of all, as a type of Christ, whose sufferings anticipate the Passion of the Redeemer. The devil removes from Job all of his possessions, his servants, and his family, just as he took from Christ His people (the Jews) and even the Apostles in His time of trial. Job was covered with boils, even as Christ was covered with wounds in the Crucifixion, and also as His Body (the Church) was subsequently wounded with persecutions. This extension of the allegory from

Christ to the Church is characteristic, and Gregory often refers both meanings to one and the same passage, by observing that what has been spoken concerning the Head (Christ) may likewise be said of the Body (the Church). The friends of Job, who speak in pride, are likened to heretics, who, coming with the pretense of helping him, attack him viciously instead. Even though this is the least convincing part of Gregory's exegesis for the modern reader, the allegory is set forth with consistency and considerable skill.

Aside from the main lines of the allegory, it is worth noting that Gregory is often attentive to details as well, and the rich incremental repetition in the poetry of Job encourages this. Eliphaz, for example, speaks eloquently and figuratively of God's vengeance against the wicked man (4:10): *The roaring of the lion, and the voice of the lioness, and the teeth of the young lions, are broken.* In commenting on this verse, Gregory asks rhetorically: "For what does he call *the roaring of the lion* but . . . the severe character of that man? What *the voice of the lioness,* but his wife's loquacity? What *the teeth of the young lions,* but the greediness of his children?" A new dimension is added, moreover, when we realize that the lion may be understood on the side of either good or evil: "Forasmuch as the nature of everything is compounded of different elements, in Holy Writ different things are allowably represented by any one thing. For the lion has magnanimity, it also has ferocity: by its magnanimity then it represents the Lord, by its ferocity the devil." Gregory sees this duality again in the eagle that hastens to the prey (9:26), where the eagle is first associated with the Incarnation, and then with the Fall of man.

A difficulty with the allegorical reading of a text, as we have seen, is the establishment of criteria in support of it. Gregory does not deal with this problem directly, but there are times when he does seem conscious of it. After having expounded Job's words for some time as applicable to Christ, for instance, Gregory, before introducing one of the most famous passages, pauses for a moment: "Now we say with justice that blessed Job uses the accents of our Redeemer and His Church, if we find anything that he says explicitly of that same Redeemer of us men; for how is it to be believed that he teaches us anything connected with Him in a figure, if he does not point Him out to us in express words? But now let him disclose to us what he is sensible of concerning Him, and let him take away from us all misgivings in our thoughts." He then quotes the memorable verse (19:25): *For I know that my Redeemer liveth,* and adds: "Let him reflect with what a weight of punishment he deserves to be stricken, if he still does not believe his own resurrection, who now knows the resurrection of the Lord which has taken place, if even he [Job] believed his own, who was still waiting for the resurrection of the Lord Jesus to be brought to pass." Thus to Gregory Christ's resurrection is not an "answer to Job" (to use Carl Jung's phrase), but a fulfillment of Job's faith that it would occur.

At times the allegorical interpretation could best be described as a case of the New Testament "drowning out" or overriding the Old Testament. This is quite understandable, of course, in view of the fact that the early Church came to a knowledge of the Old Testament only through the New. But one wonders whether, by the time of Gregory, the importance of the Gospels and Epistles in the liturgy may not have reinforced this tendency. Certainly Gregory gave sermons on the Gospels regularly—forty of them have survived—and he was undoubtedly called upon to speak on Paul's epistles almost as frequently. Perhaps these practical considerations contribute to our feeling that the vivid presence of the New Testament breaks through in his allegorical exegesis, and draws our attention from Job to New Testament narrative and in particular to the life and letters of Paul.

In the speech, for example, describing the habits of the animals, God mentions the raven (38:41) whose young ones wander about for lack of meat. Gregory likens the wandering of these young ones to the running about of eager preachers, illustrated particularly by the journeys of Paul described in the book of Acts. This idea is elaborated when we come to the calving of the hinds (39:3), *They bow themselves for the birth, and bring forth, and utter roarings,* concerning which Gregory remarks:

> For to speak of one out of many, I see Paul, like a hind, uttering roarings of great pain in his pangs of birth. For he says [Galatians 4:19], *My little children, of whom I travail in birth again, till Christ be formed in you, I desire to be with you now, and to change my voice, since I am perplexed for you.* Lo, he wishes to change his voice in his child-birth, that the voice of preaching may be turned into the roaring of pain. He wishes to change his voice, because those whom he had already brought forth by preaching, he was again bringing forth with groans in forming them anew.

In exegesis of this kind, it seems to me, the linking of the two testaments is less harmonious than it is in the other examples we have examined, where a purer typology prevails.

Although Gregory usually emphasizes one particular line of

allegorical interpretation, there are times when he tosses out several possibilities at once. Such is the case in his comment on the mountains that bring forth grass for Behemoth (40:20, Vulgate 40:15):

> By a mountain is expressed the covenant of God, as Habakkuk says [Habakkuk 3:3], *God will come from Libanus, and the Holy One from the shady and thick mountain.* . . . And this covenant is well said to be a shady and thick mountain, because it is darkened by the thick obscurities of allegories. Again, by a mountain is designated the apostate angel, as is said to preachers concerning the ancient enemy under the character of the King of Babylon [Isaiah 13:2], *Lift ye up a banner upon the gloomy mountain.* For holy preachers lift up a banner above the gloomy mountain, when they exalt the virtue of the cross against the pride of Satan, which is frequently concealed under the mist of hypocrisy.

Earlier in the discussion of exegesis I was somewhat critical of Saint Augustine's fanciful allegorizing of the Song of Solomon, but I must confess that Gregory cites his interpretation of the verse, *Thy teeth are as a flock of sheep,* with complete approval, and even matches it with a line from the description of Leviathan (41:14, Vulgate 41:5), *In a circle is the terror of his teeth:* "The teachers of errors are typified by the teeth of this Leviathan: because they mangle with their bite the life of the reprobate, and offer them, when withdrawn from the integrity of truth, in the sacrifice of falsehood." But such elaborations are rare, and while Gregory's allegorizing is not the main strength of his commentary, it is saved from excesses by his customary common sense.

The moral sense of Scripture particularly fascinated Gregory, and he devotes more space to it than to either of the other two levels of meaning. In some parts, particularly the narrative portions of Job, the moral interpretation is highly structured, and is made congruent with the events of the story. Thus Job's seven sons represent the seven virtues of the Holy Spirit (Isaiah 11:2), his three daughters are Faith, Hope, and Charity, and the great household represents "the multitude of our thoughts." When the sons feast in their houses, the seven virtues are feeding the mind. But into this tranquil scene comes the intruder, Satan. Gregory comments: "It very often happens that the old enemy craftily blends and unites himself with those good thoughts which are sown in our hearts through the instrumentality of the coming of the Holy Spirit, to disorder all that is rightly conceived. . . . But He, who created us, does not forsake us in our temptation. For our enemy, who hid himself in ambush against us, He makes easy to be discovered by us, through the illumination of

[70]

His light. Wherefore He saith to him immediately, *Whence comest thou?"*

Moreover, when a great wind smites the four corners of the house, strong temptation is shaking the four cardinal virtues; but no matter how severely the mind is disturbed by Satan's assault, reason invariably returns to reassure it, saying: *I only am escaped alone to tell thee.* Indeed, in the very occurrence of fall and recovery, a creative process is operating: "Sometimes while we are congratulating ourselves that we do everything with grave deliberation, some piece of chance takes us in the nick, and we are carried off with a sudden precipitancy; and we, who believed ourselves always to have lived by method, are in a moment laid waste with an inward confusion. Yet by the discipline of this very confusion we learn not to attribute our counsels to our own powers; and we hold to gravity with the more matured endeavors, that we return to the same as if once lost."

The moral interpretations are often ingenious and intricate, but it is in the digressions on the inner workings of the mind that Gregory is at his best. Hear his comment on the value of speaking one's mind: "For if the tongue declared with calmness the annoyance inflicted, grief would flow away from our consciousness. For closed wounds give more acute pain, in that when the corruption that ferments within is discharged, the pain is laid open favorably for our recovery." On bad teachers: "They are upheld by scholarship in the sacred Law, they deliver lessons of instruction, they fortify by testimonies every notion that they entertain; but they do not hereby seek the life of their hearers, but applause for themselves." On good and bad minds in debate: "Bad minds, if they have once broken out into the eagerness of opposition, whether what they hear from those that withstand them be right or wrong, assail it with contradictory replies: for whereas the speaker is unwelcome from being in opposition, not even what is right is welcome when he utters it. But, on the other hand, the hearts of the good, whose dislike rises not at the speaker but at the offence, in such sort pass sentence on what is amiss, as to adopt still any right things that are said." On the mixture of virtue and vice: "For often our good points are spoilt by deceit robbing us, in that earthly desires unite themselves to our right actions; oftentimes they come to nought from sloth intervening, in that, love waxing cold, they are starved of the fervour in which they began. And so because the stealth of sin is scarcely got the better of even in the very act of virtue, what safeguard remains for our security, but that even in our virtue, we ever tread with fear and caution?" And, finally, on the value of adversity: "But oftentimes Divine mercy breaks by the encounter of sudden adversity those whom it sees going into the unruliness of lawless freedom, that being crushed they may learn with what damnable exaltation they had been swollen, that being now tamed by the experience of the scourge, they might, like tame animals, yield the mind's neck to the reins of the commandments, and go along the ways of the present life at the ruler's beck."

In addition to these brief and incisive comments, Gregory sometimes allows himself a more extensive exploration of the human mind. One instance is his analysis of the psychology of the damned: "The mind of man has for the most part this thing proper to it, that as soon as ever it falls into transgression, it is still further removed from the knowledge of self. . . . Hence it is that lost sinners, whilst subject to sins to be lamented, rejoice; concerning whom it is said by Solomon [Proverbs 2:14]: *Who rejoice to do evil, and delight in the worst things.*"

The counterpart to this passage is what might be called an analysis of the psychology of salvation, a very perceptive description of the operation of conscience:

For as we do not notice how our limbs grow, our body increases, our appearance changes, our hair turns from black to white (for all these things take place in us without our knowing it), in like manner is our mind changed from itself, by the very habit of anxiety every moment of our life; and we do not perceive it, unless we sit down to carefully watch our inmost condition, and weigh our advances and failures day by day. For in this life, to stand still is in itself to go back, as it were, to our old state, and when the mind is left undisturbed, it is overpowered by an old age, as it were, of torpor. . . . Whence it is said by the Prophet, under the character of Ephraim [Hosea 7:9], *Strangers have devoured his strength, and he knew it not, but even gray hairs are sprinkled on him, and he himself was ignorant of it.* But when the mind enquires into itself, and examines itself carefully with penitence, it is renewed from this its old nature, by being bathed with tears, and kindled with grief; and, though it had been well nigh frozen with the chill of age, it grows afresh by a supply of the zeal of inward love.

Having observed the psychological character of Gregory's moral exegesis, we must now turn, finally, to a consideration of the sources of his strength as an interpreter. For there can be little doubt that the virtues we have observed in his commentary rest on solid ascetic foundations. Gregory's exegesis is inseparable from his monasticism. As has already been suggested, he sees Job as a saint of the desert, a point of view which is maintained throughout his interpretation of the book.

We see this asceticism clearly when Gregory establishes a context for Job's opening curse. He wishes to make it clear, of course, that Job is not impatient, and at the same time he wants to provide realistic psychological motivation for his moral interpretation of the speech:

> For in fact he [Job] saw his friends weeping and wailing . . . he saw them struck dumb at the thought of his affliction; and the Saint perceived that those whose hearts were set upon temporal prosperity, took him, by a comparison with their own feelings, for one broken hearted with his temporal adversity. He considered that they would never be weeping for him in despair, who was stricken with a transient ill, except they had themselves withdrawn their soul in despair from the hope of inward soundness; and while he outwardly burst forth into the voice of grief, he showed to persons inwardly wounded the virtue of a healing medicine, saying, *Let the day perish wherein I was born.*

This "healing medicine" is the ascetic's contempt of the world, the philosophy of the Desert Fathers, as Gregory makes evident in his explication: "What then is it to curse the day of his birth, but to say plainly, 'May the day of change perish, and the light of eternity burst forth!' "

Ascetic contempt for the world, although a striking feature of the Middle Ages, has not often been favorably regarded by modern historians. For one thing, it seems to be socially irresponsible. Why didn't the Essenes leave their desert caves and help the Jewish patriots cope with the Romans? Why did the Desert Fathers turn their backs on Roman civilization? Gregory himself seems at times to describe them as in retreat from society: "Holy men then are objects of scorn without, and as unworthy persons have every indignity put upon them, yet in sure confidence that they are meet for the heavenly realms, they look with certainty for the glory of the eternal world. And when they are hard pressed without in the assaults of persecution, they fall back within into the fortified stronghold of their mind; and thence they look down upon all things passing far below them, and amongst them they see passing even themselves as in the body." Thus in achieving a state of contempt for worldly affairs the ascetic is able to stand outside himself, and view this little spot of earth under the aspect of eternity.

But common sense tells us that this is not the whole story. Gregory himself, as we have seen, combined dedication to Benedict's rule with conscientious service in the Roman administration, and, when he became Pope, turned monks into missionaries. Hence, as we might have anticipated, the social side of asceticism is not neglected in his commentary:

> It is well on this point to lift up the eyes of the mind, and to see the Elect of God, who are suffering oppression without, what a fortress of strength they are masters of within. For all that is high and exalted without, in their secret view is grovelling, from the contempt they feel. For transported above themselves in the interior, they fix their mind on high, and all that they meet with in this life, they look upon as passing away far below unconnected with themselves, and so to speak, while they strive by the Spirit to become quit of the flesh, almost the very things they are undergoing, they are blind to. For in their eyes whatsoever is exalted in time, is not high. For as though set upon the summit of a high mountain, they look down upon the flats and levels of the present life, and rising above themselves in spiritual loftiness, they see made subject to themselves, within, all that swells highest without in carnal glorying.

The above passage gives us a remarkable description of the ascetic viewpoint of monasticism in the early days of Christianity. The holy men of the North African desert were regarded as Outsiders, separated from all mundane affairs, whose reputation for rigorous objectivity led the kings and princes of this world to go to them for the settlement of political differences. The archtypal desert monk, for Gregory, was Moses, who came in from the wilderness to denounce the Egyptian monarch, abasing him by the authority of the Spirit. "Thus it is that Moses, coming from the wilderness, encounters the king of Egypt with authority, saying [Ex. 10:3]: *Thus saith the Lord God of the Hebrews, How long wilt thou refuse to humble thyself before me? let my people go, that they may serve me.*"

Yet Gregory does at times seem conscious of the apparent paradox of contempt for the world combined with social responsibility. Chaucer's monk put it this way: How shall the world be served? Gregory almost seems to anticipate this question and answer it:

> But how is it that we know that most of the old Fathers at once interiorly held fast this wisdom, and outwardly administered the affairs of the world in ordinary? Do we call Joseph deprived of the attainment of this wisdom, who in the time of dearth taking upon himself the affairs of all Egypt, not only furnished provisions to the Egyptians, but by the skilfulness of his administration preserved the life of foreign people as well that came to him? Did Daniel prove a stranger to this wisdom, who, when he was made by the king of the Chaldeans in

[74]

Babylon chief of the governors, was busied with greater charges in proportion as by a higher pitch of dignity he was likewise set above all? Whereas then it is plain that very often even the good are engaged in earthly charges with no interest, we plainly see that in this way the citizens of Jerusalem sometimes render service to Babylon, in like manner as oftentimes the citizens of Babylon pay suit and service to Jerusalem. For there are some persons who preach the word of life for the displaying of wisdom alone, and they minister the succour of alms from the passion of vain-glory; and indeed the things they do seem to be proper to Jerusalem, but yet are they citizens of Babylon.

Gregory then suggests that the wisdom of ascetics in fact makes them better administrators of affairs than ordinary men, because they lack worldly ambition, and are therefore better able to bear the turmoils of business.

Along with this concern for the functional value of asceticism, Gregory occasionally expresses the more conventional kind of self-denial associated with the monastic life. In one passage, for example, he denounces lust of the flesh in the classic manner, taking as his text Job's remark (24:20), *The worm is his sweetness.* "For what is our flesh," he exclaims,

but "rottenness" and "the worm"? And whosoever pants with carnal desires, what else does he but love "the worm"? For what the substance of the flesh is, our graves bear witness. What parent, what faithful friend can bear to touch the flesh of one, however beloved, fraught with worms? . . . Nothing has so much efficacy to subdue the appetite of carnal desire, as for every one to consider what that which he loves alive will be when dead. For when we consider the corruption of the flesh, we see in a moment, that when the flesh is unlawfully lusted after, corruption is desired. Therefore it is well said of the mind of the lustful man, *the worm is his sweetness,* in that he who is on fire with the desire of carnal corruption, pants after the stink of rottenness.

This is a vivid statement of the philosophy that later produced the loathsome cadavers carved in stone, resting sardonically beneath the magnificent outer surfaces of medieval tombs.

At the same time, Gregory places restraints on the hatred of the flesh, a doctrine which at certain periods in the history of monasticism was carried to extremes. An occasion for Gregory's warning against excessive denial of the flesh is provided by a verse describing the wild ass (39:7): *He heareth not the cry of the exactor.* Here the exactor is interpreted as the belly, and there is a long discourse on gluttony, which leads to a definition of the mean between the extremes of self-indulgence and self-denial: "It is necessary," he argues, "for a man so to maintain the citadel of continence, as to destroy, not the flesh, but the vices of the flesh. For frequently, when the flesh is restrained more than is just, it is weakened even for the exercise of good works, so as to be unequal to prayer also or preaching, whilst it hastens to put out entirely the incentives of vices within itself. . . . But often, whilst we attack an enemy therein, we kill a citizen also whom we love; and often while we spare, as it were, a fellow-citizen, we nurture an enemy for battle."

These examples underline the importance of Gregory's asceticism in the shaping of his commentary on Job, particularly that part concerned with the moral level of meaning. But lest we lose sight of the forward movement of the exegesis, I wish to conclude our survey with a review of the interpretation of one complete passage: the description of the horse in God's interrogation of Job (39:19–25). First let me quote this passage in full, in a form corresponding to the text of the Vulgate which Gregory had in front of him:

> *Wilt thou give the horse strength,*
> *or wilt thou surround his neck with neighing?*
> *Wilt thou rouse him as the locusts?*
> *The glory of his nostrils is terror.*
> *He diggeth up the earth with his hoof.*
> *He exulteth boldly, he goeth on to meet the armed men.*
> *He mocketh at fear,*
> *and yieldeth not to the sword.*
> *Over him will rattle the quiver.*
> *The spear will shake, and the shield.*
> *Raging and snorting he swalloweth the earth,*
> *neither believeth he that the blast of the trumpet soundeth.*
> *When he heareth the trumpet, he saith, Vah!*
> *He smelleth the battle afar off,*
> *the exhortation of the captains,*
> *and the howling of the army.*

Since Gregory devotes a great deal of space to each of these verses, what follows here is but a bare summary of his interpretation. First, the horse is to be understood as a holy preacher, who receives strength by overcoming sin in himself, and then attains to neighing, that is, the voice of preaching for instructing others. The neighing is said to *surround his neck* in that a preacher is restrained by his own words from doing evil, even as the fighting man who has won a collar for bravery is restrained from cowardice by the collar which he wears.

The horse is roused as the locust, since holy men, like the locust, first raise themselves on their legs and then fly with their wings—

that is, first they strengthen themselves by good works in the active life, and then fly with the wings of contemplation. Moreover, again like locusts, they scarcely rise from the ground in the cool of the morning, but in the heat of the day they gladly soar aloft—in that during quiet times in the life of the Church they appear lowly, whereas in the heat of persecution they soar on high with sublime devotion to heavenly things.

The nostrils of the horse represent the preacher's foreknowledge and expectation of the Last Judgment, and *the glory of his nostrils is terror* because the wicked will rightly fear the coming doom. But the holy preacher who is conscious of good works looks forward to this day, as did Paul, for example, when he exclaimed (2 Timothy 4:6–7), *I am now ready to be offered, and the time of my dissolution is at hand. I have fought a good fight; I have finished my course; I have kept the faith.*

This horse *diggeth up the earth with his hoof* when each holy man despises the things of this world, and carefully searches his mind to dig out and remove all earthly thoughts. And when thus protected from the wrath to come by true penitence, *he exulteth boldly,* because he is neither elated by prosperity nor bowed down by adversity, and he rejoices at the prospect of enduring punishment, as did the Apostles who rejoiced *that they were counted worthy to suffer shame for the name of Jesus* (Acts 5:41). Moreover he takes the initiative against the wicked, in that *he goeth to meet the armed men.* Such was the case with Paul, who at Ephesus had to be restrained by the love of his friends and disciples from entering the riotous theater at the risk of his life (Acts 19:28–31). At the same time, each holy man must exercise discretion in his boldness, as did Paul when he escaped from Damascus by being lowered through a window in a basket (2 Corinthians 11:32–33).

The holy preacher *mocketh at fear, and yieldeth not to the sword,* when he refuses to be cowed by persecution. Thus Paul says, *Who shall separate us from the love of Christ? shall tribulation, or distress? or famine, or persecution?* (Romans 8:35). But the enemies of the righteous *have made ready their arrows in the quiver, that they may shoot in darkness at the upright in heart* (Psalm 11:2). Hence *over him will rattle the quiver* when those who failed in attacking him openly begin to wait in ambush or to threaten punishment by hints and signs. Yet at last *the spear will shake, and the shield,* as the wicked once more resort to open violence, shielding themselves meanwhile from the arrows of truth launched against them by the holy preacher.

The preacher exhibits his zeal in converting sinners even in the

[77]

midst of severe punishment; hence it is said that *raging and snorting he swalloweth the earth*, which applies well to Paul, who, after being stoned and left for dead, rose up and returned to the city, so that even death was unable to restrain him (Acts 14:19–22). And concerning the holy man who is zealous in preaching salvation it is well said, *neither believeth he that the blast of the trumpet soundeth;* for the trumpet is the voice of worldly authority, prohibiting the proclamation of the gospel, which trumpet the preacher ignores in his zeal to proclaim it.

But when the voice of worldly power is raised against him and threatens persecution, the preacher rejoices in expectation of his approaching peril and death. Hence *when he heareth the trumpet he saith, Vah!* as did Paul when he said, *I have a desire to be dissolved, and to be with Christ* (Philemon 23). Every man trembles at the thought of his death, yet the holy man goes to his suffering with confidence because he has prepared himself for the battle in advance. Thus it is that *he smelleth the battle afar off*, for he has weighed what the wicked leaders and their bestial followers are able to do against the Elect, that is, *he has heard the exhortation of the captains, and the howling of the army.*

Pope Gregory was a Roman who never set foot in Britain nor understood the English language. Nevertheless he was fondly regarded by the Anglo-Saxons as their apostle, and his influence upon them was profound indeed. Bede's *Ecclesiastical History* was greatly indebted to Gregory's *Dialogues*, Cynewulf's poem on the Ascension was inspired directly by one of his homilies on the Gospels, and his influence is to be seen throughout the writings of Ælfric. The *Dialogues* were translated into English for King Alfred by Wærferth, Bishop of Worcester, and the *Pastoral Care* was translated in part by Alfred himself. Beyond these obvious facts, Gregory's most profound contribution to Anglo-Saxon culture was, I believe, in the realm of the spirit—that militant asceticism which we have seen throughout his commentary on the book of Job. This is the spirit that dominates the moody reflections of the *Wanderer*, the stoic intensity of the *Dream of the Rood*, and the wise meditations of the Danish King Hrothgar in *Beowulf*, as we shall have occasion to observe in the next chapter devoted to the literature of the Old English period.

CHAPTER THREE

Old English Translations and Paraphrases

THE Venerable Bede, in his *Ecclesiastical History of the English People* (A.D. 731), tells how Saint Gregory first became interested in the conversion of the heathen Anglo-Saxons to Christianity:

They say that one day, when merchants had recently arrived, and many things for sale were collected in the market-place, and many people had assembled to buy them, Gregory came himself with the rest, and saw among other wares some boys put up for sale, white of body, pleasing in countenance, and also with very beautiful hair. When he saw them, he inquired, they say, from what region or country they had been brought. And he was told that they were from the island of Britain, whose inhabitants were of such appearance. Again, he asked whether the islanders were Christians, or still bound in pagan errors. He was told that they were pagans. And, drawing a deep sigh from the depths of his heart, he said: "Alas, the pity, that the author of darkness should possess men of such bright countenances, and that so graceful an outward form should contain a mind destitute of internal grace." Accordingly, he inquired again, what was the name of that nation. He was answered that they were called Angles. And he said: "Good, for they have angelic faces, and such are meet to be co-heirs with the angels in heaven. What is the name of the province, from which they have been brought?" He was answered that the people of that province were called the *Deire*. "Good," he said, "Deire; snatched from wrath [Latin *de ira*], and called to the mercy of Christ. How is the king of that province named?" He was told that he was called Ælle. And, playing on the name, he said: "Alleluia, the praise of God the Creator ought to be sung in those parts."

Whether or not this story is literally true, it may serve to remind us of the central position of Gregory the Great in the development of Anglo-Saxon Christianity. Bede interrupts his history in order to devote a lengthy chapter to his life, and defends this digression by pointing out that Gregory "converted our nation, that is, the nation of the English, from the power of Satan to the faith of Christ; and we can rightly, and should, call him our apostle." Later on Bede quotes the famous passage from the *Morals on the Book of Job* in which Gregory tells how the tongue of Britain has begun to resound the Hebrew Alleluia in praise of God. As we turn, therefore, to consider the influence of the Bible in the earliest English literature, we may well expect to see the influence of Saint Gregory manifested in the various forms of Christian literature that arose as a result of the conversion of the English nation. In order to see the literature in its context, however, we need first to review briefly the historical events leading up to this conversion.

At the time of the Anglo-Saxon invasion (A.D. 449), the British Isles were occupied by Celtic tribes that had migrated there in earlier centuries from the European continent. The first of these people probably arrived as early as 600 B.C., although the history of the early Celtic settlements is by no means clear. Traditionally it has been thought that the Gaels came first, followed some three centuries later by the Britons, but it is entirely possible that the latter were the first settlers, and that the Gaels avoided Britain completely and sailed straight to Ireland. In any case it is sufficient for our purposes to recognize two distinct Celtic groups: the Gaels, speaking a language that still survives in Ireland, the Isle of Man, and the Scottish highlands; and the Britons, whose language survives in the closely related dialects of Wales, Brittany, and Cornwall. Though these two groups had a common cultural and linguistic heritage, their language had become widely differentiated by the time of our earliest written records. Between Gael and Briton, speakers of "q" Celtic and "p" Celtic respectively, communication was difficult indeed. Thus the Indo-European numeral four (represented by Latin *quattuor*) appears in Irish as *cethir* and in Welsh as *pedwar*. It is therefore not surprising that the two groups went their separate ways in the course of later history.

The development of British civilization was deeply affected by the period of Roman occupation, which lasted from the time of the first invasion of Julius Caesar in 55 B.C. until the final withdrawal of Roman troops in A.D. 410. The Romans built roads and towns, and eventually extended a firm administrative control over the southern and central portions of the island. Hadrian's wall in the north protected peaceful citizens from raids conducted by the primitive Picts, who were reinforced at times by Gaelic settlers from Ireland, known to Bede as the "Scots." In the west, those British settlers who refused to collaborate with the Romans clung to their culture and language in the relatively uncivilized regions of Wales and Cornwall. Viewed as a whole, the Roman influence was benevolent, and did much to improve the lot of the Celtic inhabitants. Unfortunately, however, it did not prepare them for the time when the Roman legions were forced to withdraw, leaving the British to defend themselves against the increasing attacks launched by Germanic tribes from across the channel.

Bede relates the pathetic efforts of the British rulers to obtain military assistance from the Romans, who were of course unable to respond, being fully occupied at home with their own defense against the barbarian hordes. At length the British King, Vortigern, in 449, made the decision to invite tribes of Angles, Saxons, and Jutes, from the northern shores of Europe around the Jutland peninsula, to serve as mercenaries for the defense of Britain against the invaders. At first the policy seemed effective, for the new defenders quickly won a decisive victory against an enemy in the north. What happened next, however, was less reassuring: "When this [victory] was announced in their [the Saxons'] homeland, as well as the fertility of the island and the cowardice of the Britons, a more considerable fleet was quickly sent over, bringing a stronger force of armed men, which, added to the band sent before, made up an invincible army." It was not long, therefore, until the army which was supposed to defend the Britons turned against them, and the Anglo-Saxon settlement began, a century and a half before the coming of Gregory's missionaries.

As a historian Bede is remarkably balanced, as can be seen in the sympathy sometimes accorded to the Britons, and his criticism of the heathen Anglo-Saxons. Indeed one particular criticism which he records against the British has been echoed by modern historians, namely that "they never undertook the preaching of the word of the faith to the race of the Saxons or Angles who inhabited Britain with them." This criticism serves to remind us that the Britons, and indeed the Gaels also, had converted to Christianity considerably earlier than the time of the arrival of Saint Augustine in Kent. Ireland had been converted by Saint Patrick (d. 461), and the conversion of the

Britons has been attributed to Saint Illtud, a more obscure figure associated in legend with Arthur, leader of British resistance against the Saxons at the battle of Mount Badon (c. 517). Better known are Illtud's followers, Saint David and other British saints whose names have been preserved in the legends and place names of Wales and Cornwall.

The inspiration for the conversion of the Celts came ultimately from the ascetic life of the Desert Fathers of North Africa, and hence in both Britain and Ireland early Christianity was austere and monastic, unaffected by the parochial organization that was being developed in the Roman church. A visitor to Britain or Ireland in these early times would have found institutional Christianity expressed in scattered, independent monasteries, some of them very large. Indeed, a few Irish communities consisted of several hundred monks. At the same time, the missionary work of the Celtic church was carried out mainly by individual monks who lived in solitary cells along the coasts of Britain and Ireland, and whose asceticism and general style of life was very similar to that of the hermits who inhabited the slopes of Mount Sinai. One of these cells, the oratory of Saint Piran, can be seen to this day, in the sand dunes near Perranporth, Cornwall. It was preserved from the ravages of time by the encroaching sands, in which it was buried centuries ago, only to be rediscovered in modern times, virtually intact, lacking only its roof. When the site was cleared, and a modern building constructed around it to hold back the sands, a spring began to flow from the floor of the sanctuary, perhaps the very one used by Saint Piran nearly fifteen centuries ago. The traveler who stands inside this little cell should, with a little imagination, be able to pick up echoes of the services of the canonical hours recited by the saint during his lonely vigil on the Cornish coast. Men like Piran at once embodied and transmitted the spirituality of Celtic Christianity.

Against this background of Romanization and Christianization of the Celtic inhabitants, the Anglo-Saxons appear on the scene as barbaric invaders. Rapidly and fiercely they pushed westward and to the north, until they eventually occupied all of what we may now legitimately call "England" (Angle-land). The country was generally divided along tribal lines. Bede tells us that the Angles held the largest area, including the midlands and the north up to the Roman wall, the Saxons were in the south, except for the southeast corner (Kent) and the Isle of Wight, held by the smaller tribe of the Jutes. These areas, apart from their fluctuating political importance, came to define the four main dialect regions of Anglo-Saxon or "Old English" as it was spoken up to the time of the Norman Conquest (1066): Northumbrian, Mercian, West-Saxon, and Kentish. The civilizing influence of Christianity came to these regions at different times, so that during the Old English period there were several waves of cultural and literary achievement, beginning with Kent at the end of the sixth century, shifting to Northumbria in the seventh, Mercia in the eighth, and finally to Wessex under King Alfred in the ninth century. These cultural developments, of course, reflect the spread of Christianity among the various regions of the Anglo-Saxon settlement.

The Venerable Bede tells the story of the mission of Saint Augustine to King Ethelbert of Kent in 597. Augustine and his followers arrived on the island of Thanet, with interpreters brought from the Frankish nation, the homeland of the king's Christian wife, Bertha. They then sent word to the king regarding their mission, and Ethelbert met them on the island in an open field — lest the missionaries try to work magic against him. Augustine and his companions approached the king and preached the word of life to him and his followers. When they finished the king replied:

> Fair, indeed, are the words and promises which you bring; but because they are new and uncertain, I cannot give assent to them and abandon those which I along with all the nation of the English have followed for so long a time. But because you have come from far hither as strangers, and, as I conceive, have desired to impart to us also those things which you yourselves believe to be true and best, we do not wish to harm you; rather, we will receive you with friendly entertainment, and supply you with things necessary for your sustenance; nor do we forbid you to gain to your religious faith all whom you can by your preaching.

Accordingly, continues Bede, he gave them an abode

> in the city of Canterbury, which was the metropolis of his whole realm, and, as he had promised, besides seeing to their temporal sustenance, he did not withhold permission for them to preach.

The establishment of the missionaries in Canterbury gave the people of Kent an opportunity to observe their way of life and hear their message. And before long, Bede reports, several converts were found, persuaded by the simplicity of the way of life of the monks, and the attractiveness of their teaching. When at last King Ethelbert himself was baptized, the province was won over to Christianity. During all this time Pope Gregory kept in close touch with his representatives, encouraging and advising them in matters of policy. When it appeared that the mission was successful, he sent Augustine to the continent, to Arles, where he was consecrated the first Archbishop of Canterbury, spiritual leader of the newly christianized English nation. The actual territory affected, of course, did not extend beyond the borders of Kent itself; but this small beginning was destined ultimately to have a profound effect on the development of Anglo-Saxon Christianity.

Many problems concerning religious practices were raised by the conversion of Kent, and Augustine turned to Pope Gregory for advice. How should offerings be divided? Which liturgical practices should be adopted? How should thieves be punished? Gregory answered these and other questions with his customary good sense. In the last case, for example, he says that punishment should be based on "the standing of the thief." If he is simply avaricious, he should be dealt with severely; if he stole out of real need, charity should be employed. God forbid that the church should seek to become wealthy! Most important for the future of the church in England, I think, was Gregory's attitude toward the old religion. At one point he had advocated destruction of the heathen temples, but after further reflection he sent word by Abbot Mellitus, who was going to Britain, that the temples should not be destroyed. Rather, he suggested, let the idols themselves be removed, and the temples rededicated to God, so that "the nation, seeing that their temples are not destroyed, may remove error from their hearts, and, knowing and adoring the true God, may the more familiarly resort to the places to which they have been accustomed." Gregory's generosity of spirit was destined to affect not only the form of early Christian worship in England, but also, as we shall see, the scope and quality of Old English literature.

The turbulent and barbaric Angles of Northumbria were the next people to be stilled and pacified by the Christian message, through the conversion of King Edwin (617–33). As a young man Edwin had been forced into exile by the ambition of King Ethelfrith, a successor to Ælle, King of Deira. Edwin fled first to Cadfan, King of North Wales, where he may have first been introduced to the Celtic form of Christianity, and later he found refuge with the pagan king Raedwald of East Anglia. In any case it was when he was with Raedwald that he had the vision, referred to by Bede, of a stranger who prophesied victory and his restoration to the throne of Northumbria, and exhorted him to accept Christianity when the prophecy was fulfilled. Edwin promised to do so, and the stranger then placed his right hand on the exile's head, saying: "When this sign shall be given you, remember this time and our talk, and do not delay to carry out what you now promise." Having said this, the stranger vanished.

When Edwin in fact regained the throne, he married Ætheburh, Christian daughter of King Ethelbert of Kent, with the understanding that she would be free to follow the practices of her religion. With her came Bishop Paulinus, who, says Bede, was intent on converting the whole of the nation of the Northumbrians. One day, when the king was pondering whether he should accept the new religion, Paulinus came to him, and, placing his right hand on Edwin's head, he reminded him of his past victories and his promise to accept the new faith. The king was greatly impressed, and indicated his willingness to be converted, but said that he would first be obliged to consult his wise men concerning such a momentous decision. Paulinus agreed, and a council was held, which Bede reports in detail, including a famous speech by one of the king's chief advisors:

> O king, the present life of men on earth, in comparison with the time that is unknown to us, appears to me to be as if, when you are sitting at supper with your ealdormen and thegns in the winter time, and a fire is lighted in the midst and the hall warmed, but everywhere outside the storms of wintry rain and snow are raging, a sparrow should come and fly rapidly through the hall, coming in at one door, and immediately out at the other. Whilst it is inside, it is not touched by the storm of winter, but yet, that tiny space of calm gone in a moment, from winter at once returning to winter, it is lost to your sight. Thus this life of men appears for a little while; but of what is to follow, or of what went before, we are entirely ignorant. Hence, if this new teaching brings greater certainty, it seems fit to be followed.

The other counselors soon confirmed this view of the matter and it was agreed that the new religion would be adopted. Among the most zealous of the new converts was Coifi, high priest of the old religion. When it was asked who would undertake the desecration of the heathen altars and idols, he responded: "I will; for who may now more fittingly destroy the things which I worshipped through folly, as an example to all others through the wisdom truly granted to me by God?" He then armed himself and mounted a horse (contrary to the rule of the old religion) and approached the temple. The people, says Bede, seeing this, thought that their priest had gone mad. But under his leadership the idols were destroyed, and the nation of the Angles in Northumbria was converted. In this way was

[85]

laid the foundation of a cultural renaissance in the north that was destined to produce such men as Cuthbert, Wilfred, and Bede.

Edwin's reign as a Christian king, however, was cut short in 633 by his death in battle against the Anglo-Celtic alliance of the heathen king Penda of Mercia and the British king Cadwallon. It appeared for a time that Paulinus' hope for a Christian Northumbria would be shattered, since, after the death of Edwin, the kingdom was divided and its leaders reverted to paganism. But when the two kings, Osric and Eanfrid, were slain within the year by Cadwallon, a very gifted leader, Oswald, son of Edwin's predecessor Ethelfrith, became king of all Northumbria (634–42). For nearly two decades Oswald had lived in political exile among the "Scottish" monks of the island of Iona, a most important center of Gaelic missionary activity, established in the preceding century by the Irish Saint Columba (d. 596). Oswald came to the throne of Northumbria, therefore, as a Christian king, not by political persuasion, but by conviction. And it is a fact of considerable importance that his inspiration came from Celtic rather than Roman missionaries.

One of the first things that Oswald did as king was to ask the Scots of Iona to send him a bishop to strengthen his people in the faith and administer the sacraments. The monks sent him Bishop Aidan, "a man of the greatest gentleness, godliness and moderation," says Bede, "and possessing the zeal of God." The king granted Aidan the island of Lindisfarne, the holy island destined to become the most famous of the cultural centers of Northumbria. In spite of the language barrier that existed between the Celtic missionaries and their English congregations, the success of the mission was immediate. Some credit for this should go to Oswald himself, for, as Bede tells us, he not only endowed monasteries, but even served as translator for his newly appointed bishop:

> It was a beautiful sight to see the king acting there as interpreter of the heavenly word to his ealdormen and thegns when the bishop was preaching the gospel, since the bishop did not know the English language thoroughly; for the king had fully learnt the language of the Scots during his long exile. From that time there came many every day from the region of the Scots to Britain, and preached the word of the faith with great devotion to those provinces of the English over which Oswald reigned, and those of them who had received priests' orders ministered the grace of baptism to believers. Churches were built in various places; the people joyfully flocked to hear the word; possessions and estates were given by the gift of the king for the founding of monasteries; English children, as well as older people, were instructed by Scottish masters in study and the observance of monastic discipline.

[86]

From this account we can see the Celtic foundations of the Northumbrian culture which flourished from the time of Oswald and reached its climax in the life of Bede (d. 735). This was the period that produced the earliest of the surviving literature of the Anglo-Saxons, and the beginning of study of the Bible. Bishop Aidan himself provided the impetus for the tradition of scholarship and learning inevitably associated with the name of Lindisfarne. "His manner of life," remarks Bede, "was so different from the slothfulness of our times that all those who bore him company, whether clerics or laymen, had to study, that is, to be engaged in either reading the Scriptures or learning psalms. This was the daily employment of himself and all who were with him, wherever they went." His spiritual successors in the north were Cuthbert, Wilfred, and Bede; but it is also important to realize that two of his disciples, Cedd and Chad, preached to the Mercians, thus providing a basis for the cultural development of Mercia in the following century. It was from Mercia, finally, that King Alfred found scholars to assist him in his revival of learning in Wessex in the late ninth century. This chain of circumstances inevitably affected the development of Old English literature, to which we may now turn. And since Anglo-Saxon learning was focused on the Bible, it will not be surprising to find that the biblical influence on Old English literature was very strong indeed.

Glosses and Prose Translations

During the Old English period a primary scholarly task of the monks was the preservation, study, and copying of the Latin text of Saint Jerome, which was gradually taking its place as the official Bible of the church in the West. Although a few complete texts of the Scriptures survive from this time, the most important and numerous examples of manuscripts produced in the monastic scriptoriums are Gospels and psalters—the former because of their central position in the Mass, the latter because of the Psalms' liturgical importance, particularly in the office of the canonical hours. Of all the Latin manuscripts that have survived, however, the most interesting for our present purpose are those containing interlinear glosses, for in a sense these glosses represent the first systematic effort that was to result in the translation of the Bible into Old English prose. Anyone who has studied a foreign language, and found himself writing the meaning of the various words in English between the lines of his text, will have no trouble understanding how the practice of glossing

[87]

originated. And it is quite clear that the early biblical glosses were put there by English-speaking monks as an aid to understanding the Latin text which they recited daily in religious worship.

The Lindisfarne Gospels provide a good example of the practice of glossing. This magnificent manuscript, actually copied at Lindisfarne toward the end of the seventh century, contains, in addition to the Latin text of the Gospels, beautiful portraits of the four Evangelists, ornamental initials, and pages devoted to geometric designs of great intricacy and splendor. In addition the whole of the text is perfectly preserved—a rare state of affairs for a manuscript nearly thirteen hundred years old. Indeed, as has been suggested, it may be that the beautiful condition of the book owes something to its association with Saint Cuthbert.

About the time that Bishop Aidan died, in 651, the young man Cuthbert was accepted as a member of the monastic community of Melrose, where he remained for over a decade. Toward the end of his stay his devotion was such that he was made a leader, and proved to be of such holy life that when a vacancy occurred at Lindisfarne, Cuthbert was transferred there and appointed as prior (664–76). The position was a difficult one, owing to the conflict between Gaelic and Roman practices that occurred at the Synod of Whitby in 664. Of the controversy itself, which mainly involved the calculation of Easter, it is sufficient here to say that Colman, one of the spiritual successors of Aidan and a defender of the Gaelic party, was discouraged by the decision of the king, Oswy, in favor of the Roman faction, and, leaving with a number of followers, he wandered to the west and settled in Ireland. When Cuthbert arrived at Lindisfarne, he discovered that even among the monks who remained there was considerable hostility toward Roman practices, and it is therefore all the more remarkable that he was able, through patience and humility, to win the brothers over to orthodoxy during his twelve years as prior. Even though he defended the Roman practices, Cuthbert was at heart a desert father of the Gaelic school, and was restless in his role as the leader of a community. Finally, in 676 he retired from Lindisfarne and built himself a small oratory on the solitary, uninhabited islet of Inner Farne, seven miles distant from the holy island, where he remained for eight years as a hermit. Toward the end of his life he was called back to active service as Bishop of Hexham, but after two years he returned to his little island, where he died in 687.

From the stories that Bede tells it is easy to perceive that Cuthbert was greatly beloved during his lifetime; yet this scarcely prepares us for the remarkable and enduring influence that he had after his death. In addition to numerous miracles, both before and after his death, Bede tells of the miraculous preservation of Cuthbert's body on the occasion of its translation when the monks were preparing a new shrine for him in 698. From this time forth, the relics of Saint Cuthbert have had a continuous history, and among these relics was that remarkable manuscript known as the Lindisfarne Gospels.

For nearly two centuries the monastery at Lindisfarne existed with an almost constant danger of attack from the sea by Danish pirates. One particular raid, in 793, forced the monks to flee, although they were able to return after a short time. During the next century the peril increased, and, in 875, a few years after Alfred came to the throne in Wessex, Lindisfarne was abandoned. Taking with them the precious relics of Saint Cuthbert, the monks wandered through the north of England for eight years. It is indeed a miracle that the manuscript survived this period of homelessness. According to a reliable account, it was once lost overboard in a storm when the hapless monks were attempting to embark for Ireland, but was recovered unharmed at low tide. In 883, the monks were given sanctuary in Chester-le-street, which became the headquarters of Saint Cuthbert's see for over a hundred years. Finally, at the end of the tenth century, the saint was moved for the last time a few miles to Durham, where he now lies, with his relics, in the sanctuary of the cathedral.

During the time that the see of Cuthbert was at Chester-le-street, probably soon after 950, the Latin text of the Lindisfarne Gospels was given an English interlinear gloss. A note at the end of the manuscript, added about this date, informs us that the glossing was done by a man named Aldred, who was Provost of Chester-le-street in the year 970. The note reads in part:

Eadfrith, Bishop of the Lindisfarne Church, originally wrote this book, for God and for St. Cuthbert and, jointly, for all the saints whose relics are in the Island. And Ethilwald, Bishop of the Lindisfarne islanders, impressed it on the outside and covered it—as he well knew how to do. And Billfrith, the anchorite, forged the ornaments which are on it on the outside and adorned it with gold and with gems and also with gilded-over silver, pure metal. And Aldred, unworthy and most miserable priest, glossed it in English between the lines with the help of God and St. Cuthbert. . . .

Although the relics of Saint Cuthbert remain to the present day in Durham, the later history of the Lindisfarne Manuscript is obscure up to the time of its appearance in the library of Sir Robert Cotton, who bought it in the early seventeenth century. It may have been restored to Lindisfarne after the rebuilding of the priory there in the eleventh century, but in any case it probably fell into private hands at the time of the dissolution of the monasteries during the reign of Henry VIII. Eventually, in the eighteenth century, it formed part of the collection of Cottonian manuscripts turned over to the British Museum when it was founded in 1753. Along with Codex Sinaiticus, the Lindisfarne manuscript remains one of the great treasures of that museum, and a continuing object of study by students of the Bible and of the Old English language.

The other major example of Gospel books that have been glossed is the Rushworth Gospels, a Latin manuscript of about A.D. 800, with English glosses added in the latter half of the tenth century. It is likely, moreover, that these glosses were copied, at least in part, from those of the Lindisfarne Gospels, when the famous manuscript was removed for a short time in 995 by Bishop Aldhun to Ripon, before being brought finally to Durham. Two glossators did the work on the Rushworth text: Farman glossed all of Matthew and the opening of Mark, and Owun did the rest. The work of Farman is of particular value since, unlike Owun, whose dialect was Northumbrian, Farman used a Mercian dialect, surviving examples of which are relatively rare.

In addition to the glossed Gospels, a prose translation of the Gospels into West Saxon was made in the tenth century, of which there are six surviving copies. The earliest of these is a manuscript in Corpus Christi College, Cambridge, that was written about the year 1000. It is perhaps only natural that the glossing of the Gospels should be followed so quickly by a prose translation of them, but it should be pointed out also that the latter half of the tenth century was a period of intense literary activity, notably in the West Saxon dialect of the south. There are two reasons for this. First, this revival springs from the seeds of learning sowed by King Alfred at the end of the ninth century. The other, and more immediate factor, is that the literary renaissance is one of the fruits of the monastic reform of the tenth century under the leadership of Archbishop Dunstan.

To illustrate how the Gospels were glossed and translated, I have chosen the parable of the sower who went out to sow the seed, as it appears in the Gospel of Mark, 4:1–9. First I quote the passage in the

King James version, then the text and gloss of the Lindisfarne Gospels, and finally the West Saxon prose translation from the Corpus Christi manuscript.

MARK 4:1–9

Authorized Version

1. And he began again to teach by the sea side: and there was gathered unto him a great multitude, so that he entered into a ship, and sat in the sea; and the whole multitude was by the sea on the land.

2. And he taught them many things by parables, and said unto them in his doctrine,

3. Harken; Behold, there went out a sower to sow:

4. And it came to pass, as he sowed, some fell by the way side, and the fowls of the air came and devoured it up.

5. And some fell on stony ground, where it had not much earth; and immediately it sprang up, because it had no depth of earth:

6. But when the sun was up, it was scorched; and because it had no root, it withered away.

7. And some fell among thorns, and the thorns grew up, and choked it, and it yielded no fruit.

8. And other fell on good ground, and did yield fruit that sprung up and increased; and brought forth, some thirty, and some sixty, and some an hundred.

9. And he said unto them, He that hath ears to hear, let him hear.

The Lindisfarne Gospels

   & eftersona ongann læra   to   sæ
1. ET ITERUM COEPIT DOCERE AD MARE

   & gesomnad   wæs to him ðreat   menigo
   ET CONGREGATA EST AD EUM TURBA MULTA

   sua þætte in scipp   astag   gesætt   on sæ
   ITA UT   IN NAVEM ASCENDENS SEDERET IN MARI

   & all   ðreat ymb sæ   ofer   eorðo   wæs
   ET OMNIS TURBA CIRCA MARE SUPER TERRAM ERAT.

   & lærde   hia   in bispellum   menigo &
2. ET DOCEBAT ILLOS IN PARABOLIS MULTA ET

   cuoeð   to him on lar   his
   DICEBAT ILLIS IN DOCTRINA SUA.

   herað   heono eode ðe sawende/sedere to   sawenne
3. AUDITE ECCE EXIIT SEMINANS   AD SEMINANDUM.

   & miððy geseaw   oðer/sum feoll   ymb   ða stret
4. ET DUM SEMINAT ALIUD   CECIDIT CIRCA VIAM

   & cwomon   flegendo   & fretton/eton   ðæt
   ET VENERUNT VOLUCRES ET COMEDERUNT ILLUD.

sum   ec   feoll   ofer   stænes   ðer ne
5. ALIUD VERO CECIDIT SUPER PETROSA UBI NON
hæfde   eorðu   michel/menig & hræðe
HABUIT TERRAM MULTAM   ET STATIM
upp-iornende wæs/arisæn wæs
EXORTUM EST
forðon   næfde   heanisse   eorðes
QUONIAM NON HABEBAT ALTITUDINEM TERRAE.
& ða   arisen wæs/ða upp-eode sunna
6. ET QUANDO EXORTUS EST   SOL
ge-drugade/forbernde
EXAESTUAVIT
forðon   næfde   wyrtruma gedrugade
EO QUOD NON HABERET RADICEM EXARUIT.
& sum   feoll   in ðornum &   astigon/upp-eodun
7. ET ALIUD CECIDIT IN SPINIS ET ASCENDERUNT
ðornas & under-dulfon   þæt   &   wæstm   ne
SPINAE ET SUFFOCAVERUNT ILLUD ET FRUCTUM NON
salde
DEDIT.
& oðer   feoll   on eorðu   godum & salde
8. ET ALIUD CECIDIT IN TERRAM BONAM ET DABAT
wæstm   stigende   & wæxende   & to-brohte
FRUCTUM ASCENDENTEM ET CRESCENTEM ET ADFEREBAT
enne/an ðrittig   & an   sexdig   & an
UNUM TRIGENTA ET UNUM SEXAGENTA ET UNUM
hundrað
CENTUM.
& he cuœð se ðe hæfeð earo   to heranne geherað
9. ET DICEBAT QUI HABET AURES AUDIENDI AUDIAT.

West Saxon Prose Translation

1. And eft he ongan hi æt þære sæ læran. And him wæs mycel menegu to gegaderod, swa þæt he on scip eode, and on þære sæ wæs; and eall seo menegu ymbe þa sæ wæron on lande.

2. And he hi fela on bigspellum lærde, and him to cwæð on his lare,

3. Gehyrað; Ut eode se sædere his sæd to sawenne:

4. And þa he sew, sum feoll wið þone weg, and fugelas comon and hit fræton.

5. Sum feoll ofer stanscyligean, þar hit næfde mycele eorðan, and sona up eode, and for þam hit næfde eorðan þiccnesse,

6. þa hit up eode, seo sunne hit forswælde, and hit forscranc, for þam hit wyrtruman næfde.

7. And sum feoll on þornas; þa stigon ða þornas and forðrysmodon þæt, and hit wæstm ne bær.

[92]

8. And sum feoll on god land, and hit sealde uppstigende and wexende wæstm; and an brohte þritig-fealdne, sum syxtig-fealdne, sum hund-fealdne.

9. And he cwæð, Gehyre se ðe earran hæbbe to gehyranne.

These examples show that the interlinear gloss of the Lindisfarne Gospels follows the word order of the Latin exactly, and even has, now and then, a choice of two English words or phrases for a single Latin word. Thus for *sower* (Latin *seminans*), the gloss offers *sawende* or *sedere*; for devoured (Latin *comederunt*) the gloss has *fretton* or *eton*; and so forth. The prose version, on the other hand, is clearly a translation, for it does not offer alternative readings, and it follows a more natural English word order. The sentences are very simple and straightforward, and really not hard for a modern reader to understand, although perhaps easier heard than read, because of archaic spelling conventions. By modernizing the orthography, and providing an occasional synonym to explain an obsolete word, the opening verse of the prose translation reads as follows: "And eft [=again] he began them at the sea to learn [=teach]. And him was muchel [=large] many [=multitude] to gathered, so that he on ship yede [=went], and on the sea was; and all the many [=multitude] ymbe [=around, beside] the sea were on land." This is essentially modern English word order, except that we would put the object, whether direct or indirect, after the verb—that is, we would say *to learn them* (meaning to teach them) and *was gathered to him* instead of *him was . . . to gathered.* When we take into account these and other differences between Old and Modern English, therefore, it is evident that the West Saxon prose translation is a natural, direct, and clear rending of the Latin text. When read aloud, it made available to a wide audience the story of the Gospels in simple language.

The glossed Psalters that survive from the Old English period are much more numerous than the Gospels. There are fourteen in all, of which eight have the Roman version of the Psalms, and six the Gallican version. Because of differences between the two Latin texts, it is possible to detect that in certain cases the interlinear gloss of one manuscript has been copied from another, despite the fact that the gloss may be based on the Roman text, and yet written between the lines of a Gallican Psalter. This is true, for example, of the Salisbury manuscript. Even when there is no discrepancy in the Latin text used, it has been determined that most of the surviving Psalter glosses are copies, rather than independent projects. The three that seem largely original are the Lambeth, Royal, and, most famous of

[93]

all, the Vespasian Psalter, the latter important both for the early date of its glosses (ninth century), and its dialect (Mercian). On the other hand a fourth manuscript, the Paris Psalter, is unique in that it has the Latin text of the Psalms in one column, and an Old English translation in the other. In other words, it is not a glossed psalter, but a Latin text with English translation. Moreover the first fifty psalms are in prose, while the remainder are in Old English alliterative verse. The origin of the translations is obscure, but it has been suggested that the prose portion (Psalms 1–50), at least, may have been the work of King Alfred himself.

As an example of the Old English version of the psalms, let us look at the text of the Twenty-third Psalm (Vulgate 22) as it appears in the Paris Psalter, in the prose version attributed to Alfred. To facilitate comparison, I first quote the King James version.

PSALM 23

Authorized Version

1. The Lord is my shepherd; I shall not want.

2. He maketh me to lie down in green pastures: he leadeth me beside the still waters.

3. He restoreth my soul: he leadeth me in the paths of righteousness for his name's sake.

4. Yea, though I walk through the valley of the shadow of death, I will fear no evil: for thou art with me; thy rod and thy staff they comfort me.

5. Thou preparest a table before me in the presence of mine enemies: thou anointest my head with oil: my cup runneth over.

6. Surely goodness and mercy shall follow me all the days of my life: and I will dwell in the house of the Lord for ever.

The Paris Psalter

1. Drihten me ræt; ne byð me nanes godes wan.

2. And he me geset on swyðe good feoh-land: and fedde me be wætera staðum,

3. And min mod gehwyrfde (of unrotnesse on gefean): he me gelædde ofer þa wegas rihtwisnesse for his naman.

4. Þeah ic nu gange on midde þa sceade deaðes, ne ondræde ic me nan yfel: for þam þu byst mid me, Drihten; þin gyrd and þin stæf me afrefredon (þæt is þin þreaung and eft þin frefrung).

5. Þu gegearwodest beforan me swiðe bradne beod wið þara willan þe me hatedon: þu gesmyredest me mid ele min heafod; Drihten, hu mære þin folc nu is, ælc dæge hit symblað.

6. And folgie me nu þin mildheortnes ealle dagas mines lifes, þæt ic mæge wunian on þinum huse swiðe lange tiid oð lange ylde.

The Old English and King James versions are not precisely parallel, first, because the originals from which the translations were made are not exactly the same, and, second, because the Old English includes two interpretive passages (indicated by parentheses), which are not in the text of the psalm. Here is a modernization of the Old English version:

1. The Lord guides me; nor shall I lack any gift.
2. And he set me in very good pasture: and fed me beside the waters,
3. And turned my mood (from sorrow to joy): he led me over the ways of righteousness for his name.
4. Though I now go amid the shadow of death, I dread me no evil, for thou be with me, Lord; thy rod and thy staff comfort me (that is thy correction and also thy consolation).
5. Thou didst prepare before me a very broad table against the will of them that hate me: thou didst smear my head with oil; Lord, how famous is thy folk now, that each day feasts.
6. And may thy mercy follow me now all the days of my life, that I may dwell in thy house a very long time to old age.

The beginning of verse 3, which in King James reads *He restoreth my soul,* appears in the Latin Vulgate as *Animam meam convertit,* and the Psalter glosses uniformly render this *sawle min (he) gecyrde,* that is, "my soul he converted." The translation of the Paris Psalter, "turned my mood from sorrow to joy," would seem to be merely an expansion for the purpose of clarification. The other case of this kind, however, in verse 4, comes closer to being exegesis, and in fact the added words are clearly an interpretation of "thy rod and thy staff comfort me." The rod is understood to be a rod of punishment, and the staff one of support. The source for this interpretation is a commentary on the Psalms once attributed to Bede, but now regarded as the work of a later exegete, the Benedictine Ambrosius Autpertus (d. 778). Here is his comment on this verse: "*virga tua,* id est, paterna correctio tua, *et baculus tuus,* id est, auxilium tuum." The Old English passage is virtually a translation of this: "that is thy correction (correctio) and also thy consolation (auxilium)." Once established, interpretations of this kind had a long life in the Middle Ages. As late as the fourteenth century, for example, the rod of the Twenty-third Psalm understood as a rod of correction shows up in the Middle English poem, *Piers the Plowman.* One error in the Old English psalm appears in verse 5, where, instead of "my cup runneth over," the text reads, "Lord, how famous is thy folk now, that each day feasts." Here we can observe how the translator is often at the mercy of his Latin manuscript, for it would seem that in this case, instead of the word *poculum* ("cup"), his copy had *populum* ("people," "folk"). In spite of this difficulty, however, he managed with considerable ingenuity to retain a reference to the Eucharist in his translation ("that each day feasts").

In addition to these internal guides to the meaning of the text, the Old English translation included an introduction to each psalm derived, incidentally, from the commentary on the Psalms by Ambrosius referred to above. Here is the introduction to the psalm we have just been considering, put into modern English:

> David sang this twenty-second psalm, when he prophesied concerning the freeing of the people of Israel, how they would be led from the slavery of Babylon, and how they would thank God for the favors that they received on the way homewards; and also concerning his own return from his exile. And each one who sings it thanks God for his liberation from affliction, even as did the apostles and all Christian people for the resurrection of Christ. And also Christian men in this psalm give thanks for their redemption from their sins after baptism.

Thus it is evident that this translation of the psalms was carefully provided, both within and without, with a means for interpretation based on standard medieval exegesis. Is this the work of King Alfred? We cannot be sure of course, but it is satisfying to think that he may indeed be responsible for at least this prose translation of the first fifty psalms in the Paris Psalter.

The Old English period did not produce a complete translation of the Bible. In addition to the Gospels and Psalms, however, considerable portions of the Old Testament were turned into Old English. The man principally responsible for this was Ælfric, a monk who was educated in the latter half of the tenth century at the cathedral school in Winchester, where he came under the influence of Bishop Æthelwald, one of the principal leaders, along with Archbishop Dunstan, of the monastic reform. At this school Ælfric received the training and inspiration that were to make him one of the greatest of Old English scholars. His teaching and writing career began in 987 when, at about the age of twenty-eight, he was put in charge of a school at the monastery of Cerne in Dorset. Here he seems to have remained for eighteen years, and probably most of his writing was done during this period. He produced sets of sermons, called the

Catholic Homilies, a collection of lives of saints, and translations of parts of the Old Testament which have been assembled under the title of Ælfric's *Heptateuch* (Genesis through Judges). Various shorter works, not all of them yet edited, combine to form an impressive literary output written as it was in the midst of a very busy life. There are numerous letters, prefaces, sermons for special occasions, and textbooks for school use. The latter include a grammar, a glossary, and a Latin exercise for schoolboys known as the *Colloquy.*

Although it is simply an exercise, Ælfric's *Colloquy* gives us a glimpse of life in a monastic school of the tenth century. It is written in the form of question and answer, and opens with a question directed to the teacher by the students:

> We boys ask you, O Master, that you teach us to speak rightly, for we are ignorant and speak corruptly.
> What would you speak?
> What care we what we speak, unless it be correct speech, not at all idle or vain.
> Do you wish to be beaten while you learn?
> We would rather be beaten for learning than not to acquire it. But we know that you are kind and will not inflict strokes on us unless we compel you to.
> I ask you, what do you say? What job do you have?
> I am a monk by profession, and I sing the psalms seven times each day with the brothers, and I am busy with reading and song, but I would like also, in between, to learn to speak in the Latin language.
> What do your companions know?
> Some are plowmen, some shepherds, some oxherds, some also hunters, some fishers, some fowlers, some merchants, some shoe-wrights, salters, and bakers.

The substance of the *Colloquy* is then taken up with the master's interrogation of each of these professions. "What do you say, plowman? How do you perform your work?" The plowman tells how he drives the oxen to field in the cold mornings, and describes the equipment he uses in plowing. His lord is so strict that, regardless of the weather, he must plow at least an acre a day. And so it goes with all the other professions named.

Toward the end of the *Colloquy,* Ælfric inserts a bit of educational philosophy by having the teacher say:

> I ask you, why are you so eager to learn?
> Because we do not wish to be like dumb animals, that know nothing but grass and water.
> And what do you want?

We want to be wise.

In what wisdom? Do you want to be cunning or clever in lying, crafty in speech, artful, wily, well speaking and evil thinking, addicted to suave words, abounding in guile within, like a sepulchre painted without, but within full of stench?

We do not wish to be wise thus, for he is not wise who deceives himself with delusion.

But how would you?

We would be sincere without hypocrisy, and wise in turning from evil and doing good. Yet you are examining us more deeply than our age can grasp; but speak to us in our fashion, not so deeply.

At this point the teacher agrees to question them more simply, and so asks one of the boys to report on what he has been doing all day. Here we get a rare and intimate description of life in the cathedral school. The boy responds:

Last night, when I heard the bell, I arose from my bed, and went to the church, and sang matins with the brothers; afterwards we sang of all the saints, and at dawn, lauds; after this, prime and seven psalms with the litanies, and chapter-mass; then tierce, and performed the mass of the day; after this we sang sext, and ate and drank and slept, and then we arose and sang none; and now we are here before you, ready to hear what you will say to us.

When will you sing evensong or compline?

When it is time.

Were you beaten today?

I was not, because I behaved discreetly.

And how about your companions?

Why do you ask me about this? I dare not reveal to you our secrets. Each one knows if he was beaten or not.

In subsequent questions, the teacher asks what he has eaten, and then accuses him of gluttony. The boy protests and excuses himself. This *Colloquy* could have been simply a dull exercise, but Ælfric turns it into an engaging and revealing exchange:

And what do you drink?

Ale, if I have it, or water if I do not have ale.

Don't you drink wine?

I am not so wealthy that I may buy myself wine; and wine is not a drink for boys or fools, but for the old and the wise.

Where do you sleep?

In the dormitory with the brothers.

What awakens you for matins?

Sometimes I hear the bell and arise; sometimes my master awakens me sharply with the rod.

In addition to his responsibilities as a school teacher, Ælfric was in great demand as a preacher and translator, and it is this pressure

[98]

that produced his major works, including the translations from the Old Testament. The scope of his work can best be visualized by dividing it into liturgical and nonliturgical categories. The *Catholic Homilies*, for example, are essentially liturgical, that is, they were written for use in the services of the church in accordance with the calendar of seasons which we have already considered in an earlier chapter. One series of homilies begins with Christmas and ends with Advent, thus covering all the essential feasts of the *temporale* for the year. Most of these homilies are expositions of pericopes, that is, portions of the Gospels designated to be read in the mass for a particular day. A second series of liturgical homilies is designed for the *sanctorale*, which, as we have seen, is the calendar of the church as it applies to commemorations of the saints. Since Ælfric is five centuries earlier than Caxton there are naturally fewer saints than are represented in the *Golden Legend*; nevertheless there are over thirty in Ælfric's collection, and this does not include numerous homilies for days unspecified, such as "In Memory of the Saints," "On the Day of Judgment," and "The People of Israel." Taken together, Ælfric's *Catholic Homilies* provide thorough coverage, of both the seasons and the saints.

The rest of Ælfric's writing can be called nonliturgical, that is, not for explicit use in connection with a particular day, but the distinction is rather arbitrary. In this category, for example, belong the lives of the saints which were not included in the *sanctorale* mentioned above. There are more than two dozen of these—though it is difficult to be sure of the authorship of all of them—and there can be little doubt that Ælfric's monastic contemporaries found them liturgically useful, even though they are not explicitly shaped to this purpose in the versions that have survived. At this point Ælfric's writing, though technically prose, had achieved that alliterative style for which he became justly famous. Indeed, by the time he completed the lives of the saints, perhaps around the year 1000, he was an accomplished stylist, very much in demand in a nation where even the leaders were still rarely well educated.

The impetus for his translation of Genesis seems to have come from a friend of his named Æthelweard the alderman, whom Ælfric addresses in his Preface:

> You asked me, dear friend, to translate the book of Genesis from Latin into English. And when I thought it a burdensome thing to do, you said that I need only translate the book up to Isaac, Abraham's son, because some other man had translated from Isaac to the end of the

book. Now it seems to me, dear friend, that that work is very hazardous for me or any other man to undertake, for I fear that if some ignorant man reads that book or hears it read, he will think that he may live now, under the new law, as our forefathers lived in the time before the old law was ordained, or as men lived under the law of Moses.

The Preface makes it clear that Ælfric undertook the translation of Genesis with genuine concern about consequences. It is important, I think, to realize the nature of his concern, and not regard it in the same light as the fears aroused by translation of the Bible in the time of Wyclif and after. Not only must we consider the ignorance of the population in the tenth century, but also the great awe and reverence for the Bible that existed. This made for an explosive combination, and Ælfric knew it. In his homilies, he was able to give the essence of a biblical narrative and expound its meaning with clarity and force; but it was something entirely different to offer to an essentially uneducated people a translation of Genesis, as it were, stripped bare of exegesis. We have already noticed the care with which commentary was woven into the prose translation of the psalms in the Paris Psalter. It is not surprising that Ælfric should have been similarly concerned about his translation of Genesis.

Perhaps it was this issue that led Ælfric to do an English version of Alcuin's *Questions of Sigewulf the Priest on Genesis*. The Latin text has some 280 questions, which Ælfric reduces to 69, covering the first half of Genesis, the part which he agreed to translate for Æthelweard. He begins by telling who Alcuin was, how he taught in the court of Charlemagne, and how he was prevailed upon to answer the questions of Sigewulf. The questions themselves explore such issues as the nature of the universe, the Trinity as manifested in the creation, the origin and nature of man, and the origin of evil. For example: How is it to be understood that almighty God ceased his labors on the seventh day when he created all things, whereas Christ said in his Gospel, "My Father worketh even now, and I work"? The answer: God ceased then the new creation, but He renews this same universe each day and guides His handiwork until the end of the world. Question: How many rational creatures did God make? Answer: Two—angels and men. And so it continues, covering the first three ages of man, up to the time of Abraham in the middle of Genesis.

Though Ælfric does not mention Alcuin's *Questions* in his Preface to Genesis, it is very likely that he has them in mind, and he raises additional questions of his own to show Æthelweard the basis for his reluctance to undertake the translation. "Once I knew a certain masspriest," he says, "that was my master at that time, who had the book of Genesis, and he could in part understand Latin. And he said concerning the patriarch Jacob that he had four wives, two sisters and their two handmaids. He spoke the complete truth; but he did not know, nor did I then, how great a difference there is between the Old Law and the New."

Ælfric goes on to give a kind of historical perspective on the Old Testament, showing how what was right for the patriarchs may no longer be appropriate for those living under the New Law. The relevance of Genesis is then spelled out in terms of its Christological meaning: "It begins thus: *In principio creavit deus celum et terram,* which in English is, 'In the beginning God created the heaven and the earth.' It was truly so done, that God Almighty made in the beginning that which he wished of creation. Nevertheless, according to the ghostly meaning that beginning is Christ, as he himself says to the Jews: 'I am the beginning, that speak to you.'" The Spirit of God which moves over the waters is then explained as the Holy Ghost, thus completing the participation of the Trinity in creation. Other manifestations of the Trinity are next mentioned, including the appearance of the three angels to Abraham in Genesis 18, after which Ælfric comments that one may, from such examples, come gradually to realize "how deep the book of Genesis is in ghostly meaning, even though it be written with radiant words." The series of examples concludes with an exposition of Joseph as a type of Christ, and the tabernacle of Exodus as a foreshadowing of the Christian Church.

In the conclusion to his Preface, Ælfric makes an important and revealing statement about his role as a translator of Genesis:

Now the aforesaid book is very precisely composed in many passages, and yet very deeply, also, in its spiritual meaning, and it is ordered just as God dictated it to the writer Moses; and we dare write no more in English than the Latin has, nor change the order except only when Latin and English do not agree in the mode of linguistic expression. He who translates or he who teaches from Latin to English must ever arrange it so that English has its own natural order, else it will be very misleading to read for anyone who does not know the order of Latin. It is also to be understood that there were some heretics who would reject the Old Law, and some who would keep the Old and reject the New, just as the Jews do; but Christ himself and his apostles taught us both to hold the Old Law ghostly and the New truthfully in works. God made us two eyes and two ears, two nostrils and two lips, two hands and two feet, and He wished also to have two testaments placed in this world, the Old and the New, for He does whatever is pleasing to Him, and He has no counsellor, nor does any man need to say to Him: "Why doest Thou so?" We must direct our will to His ordinances, and we may not bend His ordinances to our desires. I say now that I dare not and I will not turn any book after this from Latin into English, and I bid thee, dear alderman, not to ask me to any longer, lest I be disobedient to thee, or else utter a lie. I ask now in God's name that, if anyone wishes to copy this book, he correct it carefully from the original, for I have no control whatever if, because of false scribes, it lead anyone to ruin, for then it will be his peril, not mine. The miscopier does much evil, unless he corrects his error.

Although the meaning of this conclusion to the Preface to *Genesis* has been variously interpreted, I believe that it clearly reveals Ælfric's apprehension over the whole project. The translation which follows is a clear and literal rendering of the first twenty-four chapters of Genesis, except that certain chapters, notably those containing genealogies and similar non-narrative materials, are omitted. Only rarely does Ælfric add a phrase or clause that might be construed as exegesis. A representative example would be his translation of Genesis 22, the offering of Isaac, which is very literal throughout, with one exception. In describing the preparations for the sacrifice he says, "and there he (Abraham) built an altar *in the old manner* (on ða ealdan wisan)," the latter phrase, not in the Latin, reminding us that this kind of sacrifice was proper only under the old dispensation. The same point is made in the next verse, which reads, "And he drew his sword that he might offer him *in the old manner.*" This sort of thing is quite rare, however, and it can be fairly said that Ælfric carried out his intention of producing a straight prose translation of the first half of Genesis.

What Ælfric did beyond this is not easy to ascertain. Manuscripts containing this translation also exhibit most of the rest of Genesis, Exodus, Leviticus, Numbers, Deuteronomy, and Joshua, and a homily on Judges, a circumstance which has led modern editors to speak of this collection as the Heptateuch. It is very doubtful, however, that this is all the work of Ælfric. Some see his hand only in Genesis 1–24; others would add portions of Numbers and Joshua. Judges seems authentic, but it is a homily rather than a translation. Probably the safest conclusion is that someone pieced together the Heptateuch, using other translations to fill in the gaps left by Ælfric.

One other bit of evidence, however, points to the possibility of a more ambitious plan on Ælfric's part, and that is his *Treatise on the*

[102]

Old and New Testaments. This was probably not written until after he had become Abbot of Eynsham, near Oxford, in 1005. In it he addresses another friend, Sigwerd, who, he says, has "often entreated me for English scripture." The treatise is a panoramic survey of the contents of the two testaments, in the course of which Ælfric mentions several biblical books which he "turned" (*awende*) into English. These are not in fact translations, but homilies (like that on Judges in the Heptateuch) which Ælfric composed on various occasions earlier in his career. They include Kings (i.e., Samuel-Kings), Judith, Esther, Job, and Maccabees. When these are added to the Heptateuch, a sizable portion of the Old Testament is represented. Whether Ælfric entertained the idea of collecting his biblical writings as a unit we do not know. If he did, he could scarcely have prepared a more appropriate introduction than his *Treatise on the Old and New Testaments.* In any case, it is clearly to Ælfric that we are most indebted for the Old English prose translations and homilies on the Old Testament.

Poetic Paraphrases

The most significant and revealing examples of the influence of the Bible in Old English are not to be found in the translations, but in the poetic paraphrases, which appeared long before the work of translation was even begun. The origin of this school of biblical poetry is traced back to Caedmon, whose story is told by Bede in the *Ecclesiastical History:*

> In the monastery of this abbess [Hilda] there was a certain brother specially distinguished by the divine grace, in that he used to compose songs suited to religion and piety; so that whatever he learnt by translators from the divine Scriptures, he soon after put into poetic words with the greatest sweetness and humility, and brought it forth in his own language, that is, English. By his songs the minds of many were often fired with contempt of the world and with desire for the heavenly life. . . . For he did not learn that art of singing from men, nor taught by man, but he received freely by divine aid the gift of singing. For this reason he could never compose any trivial or vain poem, but only those which belonged to religion suited his religious tongue. For he had lived in the secular habit until he was well advanced in years, and had never learnt anything of versifying; and for this reason sometimes at an entertainment, when it was resolved for the sake of merriment that all should sing in turn, if he saw the harp approaching him, he would rise from the feast and go out and return home.
> When he did this on one occasion, and having left the house where the entertainment was, had gone to the stable of the cattle which had

been committed to his charge that night, and there at the proper time had composed himself to rest, there appeared to him someone in his sleep, and greeting him and calling him by his name, he said: "Caedmon, sing me something." But he replied: "I cannot sing; and for this reason I left the entertainment and came away here, because I could not sing." Then he who was speaking to him replied: "Nevertheless you must sing to me." "What" he said, "must I sing?" And the other said: "Sing of the beginning of creation."

At this point Bede gives a Latin translation of the song, but fortunately some manuscripts preserved the English of Caedmon's song in an Old Northumbrian version:

> Nu scylan hergan   hefænricæs uard,
> metudæs mæcti   end his modgidanc,
> uerc uuldurfadur,   sue he uundra gihuæs,
> eci dryctin,   or astelidæ.
> He ærist scop   ælda barnum
> heben til hrofe,   haleg scepen;
> tha middungeard   moncynnæs uard,
> eci dryctin,   æfter tiadæ,
> firum foldu,   frea allmectig.

This song is composed in the traditional Old English alliterative form: two half-lines of two main stresses each, with alliteration occurring usually in the first three feet but not in the fourth: "*H*eben til *H*rofe, *H*aleg scepen." Here is a fairly literal modernization of the song:

> Now let us praise   the heavenly kingdom's Guardian
> The might of the Measurer   and His wisdom,
> The work of the glorious Father,   as He, of each of wonders,
> The eternal Lord,   established the beginning.
> He first shaped   for the children of men
> Heaven for a roof,   holy Creator;
> Then middle-earth   mankind's Guardian,
> The eternal Lord,   afterward prepared,
> The earth for men,   almighty Lord.

That it should take nine lines to paraphrase the opening verses of Genesis may seem surprising, but the space is required in this instance for the incorporation of a rich series of kennings, or poetic epithets, for God: the heavenly kingdom's Guardian, the Measurer, and so on. These are, of course, the biblical equivalent of the kennings such as giver of rings, whale's road, and gold friend, which go to make up the aureate vocabulary of secular Old English literature. Caedmon's originality lay in his bringing to bear this rich heritage of the Germanic scop, or minstrel, in the composition of biblical poetry.

At the same time, Caedmon's poetry was by no means theologically naïve. As Huppé has pointed out, the theme of praise here associated with the creation had already found its place in the Mass, drawing support from Psalm 19 and perhaps Job 38:4–7. And the doctrine of the Trinity, also traditionally a part of the teaching about Creation, can be seen in the references to God's might, wisdom, and work, corresponding to the Father, Son, and Holy Ghost. In this way the treasury of Old English minstrel tradition was converted to the uses of Christian poetry. Caedmon thus followed the teaching of Saint Augustine, who regarded the spoiling of the Egyptians by the Israelites (Exodus 12:35f.) as a model for the utilization of pagan cultures in the service of God (*On Christian Doctrine*, 2.40.60):

> These are, as it were, their gold and silver, which they did not institute themselves but dug up from certain mines of divine Providence, which is everywhere infused, and perversely and injuriously abused in the worship of demons. When the Christian separates himself in spirit from their miserable society, he should take this treasure with him for the just use of teaching the gospel.

According to Bede, when Caedmon informed the abbess of his dream in the stable, she ordered him to sing his song to some learned men, who concluded that he had received the gift of song by divine inspiration. They then expounded to him more of the sacred history, and he, after spending a night in composition, returned the next day and delivered what they had given him in excellent verse. "He sang," says Bede,

> of the creation of the world and the origin of mankind, and all the history of Genesis, of the exodus of Israel from Egypt and the entry into the land of promise, of very many other stories of Holy Scripture, of the incarnation of the Lord, his passion, resurrection, and ascension into heaven, of the coming of the Holy Spirit, and of the teaching of the Apostles. Also he made many songs about the terror of the future judgment, and the horror of the pains of hell, and the sweetness of the heavenly kingdom; besides very many others about the divine blessings and judgments, in all of which he endeavoured to draw men away from the love of vice and to incite them to the love and practice of well-doing.

From this we might conclude that Caedmon treated very nearly the entire Bible, and indeed the above comes very close to being a description of the surviving body of Old English biblical poetry. But scholars of the period are now agreed that the only surviving text that can safely be attributed to Caedmon himself is the Creation hymn quoted by Bede, and that the poetic paraphrases of the Bible with which we are now concerned are the work of later poets writing in the Caedmonian tradition.

Most Old English poetry was composed during the period A.D. 700–1000, and the greater part of it is either biblical or in some way explicitly religious in form or content. The specifically biblical poems are the paraphrases of Genesis, Exodus, and Daniel in the Old Testament, and a poem on Christ derived freely from the New Testament and Apocrypha with the modern title *Christ and Satan*. As would be expected, there is also a considerable body of works reflecting the liturgical needs of the church, several of these signed by Cynewulf, the one Old English poet besides Caedmon whose name we know. Representing the *temporale* is a series of three texts known by modern editors as *Christ I, II,* and *III,* dealing respectively with the Advent, Ascension, and Last Judgment. *Christ II,* based on a Latin sermon on the Ascension by Gregory the Great, is signed in runic letters near the end by Cynewulf. Representing the *sanctorale* are *The Fates of the Apostles, Andreas, Juliana,* and *Elene,* all by Cynewulf with the possible exception of *Andreas,* and two parts of the life of an Old English saint, known as *Guthlac A* and *B.*

The *Genesis* is largely a paraphrase of the first half of the biblical book, with the story of the fall of the evil angels added from apocryphal sources. This legend is developed vividly in a section of the poem (lines 235–851) based on an Old Saxon version, a fragment of which was discovered at the end of the nineteenth century in the Vatican library. This part of the poem, thought to have been composed in the ninth century, is referred to by editors as *Genesis B* to distinguish it from the earlier surrounding text, designated *Genesis A.* There is no formal separation of the two parts, however, in the Junius manuscript, where the nearly three thousand lines of *Genesis* are preserved.

The *Genesis* begins with praise of God, and a description of the heavenly hosts, followed by a brief account of the fall of the rebellious angels. The creation of man is then explained as the means chosen by God for replacing the angels who had fallen through pride. This prologue takes up over one hundred lines of alliterative verse, at which point the paraphrase of the opening of Genesis, chapter one, begins:

> Her ærest gesceop   ece drihten,
> helm eallwihta, heofon and eorðan,

rodor áræde, and þis rume land
gestaþelode   strangum mihtum,
frea ælmihtig.   Folde wæs þa gyta
græs ungrene;   garsecg þeahte
sweart synnihte, side and wide,
wonne wægas. þa wæs woldortorht
heofonweardes gast   ofer holm boren
miclum spedum. Metod engla heht,
lifes brytta,   leoht forð cuman
ofer rumne grund. Raþe wæs gefylled
heahcininges hæs; him wæs halig leoht
ofer westenne,   swa se wyrhta bebead.

Now first the eternal Lord,
The helm of all creatures, shaped heaven and earth,
Raised up the sky, and this spacious land
Established with strong power,
The almighty Lord. The earth was not yet
Green with grass; darkness of eternal night
Covered the sea, far and wide,
The wan waves. Then the glorious
Spirit of heaven's Guardian was borne over the sea
with great swiftness. The Creator of angels,
The Giver of life, commanded light to come forth
Over the spacious ground. Quickly fulfilled
Was the command of the high King; there was a holy light
Over the wilderness, as the Maker ordered.

Although some leaves are missing from the manuscript, it is evident that the poem included a description of each of the days of creation, climaxed by the creation of man and woman as described in the first two chapters of Genesis.

The description of the four rivers of paradise is interrupted by the loss of perhaps two leaves, after which *Genesis B* begins in the middle of God's warning to Adam against eating the fruit of the tree of knowledge. We are then told how God established ten orders of angels, and placed one (Lucifer) over them all. He was dear to the Lord, and secondly only to Him in power.

"Hwæt sceal ic winnan?" cwæð he. "Why must I strive?" quoth he. "There is no need for me to have a lord. I can work as many wonders with my own hands; I have enough power to fashion a better throne, higher in heaven. Why should I slave after his favor, bow to him in allegiance? I can be God as well as He. Strong comrades stand with me, who will not desert me in battle, boldhearted fighters. These brave warriors have chosen me as their lord. . . . So it seems not right to me that I should have to flatter God at all, for any benefit. No longer will I be his vassal."

[107]

Hearing this, the Lord thrust the proud one and his followers down into hell, and turned them into devils. Henceforth their leader is to be known as Satan.

Down in the abyss Satan adresses his followers:

"This narrow place is most unlike that other home that we formerly knew, high in heaven's kingdom, that my lord granted me, . . . But he has not done right to plunge us into the pit of fire, hell the hot, deprived of the heavenly realm, which he has now marked out for settlement by mankind. That to me is the greatest of sorrows, that Adam, who was made of earth, is to possess my mighty throne, live in joy, while we suffer this punishment, harm in this hell. Alas, if I had the power in my hands and could get free for one hour, just one winter's hour, then with this host, I— But iron bands surround me, a bond of chains rides me down. I am deprived of power; the hard clamps of hell have thus tightly seized me."

This is perhaps sufficient to indicate how fully the character of Satan is realized in *Genesis B*. In the same passage he goes on to exhort his followers to help him lead mankind astray. Quickly a messenger is sent to Eden to take the form of a serpent and be the instrument of temptation. Here the biblical narrative resumes in the third chapter of Genesis, but interestingly enough, there is one important scene in the Old English poem not represented in the Bible. The serpent first approaches Adam, telling him that God wishes him to taste the fruit of the tree of knowledge. With great dignity, Adam refuses the temptation, and the serpent, angry in heart, turns to Eve, with whom he is more successful. The narrative is thereby given an emphasis that accords well with medieval exegesis on the story of the Fall. When the devil persuades Eve to take some of the fruit, the poet explains parenthetically that "God had granted her a weaker mind (*wacran hige*)." In allegorical readings of the temptation, the senses are represented by the serpent, who insinuates himself into the confidence of the lower reason (Eve), which in turn corrupts the higher reason (Adam), resulting in the Fall. This was understood to be the psychological process that results in sin, a process that repeats itself in the life of every individual. It is interesting to find this idea given dramatic expression in the Old English *Genesis*.

The *Exodus* paraphrase is much briefer, amounting to less than six hundred lines, and in fact is limited to the story of the departure from Egypt as told in Exodus 12–14. It opens with the minstrel's exclamation, Hwæt! "What! We have heard far and near over middle-earth of the judgments of Moses, wonderful laws for the generations of

[108]

men . . . ," and goes on to tell how God gave Moses the power to work miracles and made him leader of the sons of Abraham to free them from bondage. The story really begins with the death of the first born of the Egyptians, which is thus described in the biblical text (Exodus 12:29–30): "And it came to pass, that at midnight the Lord smote all the firstborn in the land of Egypt, from the firstborn of Pharaoh that sat on his throne unto the firstborn of the captive that was in the dungeon; and all the firstborn of cattle. And Pharaoh rose up in the night, he, and all his servants, and all the Egyptians; and there was a great cry in Egypt; for there was not a house where there was not one dead." In the Old English poem, this event is paraphrased as follows: "Then was the greatest of nations strongly afflicted with death, old sorrows; at the fall of the treasure-keepers lamentation was renewed, festivities ceased with the loss of riches. At midnight He struck down terribly the wicked ones, many of the firstborn, slew the watchmen. The slayer moved abroad, the hostile enemy, the land darkened with the bodies of the slain; the citizens went forth, weeping was wide-spread, little rejoicing. The hands of the laughter-smiths were locked, death was let loose, and the people mourned."

Even more detailed is the poet's description of the march of Israel to the Red Sea. Even though it is not exactly appropriate to the subject, the poet uses the language of battle. Moses is called the "glorious hero," and the other people are described as a well-equipped fighting army. The war-trumpet sounds, the host of brave men moves forward to the sea. As his imagination warms to the task, the poet sees the cloud which leads Israel by day, first as a canopy to protect them from the heat, then as a billowing sail, guiding the Israelite "sailors" on their path to the shore. At night the pillar of fire gleams on their shields, and drives away the shadows, terrors of the desert night, while at the same time it threatens disobedient Israelites with a fiery death.

> The bright army shone, shields gleamed;
> The shield-warriors, down the straight road,
> Saw the banner over the army, pointing the way forward,
> Up to the seacoast, at the land's end
> Standing opposite the host. Camp was pitched;
> Weary they rested, while stewards served
> The brave ones with food, restored their strength.
> Tents of the sailors were spread over the hills
> When the trumpet sang. Then was the fourth camp,
> Resting-place of the shield-warriors by the Red Sea.

[109]

As Pharaoh's pursuing host draws near, the familiar birds of prey begin to circle the field, eager for slaughter, just as they do in Old English secular poetry. Wolves sing their dread evensong (*æfenleoð*) in expectation of a feast. The terror-inspiring advance of the Egyptian army is then described, which is halted abruptly when the pillar of cloud throws the attacking force into confusion, allowing Israel to escape. The Egyptians are drowned, and the Israelites thank God for delivering them from slavery: "They lifted up their hands in thanksgiving for safety; they were happy — they saw their deliverance; they heeded the spoils of war, bondage was broken. Among the battle-standards on the shore they began to divide the spoils washed up by the sea, the old treasure, garments and shields. They justly divided the gold and precious cloth, the treasure of Joseph, possession of men. Its former guardians, the greatest of armies, lay in the place of death."

The *Exodus* is certainly the most spirited of the Old English biblical paraphrases. Even though the poet might be considered unhistorical in depicting Israel as a fighting army, he has created an exciting narrative that does not really contradict the epic spirit of the biblical story. This is in fact one of the strengths of the Old English paraphrases: an ability to re-create the ancient text for a new audience by making a cultural "translation" of the materials.

A good example of poetry that reflects the influence of the liturgy, rather than the Bible directly, is part II of the *Christ*, signed by the poet Cynewulf, and found in the Exeter Book. It is, as we have seen, largely indebted to a homily on the Ascension by Gregory the Great. The first two sections describe Christ's farewell to the disciples and his Ascension to heaven accompanied by angels, who sing a hymn of welcome when the Lord is received in the heavenly city. The remaining three sections develop the significance of this event as expounded by Gregory. In the Ascension Christ completed the work of salvation, and thus turned aside the curse that came upon man as a result of the Fall. Hence we should praise Him for the hope that we now have. Job likened His Ascension to the flight of a bird (Job 28:7) which was invisible to those whose hearts are hardened, and who consequently do not believe that through Him mankind was exalted above the glorious hosts of heaven. Yet not only did Christ establish a place for us on high, He also granted us gifts of wisdom. To some He gives eloquence in speaking and singing. One can skillfully play the harp with his fingers, loudly before heroes he can sweep the strings. Others know the law, astronomy, composition. One gains victory in battle; another drives a ship over the salt sea; all these skills and more the Lord grants to men on earth.

The poet in the fourth section of the homily develops a traditional theme based on the Song of Solomon (2:8): *The voice of my beloved! behold, he cometh leaping upon the mountains, skipping upon the hills.* The beloved is traditionally interpreted as Christ, of course, and this is clearly brought out in our poet's paraphrase: "It shall be made known that the King of angels, the Lord great in might, shall go up the mount, leap upon the lofty downs, shall garb with His glory the hills and peaks, redeem the world, all dwellers on earth, by the noble leap." The "leaps" of Christ are six in number: conception, birth, Crucifixion, entombment, Harrowing of Hell, and, finally, the Ascension. Men, too, must leap in imitation of Christ that they may seek salvation and finally ascend to heaven, for which God be praised. The last section of *Christ II* is taken up with the terrors of judgment, in the course of which the poet, Cynewulf, signs his name in runic letters.

> þonne ᚻ cwacað, gehyreð cyning mæðlan,
> rodera ryhtend, sprecan reþe word
> þam þe him ær in worulde wace hyrdon,
> þendan ᚣ ond ᚾ yþast meahtan
> frofre findan. þær sceal forht monig
> on þam wongstede werig bidan
> hwæt him æfter dædum deman wille
> wraþra wita. Biþ se ᚹ scæcen
> eorþan frætwa. ᚢ wæs longe
> ᛚ flodum bilocen, lifwynna dæl,
> ᚠ on foldan.

Each rune stands for a word that begins with that letter:

ᚻ = Cen = the brave
ᚣ = Yr = misery (?)
ᚾ = Nyd = distress
ᚹ = Wenne = joy
ᚢ = Ur(e) = our (?)
ᛚ = Lagu = water, sea
ᚠ = Feoh = fee, wealth

The time is at hand, he says, when the *brave* (C) shall tremble, all who would find solace from *misery* (Y) and *distress* (N). Gone is the *joy* (W) of earth's jewels. For long was *our* (U) portion of life's pleasures enclosed by *water* (L), our *wealth* (F) on earth. Since each rune has a meaning, they not only spell the name CYN(E)WULF, they are also fit ingeniously into the sentiment of the passage in which they appear. The poem then concludes with a final warning of the Judgment, when there will be weeping and wailing and gnashing of teeth. The sea voyage of this life is perilous, and the deep road is storm-tossed. But God's Son gave us grace to learn where we may "moor the sea steeds, the ancient wave-horses, firmly with anchors over the side of the ship. Let us fix our hope in that haven which the Sovereign of the Skies prepared for us, in its holiness on high, when He rose to heaven." The piece thus concludes with the sea-journey metaphor, a favorite of the Old English poets, combined with a final reference to the Ascension itself.

Elene, another poem by Cynewulf, is representative of the various works reflecting the influence of the *sanctorale*. Its subject is the discovery of the true cross by Saint Helena, commemorated in the calendar on May 3. We are told of the Emperor Constantine, his dream of the cross, his victory in battle, and subsequent conversion to Christianity. His dream is particularly vivid. The night before the great battle, an angel comes to him in his sleep, and directs his attention to heaven. He sees upon the roof of the clouds the glorious cross in its beauty gleaming with ornaments, decked with gold, and gems glittering upon it. On the bright wood are shining letters: "In this sign thou shalt conquer." The emperor is so impressed by this vision that after his victory and his conversion he asks his mother, Helena, to make a pilgrimage to the holy land in search of the original cross used in the Crucifixion of Jesus. Helena goes by ship through the Mediterranean, and Cynewulf once again indulges his love of sea-journeys: "The sea-horses stood ready at the shore of the sea, ocean steeds bound by ropes, lying on the water. . . . They loaded the wave-horses with coats of mail, with shields and spears, with armored warriors, with men and woman. . . . Then they let the high ships sweep foaming over the sea. Often the sides of the ship above the water caught the blows of the waves; the sea resounded. . . . Blithe were the warriors, brave in heart; the queen rejoiced in the journey."

In Jerusalem Helena calls together men wise in the Hebrew Law and among them finds one, Judas, who, after threat of starvation and execution, agrees to search for the cross. He leads them to the hill of Calvary, and there prays to the Lord for guidance. Then he begins digging and, after some time, uncovers three crosses. At first they are unable to decide which of the three had been the one used for Jesus; but finally, at the ninth hour, a funeral passes near the spot in the city where the crosses were placed, and Judas orders the body to be brought to him. Taking each of the crosses in turn, he holds them over the body. The first two are useless, but when he lifts the third one up, the corpse stirs, and the dead person is restored to life amid the praise and thanksgiving of all the people. Thus the true cross was identified, and the Emperor, when he heard the news, ordered a temple to be built on Calvary in honor of the discovery. The cross was encrusted in precious stones, and enclosed in a silver case. Judas, who discovered it, was baptized, and took the Christian name Cyriacus.

The use of the Bible in the creation of this legend is clear enough. Even the popular antitheses of Saint Paul can be seen in the character of Judas. Just as Adam's fall finds its counterpart in Christ's redemption, or as Babylon is counterbalanced by Jerusalem, so Judas the betrayer is matched by Judas the discoverer of the cross and the convert to Christianity. When he raises the dead man, the devil is heard to exclaim: "Once I was heartened by Judas, and now once again by Judas I am humiliated!" A less obvious use of the Bible is reflected in a minor episode toward the end. At the urging of Helena, Judas searches for and finds the nails, shining like gold in the ground. Overjoyed, Helena consults a sage, asking him what disposition should be made of the nails. The wise man without hesitation tells the queen to have the nails made into a bit for the bridle of a horse belonging to the noblest of kings. He explains to her that this bridle will then assure victory for the king in battle, neglecting to point out that his strange instructions are also intended as a fulfillment of the prophecy of Zechariah (14:20): *In that day shall that which is upon the bridle of the horse be holy to the Lord.* Thus medieval exegesis plays its role in the fashioning of postbiblical legends such as that of St. Helena and the true cross.

Allegory and Wisdom Literature

Under the heading of allegory and wisdom we find miscellaneous Old English verse which shows biblical influence only in the most general sense. *The Phoenix,* for example, is a free rendering of a Latin poem by Lactantius, but it is turned by the Old English poet into a more explicit Christian allegory using the model of biblical exegesis. The first half is devoted to an account of this fabulous bird and its flight from the earthly paradise, in the course of which the poet "plants" the hidden significance he wishes to bring out. The second half expounds the meaning of the legend in the manner of biblical

[113]

exegesis. The interpretive part of the poem has sometimes been regarded as inconsistent, since the Phoenix is made to symbolize at different times both Christ and mankind. But in this the poet is simply following the pattern we have seen established in medieval commentaries, where the literal history is followed by exegesis on the allegorical and moral levels, as in Gregory's *Morals on Job*.

The Phoenix opens with a description of the garden of the earthly paradise, based on the Eden of Genesis but so thoroughly embellished with traditional features that it is scarcely recognizable: "I have heard that far hence in the east there is the noblest of lands, famous among men. Nor is that part of the world accessible to many land-dwellers in middle-earth, but it is removed, through God's power, far from evildoers." The description continues, stressing the beautiful sights, sounds, and scents of the land. It has no summer or winter, no steep cliffs, no hills or mountains. Fruits never fail, and the trees stand green on the high plain. By God's grace this garden was untouched by the flood that engulfed the world. There is neither rain nor storm, but streams well forth to water the earth. This garden, in short, reflects the innocent state of nature before the fall of man, when the ground was cursed for his sake (Gen. 3:17).

In this beautiful wood dwells the Phoenix, a bird wondrously fair, strong with feathers. From its nest it rises to greet the dawn, and twelve times each day it bathes in the cool waters of the stream. When the sun stands high in the heavens it flies aloft and sings a song more beautiful than anything heard by sons of men. At sunset it falls silent, lifts its head and listens. After a thousand years the Phoenix leaves its home in the earthly paradise and flies westward, accompanied by flocks of birds intent on serving the famous one, until he reaches the land of Syria. Here he leaves his followers and builds his nest in a tall palm tree. The nest is made of pleasant plants and blooms of the wood which the bird gathers from the surrounding country. At last when the Phoenix is perched on his nest, in the heat of summer, the nest is ignited by the sun, and the bird is consumed by the flames. Out of the ashes, however, comes a worm from which is born a new Phoenix, young and splendid in appearance. While it grows and develops its plumage it eats only a little honey-dew, which often falls at midnight. At last it flies back to the east, taking with it the remnants of bones from the funeral pyre of the old bird, which it buries in the woodland of paradise. Then the new phoenix lives out its alloted span in paradise, and at last repeats the journey to the land of Syria where it builds its final nest as before.

In the latter half of the poem the significance of the legend is explained. The Phoenix represents man, who was forced to leave Paradise and make his abode in a strange land. After the coming of Christ, man was shown how to return to the beautiful land from which he was exiled. Hence by building himself a nest of good deeds in this life, each Christian man is able, when consumed by death, to find his way to Paradise at the resurrection. "Then holy spirits shall sing, and steadfast souls shall lift up a song, the pure and elect ones shall praise the majesty of the King with voice upon voice; their praise shall rise to glory fragrant with incense, with good deeds. Then shall the spirits of men be refined, brightly cleansed in the flame of fire." The ingenuity of this kind of allegory delighted the medieval reader; yet, as we have seen, commentators usually insisted that it be responsibly developed from a sound biblical base. Our poet seems to have been conscious of his responsibilities as an exegete. "Let no man think," he says, interrupting the allegory at this point, "that I compose this song, write poetry with lying words." And in support of his interpretation of the Phoenix he turns to the book of Job, where we read (29:18), *I shall die in my nest, and I shall multiply my days as the phoenix* (Vulgate *palma*). To show that Job here refers to and awaits his own resurrection, the poet ties this verse to the famous passage beginning *For I know that my redeemer liveth* (19:25). He concludes: "Thus the sage in days of old, the prophet of God wise in heart, sang of his resurrection into eternal life, so that we might more readily perceive the famous token that the glorious bird typifies in its burning." It is a matter of some significance, I think, to see Job being invoked here by the poet to authenticate his reading of *The Phoenix*. One is reminded of the words of Gregory in his *Morals on Job:* let the man who disbelieves the resurrection blush at the faith of Job, who believed it even before it happened.

Another Old English allegorical poem is the *Physiologus,* or Bestiary, much briefer than *The Phoenix,* which describes creatures of the natural world and then expounds their significance. The work is a fragment, leading off with the panther, whale, and a bird which is apparently intended as the partridge, though the description is incomplete. The most interesting of these is the whale, whose identification with the devil may perhaps be based on Leviathan in Job.

[115]

The whale, we are told, often floats in the sea looking like an island, so much so that sailors sometimes land on him, set up camp, and build a fire. When the whale feels the fire, suddenly he dives to the sea bottom, and the men are drowned. The feeding habits of the whale are also described. When he is hungry, a pleasant smell comes from his mouth, which he opens wide. This attracts fish that swim into the huge mouth until it is full, and then the fierce jaws snap shut. These tactics are then expounded as the devil's way of enticing sinners to damnation, and the reader is finally exhorted to resist the devil's wiles and seek eternal salvation.

The wisdom literature in Old English is various, and of less importance than allegory in the tracing of biblical influences. It includes riddles, proverbs, and dialogues such as *Solomon and Saturn*, the latter a branch of the *Solomon and Marcolf* legend. Also under this heading are the poems of moral and religious instruction, such as *The Arts of Men, The Fates of Men, Doomsday,* and *The Soul's Address to the Body.* The last is perhaps typical of this category of writing, and was very popular throughout the medieval period. The soul speaks to the body and condemns it for its sins. Look what affliction you have caused me! In life you indulged yourself in pleasures, and now you are food for worms. The poem also alludes to some interesting beliefs associated with death. The soul, we are informed, must always visit the body on the seventh night, for three hundred years, unless the end of the world comes before then. In the course of his complaint, the soul remarks that it would have been better if the body had been born a fowl, fish, or animal of the earth, or even a worm, rather than a man who must answer to God at the Judgment. Behind this sentiment may linger a primitive notion of the soul's power to take up its abode in various creatures other than man. But the clear and explicit meaning of the poem is a warning to mankind that a good life is the only defence when the Judgment comes. In one of the grimmest passages in Old English, the poet provides a graphic description of the way in which worms eat their way through the corpse. In passages like this the asceticism of the Desert Fathers achieves its ultimate expression.

Elegiac and Heroic Poetry

This last heading includes some of the best-known Old English poetry: the elegies first, then *Beowulf, Judith,* and the *Dream of the Rood.* All but the last two have usually been regarded as "secular" poetry as distinct from the larger body of religious texts, and hence it may appear arbitrary to group them with religious works like *Judith* and the *Dream of the Rood*. Nevertheless it seems to me that these poems all have a style and a quality that bind them together. The traditional distinction based on subject-matter ("secular" and "religious") has a certain usefulness, but should not be allowed to obscure an important similarity in these few major poems.

The two best-known elegies, *The Wanderer* and *The Seafarer*, are preserved in the Exeter Book, and both are essentially dramatic monologues of the fleeting nature of earthly joys. The solitary spokesman of *The Wanderer* tells us that he has for years been separated from his kinsmen, and deprived of a leader by the death of his gold-friend, his lord. Few realize how cruel a sorrow it is to wander homeless, without a protector, dreaming of the joys that he used to have under the favor of his lord and friend. "It seems to him in his mind that he embraces and kisses his lord and lays hands and head on his knee, as when formerly in days of old he was near the gift-throne. Then the friendless man awakens once more, and sees before him the dark waves, sea-birds bathing, spreading feathers, frost and snow falling mingled with hail." Thus sorrow is renewed as the wanderer thinks how suddenly the lives of men are swept away. Therefore he concludes that a wise man will bide his time, not be overpassionate or anxious. As he looks around him, the speaker sees this lesson illustrated in the ruins of older civilizations — perhaps Roman remains that the poet had observed in Britain. "The wine-halls crumble, the rulers lie down, deprived of joy, the warriors have all fallen, proud by the wall. War took some, carried them on far paths; one the bird carried off over the high sea, one the grey wolf divided in death, one an earl with sad countenance hid in an earth-cave. Thus the Shaper of men laid waste this earth till the old work of giants stood empty, deprived of the laughter of castle-dwellers. . . . Where has the horse gone? Where the man? Where the giver of treasure? Where the place of feasting? Where are the joys of the hall?" All these are gone, says the wanderer, the darkness descends bringing terror to men. All earthly joys are transitory. We must therefore seek mercy and comfort from the heavenly Father, our fortress and strength. Thus the poem expresses, despite its nostalgia, a final contempt for the world together with an appeal for mercy to God in its conclusion.

The Seafarer is very similar in spirit to *The Wanderer*, but it develops a more complex interplay between the temporal and eternal longings of the speaker. It is clear, for example, that the sailor who

[117]

speaks has a genuine affection for the sea—an affection that might at first seem to undermine the expected contempt for the world. "I took my joy in the cry of the gannet," he says, "and the sound of the curlew, instead of the laughter of men, in the screaming gull instead of the drink of mead." Yet his attitude toward the sea seems to waver between affection and distrust, so much so that some readers have thought that the poem is a dialogue between two speakers. He longs to go to sea; yet he calls the sea his "paths of exile." A key paradox is at the center of the poem. When spring makes the earth beautiful, then the seafarer longs to depart on his sea-journey. "The groves put forth blossoms, the towns grow fair, the fields beautiful, the world comes alive. All these things urge the heart of the eager-minded man to a journey, who thus intends to go far on the flood-paths." The feeling described here is a genuine one; yet at the same time, as has been suggested, the passage echoes the eschatology of the Gospels (Mark 13:28–29): *Now learn a parable of the fig tree; When her branch is yet tender, and putteth forth leaves, ye know that summer is near: So ye in like manner, when ye shall see these things come to pass, know that it is nigh, even at the doors.* The recognition that the speaker's imagery has biblical echoes adds, in this case, to the significance of the poem. My heart is restless, he says, the lone-flyer screams, urging my heart to the whale-path over the stretch of seas. Thus I burn rather for the joys of the Lord than for this dead fleeting life on earth. The poem concludes with an extended passage expressing contempt for the world in the style of *The Wanderer*.

These two poems have sometimes been read as expressions of a pre-Christian spirit, a Germanic fatalism, to which pious sentiments have been added. But the reader who comes to them from the literature of the early Church must surely recognize that both poems admirably express the asceticism of Fathers such as Gregory the Great. An intense awareness of the old age of the world is everywhere apparent, and the Old English poets, along with the early Fathers of the Church, considered themselves to be living in the latter days, and looked forward to the consummation of the age in the Last Judgment. Hence the Old English elegies become clearer to the modern reader, I believe, if they are placed against an ascetic background, and framed in eschatology.

The greatest of all Old English poems is of course the *Beowulf*, named after the Geatish hero whose epic encounters with fabulous monsters provide the substance of the story. The rapid survey allowed here cannot do justice to the art and sophistication of this poem, but I would like to touch on a question that has tantalized numerous interpreters of *Beowulf* during the last century. Is this a Christian poem? If so, in what sense? At first glance one is tempted to regard it as a survival of the pagan heritage of the Anglo-Saxons. The setting is the north European home of the Germanic tribes; England finds no place in the story at all. Beowulf travels from the court of Higelac, king of the Geats, across the water to Heorot, the royal hall of the Danish king Hrothgar. The first half of the poem is taken up with Beowulf's defense of Heorot against the ravages of a monster named Grendel, and, subsequently, of Grendel's mother. Victorious over both, Beowulf receives the gratitude and gifts of the Danish king, and returns in triumph to the court of his own lord, Higelac. The second half of the poem concentrates on a single event many years later. Beowulf has become king of the Geats, and is now grown old. A fire-breathing dragon is ravaging the land, and Beowulf, in spite of his age, prepares himself for battle against it. Eleven warriors accompany him to the cave, but Beowulf goes against the dragon alone. Mortally wounded, he manages finally to kill the dragon with the help of Wiglaf, the only warrior courageous enough to come to his aid. The poem ends with a description of the funeral pyre, lamentation, and building of Beowulf's grave mound on a headland overlooking the sea.

Against the evidence of the pagan setting, however, it is often urged that the poet is nevertheless Christian in his treatment of the story. He explicitly states, at one point, that the Danes were guilty of heathen worship, that they "did not know the Lord," and it is clear that he means this as a criticism. The monster Grendel, moreover, is said to be descended from the race of Cain, thus connecting the Germanic antagonist with biblical legend. The way in which Grendel is introduced, in fact, is a good illustration of biblical influence in the handling of the narrative. The poet describes the building of Heorot, the magnificent royal hall of the Danes. To celebrate its completion, Hrothgar holds a great banquet and distributes treasures to his followers. At this point Grendel is brought into the story:

> Then the bold spirit, he who dwelt in darkness, could scarcely endure the torment of hearing every day the joyful sounds, loud in the hall. There was the sound of the harp, the clear song of the minstrel. He who could tell of the origin of men from ancient times said that the Almighty created the earth, the beautiful land encompassed by water; the Victorious One set the sun and moon as lights for the land-dwellers, and

[119]

adorned the expanse of the earth with branches and leaves; He likewise created life of all kinds that move and live. Thus the warriors lived happily in peace, until a certain fiend in hell began to perform his evil work. The grim spirit was called Grendel, famous march-stepper, who held the moors, the fen and fastness.

The contrast is clearly made between light and darkness in this scene. Forgotten is the paganism of the Danes. Their minstrel sings of the creation in the manner of Caedmon, while the fiend lurks in outer darkness. The motivation for Grendel's hatred is interesting. He cannot stand to hear the sounds of joy coming from the hall, just as for Satan, in *Genesis B*, it is the greatest of griefs to think that Adam should dwell in bliss. This is of course only a brief scene near the beginning of the poem, but in it we seem to see the influence of biblical tradition strongly at work in the poet's imagination as he gives depth and significance to the narrative.

When we consider the length of the poem, however—over three thousand lines—the biblical allusions are relatively few and far between. Hence it has been argued, with some plausibility, that the *Beowulf* is essentially a pagan poem with certain Christian additions not essential to its structure. There is one passage, however, at the mid-point of the poem, which I think tells against the theory of pagan origin. After Beowulf's victorious defense of Heorot, and just before his return home, Hrothgar addresses him in an extended speech of praise and of warning. He praises him for his heroic achievement, and warns him against the sin of pride. A man may be granted many victories in this life, he says, but he should never, because of them, allow pride to spring up within himself. If this happens, then the keeper of the soul slumbers and the slayer draws near who shoots maliciously from his bow. "Then is he struck under the helm in his breast with a bitter arrow (not knowing how to guard himself) by the crafty promptings of the accursed spirit." Thus he is robbed of the generous qualities that should govern his life and he becomes grasping and passionate in his pride. Hrothgar warns Beowulf to guard against this ambush by the devil, and choose the better part, eternal benefits (*ece rædas*). Remember that, sooner or later, age, battle, fire or flood will rob you of strength, and death will finally be victorious.

Hrothgar's use of the arrow of pride is very much in the manner of Gregory's commentary on Job 39:23, *Over him will rattle the quiver, the spear will shake and the shield:* "The heavenly soldier is often opposed by the enemy in both ways, at one and the same time, in order that he may be destroyed by some one blow. For the crafty adversary endeavors to strike at the same time, both raging openly, and lurking in ambush; in order that while the arrow is dreaded from a secret spot, the spear may be less feared before his face; or that, while he withstands the spear before his face, the arrow may not be observed when coming from a secret place." Gregory goes on to liken the spear to lust, and the arrow to pride. It is tempting to conclude that Hrothgar's sermon owes something to Gregory's exposition of the sudden ambush of pride. But the significant point to note here is the function of this centrally located passage. It places a value on Beowulf's achievements, while at the same time it establishes an important moral standard for judging his conduct when adversity strikes: "The embrace of fire, or the surge of the flood, or the grip of the blade, or the flight of the spear, or hateful old age, or the time when the gleam of the eyes shall pass away and be darkened." This, of course, is precisely the subject of the second half of the poem, which is climaxed by the fatal fight with the dragon, the final and most terrible form of the old enemy that Beowulf has to face. That he dies in killing the dragon should not be interpreted as punishment for pride. Beowulf acquits himself nobly, and is conquered only by death, which, as Hrothgar said, would be victorious at the last.

With *Beowulf* in the Cotton manuscript is *Judith*, an excellent poetic version of the Old Testament apocryphal book of that name. Its beginning is lost, but very little seems to be missing. The poem concentrates on the latter part of the story—Judith's visit to the camp of Holofernes, who commands the siege of the Israelite city of Bethulia. The poem opens with a banquet scene which is given a traditonal development. Holofernes is in the mead-hall, surrounded by his thanes. Drunk with wine, he calls for Judith to be brought to his bed. When they are left alone in the pavilion, Holofernes falls on the bed in a stupor, and Judith draws his sword. Praying to God for aid, she strikes the heathen warrior in the neck, but only wounds him. "He was not yet dead, not wholly lifeless. The fearless woman again fiercely smote the heathen hound, so that his head rolled forth on the floor." From the corpse the spirit departed to hell where it was bound forever in torment, empty of joy. Judith returns to the city with the enemy's head, and the people rejoice. As might be expected, the Old English poet gives especial emphasis to the battle that follows. The Israelite warriors make ready and march out with victory-banners against the foe, with shields ringing.

The wolf and the raven rejoice in anticipation of a feast of fated men, the horny-beaked eagle sings a song of war.

The ensuing battle occupies the remainder of the poem, which concludes with a description of the war booty given to Judith by the victorious army. This emphasis on combat is considerably greater than that provided by the biblical account. Some interpreters have regarded this as a reflection of the poet's barbaric absorption in bloodshed, but there is another possible explanation. Judith's outstanding virtue is courage in the face of overwhelming odds, a virtue also displayed by the Israelite army. Could the poet have had in mind the threat to England represented by the Danish invaders? If so, the courage of Judith may have been intended as a model for Englishmen. Indeed, some students of Old English believe that the poet may have based his characterization of Judith on a Saxon heroine, Æthelflæd, daughter of King Alfred, a notable leader of resistance against the Danes in the early years of the tenth century. Perhaps significant in this connection is the fact that Ælfric, in his *Treatise on the Old and New Testaments,* informs us that he turned the book of *Judith* into English as an example of heroism against an invader, "that you might defend your land with weapons against an attacking army." Ælfric was of course referring to one of his homilies; but it may well be that the author of the poetic *Judith* was inspired by a similar patriotism.

Our final Old English poem is *The Dream of the Rood,* a visionary poem on the cross which I think best exemplifies the merging of the heroic and the religious spirit in a single composition. The poet tells us that he had a dream one night in which he saw the cross, encompassed with light, and ornamented with gold. Gems glowed on the cross-beam, and hosts of angels surrounded it. Blessed was this victory-cross, he says, and I was stained with sins, wounded with transgressions. Yet in spite of its beauty, through the gold I could perceive blood left there by ancient suffering. Sorrows overcame me, and I was afraid at the fair sight, at times running with blood, at times shining with ornaments. But after a long time the tree of the savior spoke to me out loud. Here the cross begins to tell its own story:

> It was long ago—I still remember it—when I was cut down at the edge of the grove. Strong enemies took me and fashioned me for a spectacle, commanded me to lift up their criminals. Men bore me on their shoulders until they set me on hill, and fastened me there. Then

I saw the Lord of mankind hasten with great strength to climb upon me, nor did I dare, against God's command, bow down or shatter, when the earth began to tremble. I could have struck down the enemies, but I stood fast. Then the young Hero prepared Himself—He was God Almighty—strong and bold; He ascended the high gallows, brave in the sight of the multitude, when He would redeem mankind. I trembled when the young man embraced me; nor did I dare to bow to the earth, fall to its surface, but I had to stand fast. I was raised as a cross; I lifted up the powerful King, the Lord of the heavens; I dared not bend down. They drove through me with dark nails; in me can be seen the wounds, the open hate-wounds; and I dared not harm any of them. They mocked us both together. I was all covered with blood, that flowed from the side of the Man, when He gave up his spirit. On that hill I endured many hostile trials. I saw the God of hosts severely stretched out. Darkness covered with clouds the body of the Lord, the bright radiance; a shadow went forth, dark under the clouds. All creation wept, bewailed the fall of the King. Christ was on the cross.

The cross goes on to describe the taking down of the Lord's body, and its burial in the tomb. Throughout the remainder of the poem the heroic mood is beautifully sustained. Christ is described as "limb-weary" (*lim-werignĕ*); when they placed him on the ground, says the cross, "He rested him there a while, weary after the great strife" (*he hine þær hwile reste, meðe æfter þam miclan gewinne*). After enclosing Him in the tomb, the disciples sang a sorrow-song, the wretched ones at eventide, before they departed. Then the cross tells the history of its burial and eventual discovery, alluding to the legend of Saint Helena discussed earlier in this chapter, and exhorts the dreamer to tell the story of Christ and the cross among men. The poem ends with a meditation by the dreamer. My soul, he says, yearns to depart this life, and join those friends who have already sought the kingdom of heaven. Each day I look for the time when the cross will take me from this transitory life, bring me to the heavenly home prepared for us by Christ. This summary is no substitute for the poem itself, but perhaps it is sufficient to show that the *Dream of the Rood* is composed in the same ascetic mood as *The Wanderer* and *The Seafarer*, and at the same time draws effectively on that heroic spirit that is characteristic of the epic *Beowulf*, giving to the story of the Crucifixion a remarkable depth and power.

In view of this, it is all the more impressive to discover that the *Dream of the Rood* is one of the earliest of Old English poems, perhaps composed near the time of Caedmon himself. We know this because of the chance preservation of an eighth century stone cross, which can still be seen in the church at Ruthwell, in southwestern Scotland. On this cross are inscribed in runic letters more than a dozen lines of the *Dream of the Rood*. According to expert opinion, the date of the inscription cannot be later than A.D. 750. It is difficult for anyone to look upon the Ruthwell cross without being impressed by this ancient monument to the biblical tradition in English literature.

CHAPTER FOUR

Middle English Translations: The Wyclif Bible

T HE Norman conquest of England in 1066 accelerated the decline
of Old English culture, and the resulting gap between late Old
English and the beginnings of Middle English literature is
matched by an interruption of the work of biblical translation.
Scribes continued to copy the glosses, homilies, and translations of
the early period, but no new efforts at English translation were made
until the middle of the thirteenth century. By this time, of course,
great changes had taken place in English, so much so that we now
speak of the language employed between 1100 and 1500 as "Middle
English."

The sharpness of the break between Old and Middle English is
largely attributable to the fact that for three centuries after the
conquest England was ruled by a French-speaking aristocracy. The
Anglo-Saxon leadership was wiped out almost immediately and
replaced by Norman friends of the Conqueror. More gradually the
main officers of the English Church became French-speaking, with
the result that, by 1100, knowledge of French was a necessity for
anyone seeking advancement in either state or church. Indeed, it is in
the twelfth century that Anglo-Norman literature reached its zenith,
including among its achievements two versions of the Psalter,
translations of several other books of the Old Testament, a number of
Passion narratives adapted from the Gospels, and devotional works
such as penitentials designed for use in the confessional. The absence
of English works during this period is not surprising, because only

the wealthy French-speaking class could afford books, and in addition the English-speaking population was almost entirely illiterate. If conditions in England had not changed, it is possible that English might have become extinct, and French might have taken its place as the national language.

Important changes, however, did occur early in the thirteenth century, when the great Angevin empire built up by Henry II began to disintegrate during the reign of King John. Until then, it had been possible for the aristocracy to hold lands in both England and France, as part of a single kingdom. But in 1204 the ill-conceived policies of John resulted in the loss of Normandy, and lords of the realm had to choose between their continental and insular possessions. Although the dream of English domination of France was destined, it is true, to continue disastrously into the fifteenth century, the effective separation of the two countries had begun. Yet so strong were the cultural ties that French continued to be spoken in the English court virtually till the end of the fourteenth century. This was certainly true of Edward III's reign (1327–77), and perhaps to a lesser extent of that of Richard II, who however spoke English to turn aside the wrath of the peasants in the rebellion of 1381.

The survival of English as a literary language was assured, however, by the loss of Normandy, and the signs of this were not long in coming to the fore. Even as early as the turn of the century had appeared Layamon's *Brut*, an English alliterative version of an Old French translation of Geoffrey of Monmouth's *History of the Kings of Britain*. This was a poem very much in the style of the Old English epic, showing that English literary tradition had not been suppressed by the conquest, but had simply gone underground and been kept alive by a continuous oral tradition. Of course the influence of French poetry had begun, and we find in English texts a mixture of alliteration and rhyme which illustrates this; but it is evident that the English poetic tradition was consciously cultivated as a separate cultural entity, especially in the fourteenth century, the most flourishing period of Middle English literature.

Undoubtedly an important factor in the rather sudden emergence of English literature in the fourteenth century was the Hundred Years' War with France, which was initiated by Edward III in 1337, and which continued intermittently until nearly the middle of the fifteenth century. During this time French became in effect the language of the enemy, completing the separation of the two cultures that had begun with the loss of Normandy. Thus Chaucer imbibed French influences in the cultural atmosphere of the English court, but by 1370 there were good grounds for the choice of English as the vehicle for his poetry. In the North and West of England, there developed the poetry of the alliterative revival, spanning the latter half of the fourteenth century, which was largely independent of London. Chaucer was probably not in touch with it. He uses the French rhyming couplets, and has his parson remark, in *The Canterbury Tales,* "I can not rum, ram, ruff by letter." Yet the poetry of the alliterative revival forms a substantial part of the literary heritage of the fourteenth century. The canon of English poetry gains immensely by the survival of such poems as the *Pearl* and *Piers the Plowman.*

In the present chapter, however, we shall be concerned with more or less direct translations of the Bible, dealing first with the surviving efforts of individuals in the thirteenth and fourteenth centuries, and then turning to the first complete translation, the Wyclif Bible. At the same time, because of the quantity of the surviving texts, we will not deal directly with the large body of devotional and liturgical materials. Compendiums like *The Northern Passion,* and *The South English Legendary* were important and influential in their day, but they must remain peripheral to our main interest, the translation of the Bible and its literary influence.

Old Testament

The earliest biblical translation of the Middle English period is *Genesis and Exodus,* a metrical version in rhyming couplets. Its main source is Peter Comestor's *Historia Scholastica,* though it occasionally draws on Josephus, *Antiquities of the Jews,* for details. In spite of the title, the poem actually covers the narrative portions of the entire Pentateuch, and finishes with the death of Moses at the end of Deuteronomy. The date of composition is generally agreed to be around 1250, confirmed by the language and orthography of the manuscript. It is evident, for example, that the author had used the old runic letter for *w*, which resembles a *p*, whereas the copyist, who may have been used to Anglo-Norman texts, did not always transcribe it properly. Indeed, he sometimes mistook an ordinary *p* for the rune, so that we occasionally find Pharaoh written Wharaoh. As a whole, however, the text of over four thousand lines presents few problems, and is written in a dialect of the northern part of Norfolk.

[127]

There is a brief Prologue (1–34), followed by sections on Genesis (35–2,536), Exodus (2,537–3,628), Numbers (3,635–4,118), Deuteronomy (4,119–54), and finally a short conclusion (4,155–62).

One ought to love that poetry, says the author, which shows the layman who is not learned in book how to love and serve God, and thus achieve eternal bliss. This song is drawn from Latin into English, and Christian men should be as fain as birds at the sight of dawn to hear this tale in the native speech. I will tell how Lucifer deceived mankind and held them tied in Hell's bag until God clothed Himself in manhood and undid the fiend's power. Then, after a brief invocation, the poet begins with the creation:

> In firme bigining of nogt
> Was hevene and erðe samen wrogt.
> Ðo bad god wurðen stund and stede,
> Ðis middes-werld ðor-inne he dede.
> Al was ðat firme ðhrosing in nigt,
> Til he wit hise word made ligt.

Here is the same passage in literal modern English:

> In first beginning of nought
> Was heaven and earth together wrought.
> Then bade God to exist time and place,
> This middle-world therein he put.
> All was that first chaos in night,
> Till He with his word made light.

With the description of the creation from Genesis the poet includes (from *Historia Scholastica*) a definition of the Trinity, and an account of the creation of the angelic orders and the fall of Lucifer, in preparation for the later temptation scene.

The six days of creation follow the text of Genesis rather closely, with occasional additions from the *Historia*. According to the Bible, for example, on the second day *God made the firmament, and divided the waters which were under the firmament from the waters which were above the firmament: and it was so* (Gen. 1:7). This of course is the view of ancient cosmology; the sky is blue because of the blue waters above the firmament, while other waters lie contained beneath the earth. The only time that these waters were released was on the occasion of the great flood (Gen. 7:11): *the same day were all the fountains of the great deep broken up, and the windows of heaven were opened.* The Bible itself offers no details, but the *Historia*, which our translator is following, does seek to explain how the waters of the firmament are restrained. On the second day, he says, this middle-earth was all locked and surrounded when God bade the firmament to extend all about the sky, enclosing us with frozen water, a wall of ice, called heaven's roof. No fire can yet melt that ice, and until Doomsday all middle-earth shall be enclosed in it.

As the story of Genesis unfolds, we notice additions and bits of vivid detail lovingly interspersed in the narrative, like the marginal ornamentation of medieval manuscripts. When God created the animals, they were all tame and at the service of man before he sinned; after the Fall lions and bears began to attack him, and even little flies showed no awe of him. Thus he lost control of the greatest and the smallest, retaining his hold over those in the middle of the spectrum (e.g., domestic cattle). Jubal, inventor of the art of music (Gen. 4:21), hearing that the world would be devastated by water and fire, wrote all his wisdom on two tablets, one of tile and one of brass, to withstand destruction by fire and water, respectively. The boast of Lamech (Gen. 4:23–24) was interpreted to mean that Lamech actually slew Cain in a hunting accident, and this episode is briefly but vividly set forth. The arrow hit Cain unawares, says the poet, and "with that he grunted and stretched and died." The rainbow which God produces after the flood (Gen. 9:13) is described as blue and red; the blue betokens the waters of the flood, which will not be released again, and the red betokens the fire that will come at the end of the world. This fire will flame as high as did the waters of the flood, and beginning forty years before Doomsday, the rainbow will cease to appear. According to the Bible (and the *Historia* too, incidentally), Joseph was sold for twenty pieces of silver by his brothers (Gen. 37:28); for fairly obvious allegorical reasons, our poet has him sold for thirty pieces of silver.

In Exodus the life of Moses is greatly expanded from apocryphal sources. The daughter of Pharoah, unnamed in the Bible, is called Teremuth. One day Teremuth brought her adopted son, Moses, before Pharoah, who was very fond of him. Taking his crown, with its image of the Egyptian god Ammon, Pharoah placed it on the child's head. Promptly little Moses seized the crown and threw it upon the ground, shattering the image. This incident was witnessed by the "Bishop" of Heliopolis, who exclaimed, "If this child is allowed to thrive, he shall be the ruin of Egypt!" At this point Moses' life seemed in danger, but one of the counsellors said that it was the thoughtless deed of a child, and offered to prove it by giving him some hot coals to see what he would do with them. Moses took the coals and foolishly touched them with his tongue, thus demonstrating his childishness and saving his life. We are also given to understand that this is why Moses later excused himself before God by saying, *I am slow of speech, and of a slow tongue* (Ex. 4:10).

By the time that Moses grew to young manhood, he was renowned throughout Egypt for beauty and strength. When the country was invaded by Ethiopia, the people asked Moses to lead them and he agreed to do so, but only after Teremuth had been reassured by the authorities that faith would be kept with him. A surprise attack was launched, the Egyptians were victorious, and they pursued the enemy to Sheba. Here Moses laid siege to the city, but it held out against him until the princess Tarbis, daughter of the Ethiopian king, yielded the city to him. "Love compelled her," says the poet, "that is why she did it." Thus Moses was victorious through love, and became all powerful in Ethiopia. In response to the entreaties of Tarbis, Moses tarried there, although he wished privately that he might return to Egypt. Too courteous simply to walk out on the lady, he decided to resort to a trick. Being wise in astronomy, Moses carved two images made of precious stones, so engraved and designed that the one caused a person to remember, the other to forget. He set them in two rings of gold, giving her the one conducive to forgetting, while he took the one that would cause him to remember. The princess faithfully wore the ring, and soon forgot her love for Moses, and he was able, with her permission, to return to Egypt. The biblical story then resumes with Moses' slaying of the Egyptian overseer (Ex. 2:11ff.). Such digressions indicate that motifs from medieval romance are beginning to affect the traditional form of the biography of Moses. The Ethiopian princess has much in common with Blancheflor, the lady of Belrepeire who is rescued from a besieging army by Percival, in the *Story of the Grail* by the twelfth century poet, Chrétien de Troyes.

The account of the departure from Egypt follows the biblical text rather closely, except for a single digression. According to the Bible, Joseph made his sons swear to takes his bones with them when they left Egypt (Gen. 50:25), and Moses remembered to do this (Exodus 13:19), but no details are given. Our poet's considerable interest in burial customs can be seen in a digression on that subject near the end of Genesis (2,441–74), and in his account of the Exodus he pauses to tell us how Moses located the bones of Joseph. As Israel was about to leave Egypt, Moses suddenly remembered the promise that had been made to take the bones, but to his dismay he discovered that the Nile had flooded and Joseph's grave was now covered with water. Undaunted, Moses had a gold rod fashioned and inscribed with the name of God, and placed in the river. Miraculously it floated along until it stopped over the place where the grave was hidden. There they dug and cast up the bones, some whole and some broken. Moses had all the bones carefully enclosed in a container and took them with him on the journey from Egypt.

One of the more puzzling passages in the book of Numbers describes how Moses, in response to complaints about lack of water, strikes a rock which brings forth water, only to be rebuked by the Lord (Num. 20:10–12): *And Moses and Aaron gathered the congregation together before the rock, and he said unto them, Hear now, ye rebels; must we fetch you water out of this rock? And Moses lifted up his hand, and with his rod he smote the rock twice: and the water came out abundantly, and the congregation drank, and their beasts also. And the Lord spake unto Moses and Aaron, Because you believed me not, to sanctify me in the eyes of the children of Israel, therefore ye shall not bring this congregation into the land which I have given them.* The exact nature of Moses' failure is not made clear in the biblical text, and our poet tries to solve the problem by emphasizing the fact that Moses struck the rock twice. "I think," he says, "that Moses acted despondently (*frigtlike*). Once he smote there on the stone, and failed to see the water run; the second time he corrected his attitude [literally turned his thought, made it better and more docile], and did not fail. Then the water flowed there great and strong, so that all the folk and cattle had enough." He does not mention God's rebuke, nor His decision that Moses and Aaron shall not enter the promised land.

Nearly 150 lines are devoted to a lively retelling of the story of Balaam, and the frustration of his attempt to curse Israel (Num. 22–24). The Bible is followed very closely except at the end. Instead of having Balaam simply complete his blessing of Israel and depart, as he does in the biblical version, our poet (following the *Historia*) has Balaam advise Balak, king of the Moabites, how he may be able to do injury to Israel. "Take your young women," he suggests, "fair to see and soft to touch, those that are bright of hue and glad in speech, and have them march out to meet these men; so that when they come they will brew heart-burn with wine and beauty and seductive bodies, with soft and lovely words, to turn them from fear of God to the gods of thy land and our law. There is no hope unless you can turn their thought, for war and weapons will not help."

[131]

This advice of course derives from events related in Numbers 25, which tells of Israel's whoredom with the daughters of Moab, and their worship of the Moabite gods.

At various times, especially in the fourteenth century, other parts of the Old Testament were translated into Middle English. Occasionally these were set pieces for use in connection with devotions, like the passages from Job (sometimes called "petty" or "little" Job) used for the lessons of the *dirige*, "full profitable to stir sinners to compunction." More often we find collections of the Wisdom of Solomon, or extracts from Old Testament narrative like the story of Adam and Eve, interwoven with legends of the holy cross. There is, however, one very extended metrical paraphrase of the Old Testament, written near the end of the fourteenth century in a northern dialect, and covering the Pentateuch (except Leviticus), Joshua, Judges, Ruth, the four books of Kings (Samuel and Kings in the Authorized Version), Job, Tobias, Esther, Judith, and parts of Maccabees. It is followed in the manuscript by a brief prose *sanctorale*, or collection of saints' lives. From a literary point of view this huge work is clearly inferior to the earlier *Genesis and Exodus* discussed above, but it has occasional details of interest. In retelling the story of David and Bathsheba, the author remarks that David, after God had censured him and assigned his punishment, composed the Psalm, *Miserere mei deus* (Ps. 51, A.V.). This is a nice touch, found elsewhere in an Old French paraphrase of the Bible, and in the first of the Cornish miracle plays, *Origo Mundi*, but not, as one might expect, in the *Historia Scholastica*.

Another incident in the life of David receives elaboration at the hands of the author of the metrical paraphrase. The Bible tells of David's playing the harp for Saul whenever the king was seized by an evil spirit. Normally he would be refreshed by the music (1 Sam. 16:23), but on one occasion (1 Sam. 18:11–12) he hurled a javelin at David, apparently just missing him. We are not told anything more than this. But the author of the English paraphrase brings Michal, daughter of Saul, into the story. She is of course destined to become David's wife (1 Sam. 18:27), and can be expected to be anxious for his welfare. Thus we are told that when she saw her father the king aiming his spear at David she shouted a warning:

> Then Michal cast a cry
> And David turned him soon.
> Fast home he gan him hie,
> God would not it were done.

Although details of this kind lend interest to the story, the poem as a whole is lacking in inspiration, flaring into life only occasionally, as it does near the end in the narrative taken from the apocryphal book of Maccabees.

In the Old Testament pieces that I have mentioned thus far, the didactic purpose is quite evident, and it is probably safe to assume clerical authorship for all of them. Indeed in some cases it is possible to detect an anxiety on the part of the author to persuade his reader or listener to abandon the popular literature of the day and give his full attention to the biblical story, which is good for his soul. In some of the comments of clerical authors we can recognize a serious concern about the popularity of secular entertainment, as in the following extended title of a religious tract: "A little treatise of divinity to turn man from romances and jests, wherein he loses much of his time . . . , and to give him instead thing that is profitable both to life and to soul." Another example occurs in the prologue to a Passion narrative: "Hear now a little tale that I will tell you, as we find it written in the gospel. It is not of Charlemagne nor of the Twelve Peers, but of Christ's passion that He suffered here." Even if we did not know it from other evidence, it would be possible to deduce from these and other such statements that clerical authors were feeling the pressure of competition from secular literature. The composers of this secular literature, apart from a few major court poets, were the professional minstrels, popularizers of romance throughout western Europe in the Middle Ages. Already we have seen, in the thirteenth century *Genesis and Exodus,* that the influence of romance is clearly evident in apocryphal additions to the life of Moses. But did the minstrels themselves ever turn to the Bible for narrative materials to add to their repertoire? There is good evidence that they did. Two poems drawn from the Old Testament, *Jacob and Joseph* and *Susannah,* are fine examples of the art of medieval minstrelsy.

The earlier of the two is *Jacob and Joseph,* composed soon after 1250, which tells the story of Joseph in Egypt from the time he is sold by his brothers until the reunion with his father Jacob (Gen. 37–46). It follows the Bible in its main outlines, but compresses and alters some details of the narrative. Potiphar buys Joseph, as in Genesis, but then he gives him immediately to Pharaoh, and it is the queen, not Potiphar's wife, who falls in love with him. The cat-and-mouse game that Joseph plays with his brothers in Genesis is virtually eliminated in the poem, and the character of Joseph is consequently made more attractive. He does not accuse his brothers of being spies, and, although he does plant the cup in one of his brothers' sacks and accuses them of stealing it, he does not require them to leave a hostage, but merely to give their word that they will return with Benjamin. Finally, the earlier death of Rachel is ignored. Jacob had said (Gen. 37:10), *What is this dream that thou hast dreamed? Shall I and thy mother and thy brethren indeed come to bow down ourselves to thee to the earth?* By keeping Rachel alive, the poet allows the complete fulfillment of Joseph's dream. Most of these details can be found in earlier sources. Josephus (the Jewish historian) keeps Rachel alive, and in French versions of the Old Testament Joseph is given to Pharaoh and tempted by the queen. But our author is not slavishly following any one source, and his construction of the story shows much originality.

The poem has 538 lines—about half as long as the "Gest of Robin Hood"—and is composed of rhyming couplets in long lines of six or seven stresses, with occasional alliteration, as can be seen in this couplet:

> Iacob liuede in londe, and louede Godes lawe,
> So dude Ysaac his fader, bi his lifdawe.
>
> (Jacob lived in land, and loved God's law,
> As did Isaac his father, in his life-days.)

The number of syllables in a line varies considerably. If it were not for the rhyme, the resemblance to Old English alliterative verse would be very noticeable. As in the above example, there is usually a pause or caesura in mid-line, suggestive of the regular break found in the alliterative long line. There is some evidence indeed that the pattern of rhyming couplets is imposed on a strong habit of alliterative composition. Thus we find a few lines where the normal alliterative pattern, aaax, is reversed and becomes xaaa, apparently because of the demands of the rhyme. An example would be line 9: "Þat is þe soule ful loþ, and lef þe licame" ("That is loath to the soul, and lief to the body"), where "licame" rhymes with "game" in the next line. The normal alliterative form of the line would have been: "Þat is þe licame ful lef, and loþ þe soule." Nevertheless the verses are skillfully put together, and the general effect of the poem as a whole is very pleasing.

The tactics of the minstrel are evident in the opening lines of *Jacob and Joseph*, as the reciter seeks to get the attention of his audience. Conspicuously absent is any appeal to piety; the story is told for its

[134]

own sake. Would you now hear words very good, asks the minstrel, of a patriarch after Noah's flood? (I don't intend to tell you of the flood, but of a patriarch named Jacob). Once men loved a merry song, games, and fair tale; now they'd rather go to the alehouse, stretch out the girdle and enlarge the belly, come early and sit long. But that is loathsome to the soul, and dear to the body; unless we give it up, it will be an evil game. To fill our belly is of little profit, and then to lie sleeping, like a young pig. Thus fared our elders in Noah's days, with food and drink they filled their stomachs; and with gluttony they went completely mad; therefore the Lord sent Noah's flood. Then they could drink until they were full—but in great numbers they floated, by ditch and by pool. There is a moral here, but it is camouflaged with wit, and its purpose is not the salvation of souls but the riveting of the listeners' attention. It would seem from the minstrel's approach that his audience is having dinner. By the time he finished his prologue, one imagines that the conversation and sounds of eating and drinking had largely subsided.

The story begins by following Genesis 37 very closely. Joseph tells his dreams, and his brothers hate him as their worst enemy. When Jacob sends him to the fields to look for his brothers, they seize him and cast him into a pit. Then Reuben leaves (cf. Gen. 37:29–30); he could not for pity, says the poet, remain at the pit. The rest of the brothers sit down to eat, laughing and joking, while Joseph lies in the pit, wringing his hands. Without the restraining presence of Reuben, the brothers seem on the verge of drawing Joseph up and slaying him (alas! that between brothers there should be such hatred!), when they see two merchants coming from Gilead, their asses laden with hides and fur (rather than the spicery and balm and myrrh borne by the camels of Gen. 37:25). At the suggestion of Judah, they sell Joseph to the merchants.

The biblical account of Joseph's journey to Egypt is given in a single verse (Gen. 37:36): *And the Midianites sold him into Egypt unto Potiphar, an officer of Pharaoh's, and captain of the guard.* In the poem this verse is expanded into a passage of thirty lines. When the merchants bring him over the sea-strand to Egypt, the little boy ("youngling") weeps when he first hears the strange Egyptian language. As they approach the town Joseph sees castles high and proud, streets wide and long, many a fair hall and bower. As the merchants lead Joseph up and down, offering him for sale, knights and bold townsmen, maidens and ladies come into the street to look

[135]

at him. To them he looks like an angel from heaven. Soon tidings of Joseph reaches Potiphar the steward, who comes with a noble company. As soon as he sees the boy he alights from his steed, unfolds his mantle, unlocks his coffer and casts out gold, more than the price demanded by the merchants. Then lifting Joseph up on his steed, he rides off. Meanwhile, the brothers sprinkle blood on Joseph's coat, and take it to Jacob, who concludes that he has been killed by some evil beasts. Jacob and Rachel mourn for their son.

The queen's effort to seduce Joseph follows the biblical story of Potiphar's wife very closely. An occasional change here and there seems designed to provide a sense of immediacy or local color. For example, the Bible makes no mention of Potiphar's whereabouts during the seduction, but in the poem we are told that the king (i.e., Pharaoh) has gone to the wood to shoot with his bent bow, and the queen, taking advantage of his absence, sends for Joseph. Returning from the wood "with blowing horn," the king hears the queen's cry and her false accusation, and Joseph is imprisoned. After the dreams of the butler and the baker, at last the dream of Pharaoh himself is interpreted by Joseph, who is freed from prison and presumably given charge of the country and its granaries as in Genesis 41 (a leaf of the MS is missing at this point). When the famine strikes, Jacob sends his sons to Egypt for grain, all except Benjamin, the youngest. "If Joseph had remained at home," says Jacob sadly, "he would still be alive; for the love of Joseph I will never be happy."

The journey itself to Egypt gets no attention from the biblical narrator (Gen. 42:5), but, as was the case earlier with Joseph's journey, in the poem a rather lengthy passage is devoted to it. The brothers travel day and night until they reach Egypt. When they arrive, they see much bliss and joy, great barns piled high with grain. Food and drink are plentiful, in spite of the famine. As they are walking along, a minstrel overtakes them, bearing his harp on his back. "Whence come ye, young men?" he asks. "It seems by your asses that ye would buy corn. I will bring you to the drawbridge; there the most gracious man alive will lodge you tonight and make you full blithe. Ye seem foreign men and all freeborn—tonight many a knightly youth shall kneel before you!" The minstrel brings them to the castle and speaks to the porter, who lets them in. There they see great riches, and at last Joseph himself sitting in hall, as if he were a king.

The meeting between Joseph and his brothers follows the biblical story, but is told in a different spirit. In Genesis Joseph recognized his brothers immediately, *but made himself strange unto them, and spake roughly unto them* (Gen. 42:7) and proceeded to accuse them of being spies. In the poem, the brothers come into the hall, and before Joseph's feet they fall on their knees. "Rise up," says Joseph, "stay not on your knees but tell me very fairly what your will is." The brothers explain that their father has sent them for grain. "What is your father's name?" asks Joseph, as if from idle curiosity ("as if it were his game"). "Our father is called Jacob, our mother Rachel." With that very word he knew them full well. So happy is Joseph to learn that his father is still alive, that he has to leave the hall so that his brothers cannot see him weep. Returning to the hall, Joseph himself pours water for the brothers to wash their hands. After an ample dinner, rich wine is brought, and Joseph asks the brothers to sing in Hebrew, which they do. Not since he came into Egypt was Joseph so glad. Then follows the episode of the planted cup, and the promise exacted from the brothers to return with Benjamin. Jacob is grieved to learn of this, but releases the child to them for the return journey to Egypt.

"Lord," says Joseph, "I thank thee for it; now the eleven stars have come to me. If I could have my father and my mother, then I'd have surely the sun and the moon." He then reveals his identity, kisses each of his brothers, and tells them to fetch Jacob and Rachel. When Jacob heard that Joseph was alive, never was a father so blithe. He cast away his crutch, seized his mantle, and fairly platted his hair with a silken string. He took his beaver hat, that was covered with pall: "Of woe and of sorrow now I am all free, for now it seems to me that I can fly like an eagle, for the love of Joseph, my dearest child." Jacob rode singing, "For the love of Joseph, now I am young and wild!"

When Joseph hears that his father is approaching he goes to meet him accompanied by many knights, "with harp and with pipe, with joy and with song." The minstrel then concludes his story with an aphorism which well expresses his purpose: "The bliss is very sweet that comes after woe; well is the man alive who can escape his cares." And the closing benediction reminds us of the audience that it has been his constant aim to please: "Come never to this house worse tidings (than this story), but rather (may you have) all the greatest of honor and Christ's blessing. Amen."

The hand of the minstrel is visible, not only in the vitality of the narrative, but in the ornamental and structured use of repetition, a

[137]

feature commonly associated with oral literature. In its simplest form, repetition is used to underscore a pathetic situation, as when Joseph has been thrown in a pit by his brothers:

> Joseph sits in a pit with full sorry mood,
> His brethren laugh loud, that game they think good.
> Now Joseph sits in pit and wringeth his hand—
> Away, that between brethren such hatred be found!

Or again, to describe the crowded streets of the town where Joseph was offered for sale:

> Thither came knights and burgesses bold,
> They came into the street Joseph to behold.
> Ladies of bowers and maidens free
> Came into the street Joseph to see.

Or to express Pharaoh's perplexity over his dream:

> Hereon the king thinketh by night and by day,
> Knoweth not for his life what he do may.
> Hereon the king thinketh by day and by night,
> There could of this thing advise him no wight.

When the brothers first go to Egypt for grain, they are impressed by the prosperity of the country despite the famine:

> Much was the bliss and much was the game
> In water and in land, of wild and of tame.
> Much was the bliss that they there saw,
> Barns full rich and grain full high.
> Much was the bliss after their swink
> That they there found of meat and of drink.

Repetition is also used as a part of the narrative structure, a device very useful in oral recitation, both in aiding the minstrel's memory, and in helping the audience to keep the story straight. Identical transitions are repeated, for example, to underline the several journeys of the brothers:

> Fair fareth these young men by day and by night,
> Unto Egypt land then they come aright.

After pledging to return with Benjamin, the brothers depart:

> Fair fareth these young men by day and by night
> To their father Jacob then they come aright.

The first of these couplets is repeated when they return to Egypt with Benjamin, and the second when they go back again to bring Jacob

[138]

their father. These journeys are thus given a clarity and symmetry which aid in the comprehension of the narrative. Without being obtrusive, the technique is visible elsewhere on a smaller scale:

> Now he sits in hall, Jacob the old man,
> And his sons all from field come home.

On this occasion Joseph describes his dreams and earns the enmity of his brothers. Later this couplet is repeated:

> Now he sits in hall, Jacob the old man,
> And his sons ten from field come home.

This time Joseph is missing, and the brothers show their father his bloody coat. Some repetitions, of course, are simply formulaic: Jacob sits in hall on numerous other occasions; there is much swooning and wringing of hands; Joseph is more than once described as "hende and fre" (courteous and straightforward). Even at this early date certain conventional phrases can be recognized: the halls and bowers of Egypt are "white as any lily, bright as any flower"; Joseph diplomatically unfolds the arms of the queen "with his white fingers," and with the same white fingers he pours water for his brothers to wash their hands; and Jacob dresses in a beaver hat for the journey to Egypt.

A final example of the minstrel's technique can be seen in his handling of the prison episode. We are told that the butler and baker are betrayed and cast into prison with Joseph:

> And in the prison they lie with full much wrong;
> They have no bliss of harp nor of song,
> Of old nor of young, of friend nor of kin,
> They would rather be dead than to live so long.

Later, when Joseph interprets the butler's dream favorably, saying that he will be restored to his office, he adds:

> "And when men serve the king with harp and with song,
> Think on poor Joseph that lies here with wrong."

But when the butler was freed, he forgot about Joseph:

> Who in the prison lies, with full much wrong;
> He has no bliss of harp nor of song,
> Of old nor of young, of friend nor of kin,
> He would rather be dead, than to live so long.

By this kind of parallelism the minstrel is able to emphasize the ingratitude of the butler, and the deepening gloom and injustice of

Joseph's imprisonment. More important, the general effect of this technique is to provide the kind of symmetrical narrative best suited to oral recitation. In this respect *Jacob and Joseph* is a remarkable example of the minstrel's art, and deserves more attention from literary historians than it has hitherto received.

A better-known and much later example of minstrelsy is *Susannah*, an alliterative poem composed about 1400, which tells the "History of Susanna," an apocryphal addition to the book of Daniel. Susannah, the wife of a prominent Jew in Babylon, was accustomed to bathing in a pool in a walled garden behind the house. Two evil elders saw her there one day, and decided on a plot whereby they might satisfy their lust at her expense. Waiting until she was alone, they rushed up to ravish her, threatening that if she cried out, they would swear they had caught her with a young man who escaped as they entered the garden. The word of two witnesses was sufficient to convict her of adultery, of course, and this meant that she would be stoned to death. But without hesitation Susannah cried out, and the elders carried out their threats. Susannah was tried, convicted, and sentenced to death. Before the sentence could be executed, however, young Daniel interrupted the proceedings, challenged the verdict, and offered to prove his appeal before the court. Taking the elders aside separately, he asked each of them to name the tree under which he saw Susannah with the young man. "A mastick tree," said one; "a holm tree," replied the other. At this contradiction in the testimony the assembly cried out, and the elders, convicted of false witness, were sentenced to death. Susannah was freed and restored to her husband. From that day forth Daniel's reputation was very great in the sight of the people.

The English *Susannah* is much more ornate than *Jacob and Joseph* for it is composed in twenty-eight thirteen-line stanzas having a highly elaborate form. The first eight lines of each stanza, in addition to alliteration, have a rhyme scheme *abababab*, and then comes a short bob and wheel, rhyming *cdddc*. For the most part the poem follows the biblical text very closely, but occasionally expands on it, as in this description of Susannah's garden:

> In the season of summer with Sybil and Jane,
> She went to her garden, that glade so green,
> Where lindens and laurels leaned in the lane,
> The sabine and cypress and sycamores sheen,
> The palm and the poplar, the pear and the plane,
> The juniper gentle joining between,

> The rose ragged in root, richest in rain,
> Bound with bramble, thriving to be seen,
>   So tight.
> There were popinjays prest,
> Nightingales upon nest,
> Blithe birds of the best
>   On blossoms so bright.

Perhaps because of its stanzaic structure, *Susannah* has very few repetitions or echoes to enhance its narrative symmetry. One case does occur at the beginning of stanzas XII and XXI. The wicked elders have just threatened Susannah, and the poet introduces her silent meditation on the alternatives with the line, "Then Susan was sorrowful and said in her thought. . . ." Later, when she has been sentenced to death, her public prayer to God is introduced, "Then Susan was sorrowful and said in high. . . ."

The poet is particularly interested in Susannah as a forlorn victim of injustice on the model of the folktale of the Accused Queen, as we find in Chaucer's portrait of Constance in the "Man of Law's Tale." Both poets emphasize the pathos of the heroine's situation. A good example of this in *Susannah* is the stanza describing her interview with her husband just after she has been condemned to death:

> She fell flat on the floor when she found her husband,
> And spoke to that spouse, kindly and couth:
> "I have never annoyed you nor would I offend
> In word or in work, in age or in youth"
> (She kneeled on her knees and kissed his hand)
> "Since I'm condemned, I dare not disparage your mouth."
> Was never sorrier sight by sea nor by sand,
> Nor a more sorrowful man by north nor by south,
>   Than there.
> They took the fetters from her feet
> And oft kissed he that sweet,
> "In other world shall we meet" —
>   Said he no more.

There is no basis for this episode in the biblical text, yet it is introduced here by the poet with considerable tact and skill. The *Susannah* is not a major poem, of course, but it deserves an honored place, along with *Jacob and Joseph,* among the contributions of minstrelsy to the biblical tradition.

The Psalter

The popularity of the book of Psalms continues unabated in the Middle English period, as is attested by such magnificent manuscripts of the Latin text as the Luttrell, Tickhill, and Queen Mary's Psalters, all produced in the fourteenth century. In Middle English, however, translation becomes more important than the glossing that predominated in Old English manuscripts. Apart from condensations and extracts, there are three separate translations of the Psalms in Middle English. The earliest is the so-called Surtees Psalter, a metrical translation of the early fourteenth century. Next is the English Psalter, including a commentary, by Richard Rolle, Hermit of Hampole, who died in 1349. His translation was probably made during the last ten years of his life. The third is a West Midland prose psalter, of the middle of the fourteenth century, perhaps slightly later than Rolle's. The Surtees Psalter is composed in rhyming couplets, as can be seen in this passage from the Twenty-third Psalm (Vulgate 22):

> Lord me steers, nought want shall me;
> In stead of food there me locked He.
> He fed me over water of food,
> My soul he turneth into good.
> He led me over paths of righteousness,
> For his name that so holy is.
> For if I go amid shadow of dead
> For Thou with me art, evil shall I not dread.

The archaic verse looks stiffer in modern spelling than it actually sounded, but it still must be admitted that this metrical translation is largely uninspired.

The West Midland prose psalter is by comparison much freer and more attractive:

> Our Lord governeth me, and nothing shall defail me; in the stead of pasture he set me there. He nourished me in the water of baptism; he turned my soul from the fiend. He led me in the paths of rightfulness for his name. For if that I have gone amidst of the shadow of death, I shall not doubt evils; for thou art with me; thy discipline and thine amending comforted me. Thou madest ready grace in my sight against them that trouble me. Thou makest fat my head with mercy; and my drink, making drunk, is full clear. And Thy mercy shall follow me all days of my life, and that I wone [=dwell] in the house of our Lord in length of days.

Because the psalm is so familiar, it is easy to see how this translation has been affected by the commentaries. The *still waters* of the scriptural text have become "the water of baptism" (water of fyllyng); the speaker's soul is not simply turned to good, but turned "from the fiend"; *thy rod and thy staff* are now "thy discipline and thine amend-

[142]

ing"; the Lord makes him ready, not a table, but grace, and anoints his head with mercy rather than oil. Many of the psalms in this prose translation are similarly affected by exegesis, and it would be difficult for the casual reader to recognize where text leaves off and commentary begins. Except for this feature, the West Midland psalter is a reasonably faithful translation, and a pleasure to read.

The best known of the psalters is the English version with commentary, translated by Richard Rolle. The source for this work was the *Glossa major* on the Psalms by Peter Lombard, but with changes and additions by Rolle himself showing considerable originality, and indicating Rolle's abiding interest in the importance of the Psalms for the spiritual life of the mystic. Rolle was born around 1300 in the north of England, studied briefly at Oxford, but soon returned home on fire with determination to lead the solitary life of a hermit. During his lifetime of devotion to mystical experience, he wrote several treatises that were at once guides to the spiritual life of the mystic and biographical records of his own religious pilgrimage. His numerous scriptural commentaries had a similar orientation. They include expositions of Job (actually the nine readings from Job in the Office of the Dead), Lamentations, the Lord's Prayer, the Apostle's Creed, the Virtuous Woman (Proverbs), the Song of Solomon (Canticles), the Psalter, and the Apocalypse (Revelation). Most of these are in Latin, but in addition to Rolle's own English version of the Psalter, some of the other Latin commentaries were later translated by his followers.

A brief look at his "Encomium of the Name of Jesus," a commentary on a phrase from the Song of Solomon: *thy name is as ointment poured forth* (1:3), will illustrate Rolle's style as a scriptural commentator. From these few words of sacred text Rolle builds a lyrical exegesis that exemplifies his life-long devotion to the name of Jesus. Oil, he explains, is a token of salvation, and Jesus means "savior"; therefore "oil outpoured is Thy Name" means "Jesus is Thy Name." This is the name which is highest of all, without which no man hopes for salvation. It is sweet and joyful, giving veritable comfort to the heart of man. Verily the Name of Jesus is in my mind a joyous song and heavenly music in mine ear, he continues, and in my mouth a honeyed sweetness. Wherefore no wonder I love that Name which gives comfort to me in all my anguish, I have set it in my mind, I have set it as a token upon my heart, as a token upon my arm. For love is strong as death. The Name of Jesus has taught me to sing, and has inflamed my mind with the heat of uncreated light.

Therefore I sigh and cry: "Who shall show to the beloved Jesus how I languish for love?"

In passages like these one can perceive that Rolle's praise of the Name of Jesus is deeply interfused with poetry from later chapters of the Song of Solomon (see 5:8 and 6:6). This is particularly evident in the climax of the "Encomium": I went about, covetous of riches, and I found not Jesus. I ran in wantonness of the flesh, and I found not Jesus. I sat in companies of worldly mirth, and I found not Jesus. In all these I sought Jesus, but I found him not. For He let me know by His grace that He is not found in the land of softly living. Therefore I turned another way, and I ran about in poverty, and I found Jesus, poorly born into the world, laid in a crib and lapped in clothes. . . . Therefore Jesus is not found in riches but in poverty, not in delight but in penance, not in wanton rejoicing, but in bitter weeping, not among many, but in solitude. Throughout this passage run the echoes of the Song of Solomon: *By night on my bed I sought him who my soul loveth: I sought him, but I found him not. I will rise now, and go about the city in the streets, and in the broad ways I will seek him whom my soul loveth: I sought him, but I found him not. The watchmen that go about the city found me: to whom I said, Saw ye him whom my soul loveth? It was but a little that I passed from them, but I found him whom my soul loveth: I held him and would not let him go. . . .* (SS 3:1–4). Thus Rolle's commentary on the Canticles is of a very special kind. Based on the conventional allegorical reading of the sacred text, it is nevertheless highly individual in mystical thought and lyrical expression.

Compared with the "Encomium of the Name of Jesus," Rolle's English psalter is much more restrained exegesis—partly, of course, because it is in the main a translation of Peter Lombard. But in the prologue Rolle makes it clear that his interest in the Psalms is closely associated with his mystical experience. "Great abundance," he begins, "of ghostly comfort and joy in God comes in the hearts of them that say or sing devoutly the psalms in praise of Jesus Christ. They drop sweetness in man's soul and pour delights in their thoughts and kindle their wills with the fire of love, making them hot and burning within, and fair and lovely in Christ's eyes. And them that last in their devotion he raises into contemplative life and oft time into sound and mirth of heaven." He goes on to quote praise of the Psalms by Saint Augustine and Cassiodorus, and then, after translating the Lombard's preface, he concludes in his own words:

In this work I seek no strange English, but lightest and commonest and such that is most like unto the Latin, so that they that know not Latin, by the English may come to many Latin words. In the translation I follow the letter as much as I may, and where I find no proper English I follow the wit of the word, so that they that shall read it, need not dread error. In expounding I follow holy doctors, for it may come into some envious man's hand that knows not what he should say, that will say that I wist not what I said, and so do harm to him and to others if he despise the work that is profitable to him and others.

This concern for orthodoxy, by the way, turned out to be prophetic, for, only a few decades after Rolle's death in 1349, the Lollard followers of John Wyclif were producing a new edition of his English psalter with heretical additions. Nearly forty manuscripts of the psalter survive, and half of them are copies of the Lollard version.

Each of the psalms in Rolle's translation is divided into verses, and under each verse we find, first, the Latin text; second, a fairly literal translation of the verse; and third, a commentary in English. In the following example I omit the Latin text, and give the English translation followed by the commentary. Once again, for the sake of comparison, we choose verses from the Twenty-third Psalm (Vulgate 22).

> 1. *Lord governs me, and nothing shall me want; in stead of pasture there he me set.* The voice of a righteous man: Lord Christ is my king, and therefore nothing shall me want; that is, in him I shall be secure and sufficient, for I hope in him ghostly good and endless. And he leads me in stead of pasture; that is, in understanding of his word, and delight in his love, where I am certain to be filled; there, in that stead, he set me to be nourished to perfection.
> 2. *On the water of refreshing forth he me brought; my soul he turned.* On the water of grace are we brought forth, that makes us to recover our strength that we lost in sin, and refreshes us to do good works. My soul he turned; that is, of a sinful wretch he made it righteous, in waxing of love and meekness. First he turns our soul to him, and then he leads and feeds it. Ten graces he tells us in this psalm, the which God gives to his lovers.
> 3. *He led me on the streets of righteousness for his name.* That is he gave me endurance in his biddings, and rooted me, and made me perfect in charity. For the streets of righteousness are his straiter counsels, the which are not kept but by a few that are perfect. Therein he led me, not for my merit, but for his name, that is Jesus, that he be loved and praised.
> 4. *For why, if I had gone in midst of the shadow of death, I shall not dread ills, for Thou art with me.* Great virtue is in man when he dreads no ill that may fall, for he endures the worst. If I had gone in midst of the

shadow of death, that is, though I were dwelling among them that neither have knowing of God nor love; or in midst of this life, that is shadow of death, for it is black with murkiness of sins and it leads to death; and evil men, among whom good men dwell, bear the figure of death, that is, the image of the devil, for him they follow in sin. But if I go among all there I shall not dread ill, privy nor open, for Thou art with me in my heart, where I feel Thee, so that after the shadow of death I be with Thee in very life.

5. *Thy wand and Thy staff, they have comforted me.* Soothly I shall dread none ill; for thy wand, that is thy light discipline that chastises me as thy son, and thy staff, that is thy stalwart help, that I lean me to, and that holds me up, they have comforted me, teaching me what I should do, and holding my thought in thee, that art my comfort.

New Testament

If we included all the legendaries and Passion narratives of the Middle English period in our survey, we would quickly see that the New Testament far overshadows the Old in the attention it has received. These narratives are significant as testimony to a strong tradition of piety in the later Middle Ages, but they often stray far from the biblical text or simply recapitulate materials that are dealt with elsewhere in this study. Hence there is room here for only brief mention of specific efforts at translation of parts of the New Testament. These include harmonies of the Gospels, separate gospel commentaries, a stanzaic Life of Christ, versions of the Pauline and Catholic Epistles, and a translation and commentary on the Apocalypse. The variety of New Testament selections is well illustrated by the contents of a single manuscript in Magdalen College, Cambridge (Pepys 2498). This manuscript, dating from about 1400, contains a harmony of the Gospels, a treatise on divinity, a commentary on the Ten Commandments, the Apocalypse in English, the West Midland Prose Psalter, a piece entitled "The Recluse," a complaint of Our Lady, and an English version of the Gospel of Nicodemus from the New Testament apocrypha. The gospel harmony shows signs of having been translated from a French original, and is a Diatessaron, that is, it does not present parallel texts, but blends all four Gospels into a single narrative. The Apocalypse used to be attributed to Wyclif, but has been shown to be simply a translation of a thirteenth century Anglo-Norman Apocalypse, several translations of which survive in Middle English.

Perhaps the most influential of all these New Testament pieces is the stanzaic Life of Christ, composed by a monk of Saint Werburgh's Abbey, Chester, about the middle of the fourteenth century. It is based on *The Golden Legend,* that is, it puts together the feasts of the *temporale* so as to form a life of Christ, adding further materials from the *Polychronicon,* a universal history which will be discussed in chapter VI. The result is a poem of considerable merit, designed to set forth the contents of the Gospels for the unlettered. "A worthy person asked me," says the author, "to show certain things that he saw written in Latin, that he might know in English tongue of Jesus Christ's nativity and his deeds in order, in which he might by good authority fully trust and know." This poem, as its editor has shown, is one of the sources used by the author of the Chester cycle plays, composed about 1375.

The nearest thing to a New Testament translation among the texts we are considering is the collection edited in 1902 by Anna C. Paues, containing most of the Catholic and Pauline Epistles, together with parts of Acts and the beginning of the Gospel of Matthew. Whether these texts represent a single translation project is not clear, and later scholars have questioned the unity of Miss Paues's edition on these grounds. The portions of Acts and Matthew are in a Midland dialect, whereas the Epistles appear to be Southwestern, with the possibility of Kentish influence. The Epistles, in any case, are the heart of the collection, and they would perhaps be better known if they had not been overshadowed by the Wyclif Bible itself. Here is the anonymous translator's version of a famous passage from one of Paul's letters (1 Cor. 13:1–7):

> If that I speak with men's tongues or with angel's tongues, and I have not charity, I am made as brass that soundeth, or a cymbal that soundeth. And if I have every prophecy, and know all privities, and if I have every cunning and every faith, so that I may move hills from their places, if I have no charity, I am nought. And if I deal all my chattels into poor men's living, and give my body to burn, and I have no charity, it profiteth me nothing. Charity is patient and benign; charity hateth no man, nor does not wickedly, nor is not blown with pride; he is not covetous, he seeketh not his own things, he is not wrathful, he thinketh no evil, and joyeth not upon wickedness, but joyeth to truth; all things he suffereth, all things he believeth, all things he hopeth, all things he abideth.

As this passage shows, the translation of the Epistles is a bit stiff because of the effort to be literal, but nevertheless the version reads well and is not at all difficult to follow. Even more interesting, however, is the prologue found in two manuscripts of the Epistles. It begins with a summary of the Creation and Fall as set forth in Genesis, followed by a dialogue between the translator and an anonymous "brother" who urges him to make the translation. "You must teach us unlettered men," says the brother, "the truth of what is pleasing to God, and what displeases him." "Brother," replies the translator, "I know well that I am holden by Christ's law to perform thine asking; but natheless we be now so far fallen away from Christ's law, that if I would answer to thine askings I must in case underfong [=under-go] the death. And thou wost well that a man is holden to keep his life as long as he may." To this objection the "unlearned" brother makes an eloquent reply, proving from scripture the obligation to put oneself in peril to help others. "Brother," responds the translator, "thou hast aghast me somewhat with thine arguments. For though thou hast not been among clerks at school, thy skills [=arguments] that thou makest be founded in love that is above reason that clerks use in school; and therefore it is hard for me to again-stand [=withstand] thy skills and thine askings." He then goes on to answer questions from his companions, who now include a "sister," and he discourses at length on the giving of the Commandments at Sinai, and the moral and ceremonial laws. Suddenly the dialogue breaks off in the middle of a sentence, as the translator is explaining the regulations set forth in Leviticus. As a prologue to the New Testament Epistles, this is certainly a curious performance. Miss Paues regards this translation as orthodox in origin. But Miss Margaret Deanesly may be right in observing that its date (ca. 1388) and the tone of its prologue suggest that this version of the Epistles may be the work of a Lollard sympathizer, in the days when the Church was beginning to discourage independent efforts to translate the Scriptures into English.

The Wyclif Bible

Although our survey shows that parts of the Bible were being translated, for devotion or entertainment, throughout the Middle English period, none of these efforts quite prepares us for the Wyclif Bible, which makes its dramatic appearance, like a mountain among foothills, in the last decades of the fourteenth century. Nothing on the scale of this translation had been attempted before in England, even by Ælfric in the Old English period. It was the first and only complete Bible in English made during the Middle Ages. The inspiration for this project came from John Wyclif, Oxford scholar, theologian, Church reformer, and heretic. Wyclif was born in Yorkshire around 1330, and came to Merton College, Oxford, in 1356. He received his Master of Arts at Balliol in 1360, and eventually obtained the Doctor's degree in 1372. For a time he served as Warden of Canterbury College, but had to resign when it was decreed that only a member of the regular clergy (i.e., a monk) could hold that position. From about 1370 until his departure from Oxford in the summer of 1381, he rented rooms in Queen's College. The last three years of his life were spent in his own parish of Lutterworth, to which he retired after his teachings on the Eucharist were condemned at Oxford in 1381. Wyclif himself escaped trial as a heretic, but his disciples, the Lollards, were sharply attacked by the Church during the decades following Wyclif's death. Finally in 1407, Archbishop Arundel issued a series of Constitutions against Lollardry, of which number VII reads in part as follows:

> Therefore we decree and ordain that no one shall in future translate on his own authority any text of holy scripture into the English tongue or into any other tongue, by way of book, booklet or treatise. Nor shall any man read this kind of book, booklet or treatise, now recently composed in the time of the said John Wyclif, or later, or any that shall be composed in future, in whole or part, publicly or secretly, under penalty of the greater excommunication, until that translation shall be recognized and approved by the diocesan of the place, or if the matter demand it, by a provincial council.

The controversy surrounding the Wyclif Bible has continued, centuries after the event, in the attempt of modern scholars to assess its significance. On the one hand there are those who see Wyclif as a prophet of the Reformation, whose actual influence, indeed, was one of the forces that produced it. Others are inclined to defend the Church, saying that heresy was being condemned, not translation of the Bible as such, and that if an orthodox churchman had produced this version, it would not have been condemned. My own view is that this issue, which had already arisen frequently in the history of the Church, is inevitably affected by circumstances and conditions existing at the time it appears. The concern of Ælfric, for example, about the consequence of making a translation of the bare text of Genesis, is a legitimate case of the scholar's sense of responsibility. The anxiety of Archbishop Arundel, on the other hand, is compromised by the legitimacy of Wyclif's criticism of the Church. The use of "God's law," as the Lollards called it, as a weapon against the Church no doubt seemed intolerable at the time, but it was probably the only effective means available to individuals attempting to reform a ponderous and largely intractable institution that had grown old and wealthy. More might be said on the issues of this contro-

[149]

versy, but it is more profitable, I believe, to consider now the nature and contents of the Wyclif Bible itself, and to explore the circumstances surrounding its composition.

In spite of Arundel's prohibition, some 230 manuscripts of the Wyclif Bible survive to attest its popularity before the invention of printing. For the most part these manuscripts fall into two groups, showing that there were in fact two versions of this Bible. The smaller group of manuscripts forms what is now known as the Early Version (EV), and the other, much larger group constitutes the Later Version (LV). A comparison of the two quickly reveals a significant difference between them: the Early Version is painstakingly literal in its rendering of the Vulgate, even to the extent of following the word order of the Latin, while the Later Version is freer and more idiomatic, a much more readable translation. It would seem, therefore, that this was deliberate; that the translators regarded the first literal version as a necessary prelude to the making of the second one. In any case, let us now look at some examples of this Bible in both versions, beginning with Psalm 15 (Ps 14, Vulgate). In this one instance I will give the original spelling of the texts (except for obsolete letters), for purpose of illustration; in subsequent examples the spelling will be modernized.

PSALM XIV

Early Version

1. Lord, who shal duelle in thi tabernacle; or who shal eft resten in thin holy hil?
2. That goth in withoute wem; and werkith ryghttwisnesse; that speketh treuthe in his herte.
3. That dide not trecherie in his tunge; ne dide to his neghebore euel; and reprof toc not agen hise neghboris.
4. To noght is broght down in his sight the malice doere; forsothe the dredende the Lord he glorifieth; that swereth to his neghebore, and desceyveth not.
5. That his monee gaf not to usure; and giftis upon the innocent toc not. He that doth these thingus, shal not be moved in to without ende.

Later Version

1. Lord, who schal dwelle in thi tabernacle; ether who schal reste in thin hooli hil?
2. He that entrith with out wem; and worchith rightfulnesse; which spekith treuthe in his herte.
3. Which dide not gile in his tunge; neither dide yuel to his neighbore; and took not schenschip agens hise neighboris.

[150]

4. A wicked man is brought to nought in his sight; but he glorifieth hem that dreden the Lord; which swerith to his neighbore, and disseyueth not.
5. Which gaf not his money to usure; and took not giftis on the innocent. He that doith these thingis, schal not be moved with outen ende.

Differences between the two versions are particularly well illustrated in verse 4, where the Early Version has, "To nought is brought down in his sight the malice doer," which the Later Version converts to a more natural English word order: "A wicked man is brought to nought in his sight." Also the participial phrase of EV, "forsooth the dreading the Lord he glorifieth," is made an independent clause in LV: "but he glorifieth them that dread the Lord." Thus it is easy to see why the Later Version proved to be the more popular, even though it perhaps owed its scholarly character to groundwork that went into the making of the Early Version.

On the whole, however, the Early Version reads well in spite of its literalness. In the following examples, one each from the Old and New Testaments, I will quote the Early Version, followed by a brief résumé of the main changes introduced in the Later Version of the same passage. The spelling in these examples is modernized.

GENESIS 22:1–14 (EV)

After that these things were done, God tempted Abraham, and said to him, Abraham! Abraham! He answered, I am nigh. He said to him, Take thine only gotten son, whom thou lovest, Isaac, and go into the land of vision, and there offer him into sacrifice all burnt, upon one of the hills which I shall show to thee. Then Abraham on the night with rising, dight his ass, leading with him two young men, and Isaac his son; and when he had ɪ.ewed his wood into burnt sacrifice, he yede [=went] to the place which commanded him God. And the third day, the eyes heaved up, he saw a place afar; and said to his children [the young men], Abideth here with the ass, I and the child unto thither going, after that we have honored, we shall come again to you. And he took the wood of the sacrifice, and put upon Isaac, his son; he forsooth bare in his hands fire, and a sword. And when they two yede together, said Isaac to his father, My father! And he answered, What wilt thou son? Lo! he saith, fire and wood, where is the sacrifice of that that shall be burnt? Abraham said, God shall purvey to him, my son, the sacrifice of that that shall be burnt. Then they yede together, and came to the place whom God showed to him, in the which he builded an altar, and above made the wood; and when he had bound Isaac, his son, he put him in the altar, upon the heap of wood. And he stretched his hand, and took the sword, that he might offer his son. And lo! the angel of the Lord from heaven cried, saying, Abraham! Abraham! The which answered, I am nigh. And he said to him, Stretch thou not thine hand out upon

[151]

the child, and do not any thing to him; now I have known that thou dreadest God, and thou hast not spared to thine own gotten son for me. Abraham heaved up his eyes, and saw behind his back a wether among thorns, tied by the horns, whom taking to offered burnt sacrifice for the son. And he cleped [=called] the name of the place, The Lord seeth; wherefore yet this day it is said, In the hill the Lord shall see.

The Later Version revises the word order and syntax, though not extensively. "Then Abraham on the night with rising" becomes "Therefore Abraham rose by night"; "the place which commanded him God" is changed to "the place which God had commanded to him"; "I and the child unto thither going" becomes "I and the child shall go thither"; and so forth. In one case the meaning of the original is made more explicit: "the sacrifice of that that shall be burnt" in revision reads "the beast of burnt sacrifice." Most frequent of all in this passage are the actual changes in translation of individual words. "Tempted" in the Later Version is "assayed," "nigh" is "present," "dight" is "saddled," "wood" is "trees," "heaved up" is "raised," "honored" is "worshipped," "stretched" is "held forth," in one instance "sacrifice" is "offer," and, finally, "a wether among thorns, tied by the horns" becomes "a ram cleaving by horns among briars." Of particular theological interest is the change in Genesis 22:1 from "God tempted Abraham" to "God assayed Abraham," a revision perhaps made in the light of teaching in the New Testament Epistle of James (1:13): "Let no man say when he is tempted, I am tempted of God: for God cannot be tempted with evil, neither tempteth he any man." In general the result of the change is an improvement, but not always. It is not easy to see, for example, why "trees" was substituted for "wood" to be used in the offering. Yet in the final analysis the Later Version is certainly clearer and more readable. Now let us look at one more passage, this time from the New Testament.

LUKE 2:1–14 (EV)

Forsooth it was done in those days, a mandment went out from Caesar August, *or noble,* that all the world should be described. This first describing was made of Cyrenius, justice of Syria. And all men went, that they should make profession, *or acknowledging,* each by himself unto his city. Soothly and Joseph stied [=went] up from Galilee, of the city of Nazareth, into Judaea, into a city of David, that is cleped [=called] Bethlehem, for that he was of the house and meyne [=family] of David, that he should acknowledge with Mary, with child spoused wife to him. Soothly it was done, when they were there, the days were fulfilled, that she should bear child. And she childed her first born son, and lapped him in clothes, and put him in a cratch [=crib], for there was not place to him in the common stable. And shepherds were in the same country, waking and keeping the watches of the night on their flock. And lo! the angel of the Lord stood beside them, and the clearness of God shined about them; and they dreaded with great dread. And the angel said to them, nill ye [=do not] dread; lo! soothly I evangelize to you a great joy, that shall be to all people. For a savior is born today to us, that is Christ the Lord, in the city of David. And this is a token to you: ye shall find a young child lapped in cloths, and put in a cratch. And suddenly there is made with the angel a multitude of heavenly knighthood, herying [=praising] God, and saying, Glory be in the highest things to God, and in earth peace be to men of good will.

Differences between the two versions are fewer in this passage. "Mary, with child spoused wife to him," becomes "Mary, his wife, that has wedded to him," a decided improvement. "Caesar" is "the emperor," "stied up" is "went up," "childed" is "bare," and "put" is "laid." The hellenism in "I evangelize to you great joy" is avoided in the revision with "I preach to you a great joy." Another noteworthy feature of this passage is the doublet as in "august, *or noble*," and "profession, *or acknowledging*," offering two translations of the same Latin word. These are not retained in the Later Version, which in both cases chooses the first of the two words. The use of doublets, however, is not characteristic of the Early Version in its original form; the two in this passage, for instance, do not occur in Christ Church, Oxford, manuscript 145, the best of the EV manuscripts. It therefore seems likely that the doublets were added in the course of recension of the Early Version, independent of the making of the later translation. But of course certainty in these matters is impossible; among so many manuscripts there is bound to be some contamination between versions in the course of scribal transmission of the text.

One further irregularity in the passage from Luke concerns the famous verse which in the King James version reads (Luke 2:7), *there was no room for them in the inn.* The Early Version has instead, "there was not place to him in the common stable" (Vulgate: *non erat eis locus in diversorio*). This seems to deny the traditional view of Christ's birth in a stable, a view first popularized by the friars in order to emphasize the poverty of the Savior as a precedent for their own vow of poverty. In view of the hostility that developed at Oxford between the friars and the secular clergy (which included Wyclif), it is tempting to see a bias against the fraternal orders in this peculiar translation. Because of this possibility, it is all the more interesting

[153]

to note that the Later Version restores the traditional meaning of this verse: "there was no place to him in no chamber." This accords well with the view that the Early Version was made at Oxford, and the Later Version in some other locality, away from the university and its influence.

About the circumstances surrounding the composition of the Wyclif Bible surprisingly little is known. Archbishop Arundel, writing to Pope John XXII in 1412, remarks that John Wyclif, "of cursed memory," devised "the expedient of a new translation of the Scriptures into the mother tongue." Of about the same date is the passage in a continuation of Henry Knighton's *Chronicle*, which reads in part: "This master John Wyclif translated into English (not, alas, into the tongue of angels), the gospel which Christ gave to clerks and doctors of the church . . . , whence, through him, it [the gospel] is become more common and open to laymen and women who are able to read, than it is wont to be even to lettered clerks of good intelligence. Thus the pearl of the gospel is scattered abroad and trodden under foot of swine, and what is wont to be the treasure both of clerks and laymen is now become the jest of both." There is finally the testimony of John Hus, writing in Prague in 1411, who states: "It is said by the English that Wyclif himself translated the Bible from Latin into English." In spite of all this evidence, which seems conclusive, the fact remains that not one of the 230 manuscripts of the Wyclif Bible attributes the translation to Wyclif himself. This has led some scholars to question his connection with it. On the other hand it should be added that, with two exceptions, the manuscripts contain no attribution of authorship at all, which should not be surprising in view of the hazards involved in mere possession of a copy of this Bible after the prohibition of 1407.

One of the manuscripts of the Early Version containing an attribution of authorship is in the Cambridge University Library (MS Ee. 1. 10), which has the following note inserted at verse 20 of Baruch, chapter 3: "Here endith the translatioun of N, and now bigynneth the translacioun of J and othere men." This would of course be hopelessly enigmatic, were it not for a note at exactly the same point in a manuscript in the Bodleian Library (MS Douce 369), which reads: "Explicit translacionem Nicholay de herford." Thus the "N" referred to in the Cambridge manuscript is quite clearly Nicholas Hereford, a colleague of John Wyclif at Oxford. Unfortunately we are left in the dark as to the identity of "J and other men." The most that can be

[154]

said from manuscript evidence, is that the Early Version was made by Nicholas Hereford, J. ____, and other men, and this is about as far as most modern writers on the subject have ventured to go. There is indirect evidence, however, of a very interesting kind, which I would like to bring to bear from the following account of the circumstances surrounding the making of the Early Version of the Wyclif Bible.

The evidence points to Queen's College, Oxford, as the meeting place and the probable working quarters of the scholars involved in the translation. Among those studying and living at Queen's in the 1360s were Nicholas Hereford, whose name appears as translator of EV in the Douce manuscript; William Middleworth; and John Trevisa. All three of these men, incidentally, were ordained to the priesthood by Simon Sudbury, Bishop of London, on June 8, 1370. Wyclif himself rented rooms in Queen's as early as 1363–64, and he is listed as paying rent again there in the seventies and finally in the year 1380–81.

In 1376 Thomas Carlisle was elected provost of the college, but this election was disputed, and resulted in the expulsion of several scholars including the former provost, Henry Whitfield, along with Trevisa, Middleworth, and several other fellows. On May 13, 1378, an indenture was drawn up in the presence of the Sheriff of Oxford, containing a list of charters, books, and other goods which the expelled scholars are said to have carried off and stored "in diverse places in the town."

Unfortunately we cannot be sure how this controversy ended. If we are to believe Anthony Wood, seventeenth century Oxford historian, Whitfield himself restored the stolen property to Carlisle. We do know that a pardon of outlawry was granted to William Middleworth (for not appearing to render chattels to Carlisle) on May 1, 1380. By this time Whitfield had become Archdeacon of Barnstaple and seemed to harbor no malice. Middleworth was again in good standing, remaining as a fellow until 1383, and later renting rooms in the college in 1385–86 and 1394–95. And the last reference to John Trevisa in the Long Rolls of Queen's College, for the period of this controversy, appears under the year 1378–79. We have no certain knowledge of his whereabouts or activities from 1378–79 to 1382–83. Subsequently he is recorded as having rented rooms at Queen's College for four years from 1383 to 1387, and again for two years during the period 1394–96. From all these dates it is evident that the backbone of resistance was broken in 1378 or 1379 and that the stubborn group had dispersed or submitted by the summer of 1380. Wyclif and Hereford are not mentioned in the dispute because they were not fellows of the college, but simply rented rooms there during the controversy. Both scholars appear to have left the college some time in 1380–81.

What were these scholars doing at Queen's during the time of the controversy? Wyclif, we can be sure, was busily engaged in writing some of his numerous controversial pieces, particularly his treatise on the Eucharist, completed in 1379. Nicholas Hereford was doing his share of the translation of the Bible. What program of study were the other scholars pursuing? It is tempting to conclude, somewhat grimly, that their time was fully occupied in legal maneuvering. On the other hand, the very controversy discussed above supplies some valuable evidence of their scholarly interests. I refer, of course, to the indenture drawn up in the presence of the Sheriff of Oxford on May 13, 1378. This indenture begins with a list of the possessions of the college which the rebels were turning over to Carlisle: (1) the seal, (2) seven indentures concerning the choice of books of the college (1372), (3) a gilded silver chalice, etc. But the most important part of the indenture is its list of books which the southerners had carried off. These books are listed by title, and even identified, with great precision, by the opening word or phrase of the second folio of each.

It was a rare good fortune that preserved this list, for these books are of the utmost importance in revealing what the expelled scholars were working on. Of the twenty-four books listed, at least eight are of particular interest for the present discussion. They are:

1. A Latin text of the Bible.
2. A Latin grammar and dictionary.
3. Gregory's *Morals on the Book of Job.*
4. A Concordance to the Bible.
5. Commentary on Matthew, attributed to Saint John Chrysostom (*Opus Imperfectum*).
6. Commentary on Proverbs (in part) by Nicholas of Lyra.
7. Commentary on the Psalter by Nicholas by Lyra.
8. Commentary on Genesis.

This list indicates that Nicholas Hereford was perhaps not the only one working on a translation of the Bible in Queen's College. Indeed, I suggest that among the scholars at Queen's in the 1370s were the men who translated the Early Version of the Wyclif Bible: at the very least these would include Wyclif, Hereford, Middleworth, and Trevisa.

The presence of Trevisa in this group is particularly suggestive. One of the other manuscripts named by the sheriff (but not listed above) was a Latin text of Higden's *Polychronicon,* a work which Trevisa translated in 1387. Nearly a century later the English printer, William Caxton, published an edition of Trevisa's translation of the *Polychronicon* (1482) in the prologue to which he listed some of Trevisa's other translations. One of these, according to Caxton, was "the byble." Thereafter the statement appears repeatedly in connection with Trevisa's name. The translators of the King James Bible of 1611, for example, mention it in their preface to the reader: "Much about that time, even in our King Richard the seconds dayes, John Trevisa translated them [the Scriptures] into English, and many English Bibles in written hand are yet to be seene with divers, translated as it is very probable, in that age." Modern scholars have either tended to reject this assertion, or to assume that it means Trevisa made a separate translation. This, I think, overlooks the evidence I have just presented on the controversy at Queens. There is no need to assume the existence of a biblical translation by Trevisa now lost.

To the suggestion that Trevisa was one of the Wycliffite translators, however, it may be objected that he was not a follower of Wyclif. This is perfectly true. Trevisa was not a Wycliffite, if by that term we mean a man who accepted all the reformer's doctrines and simply followed where he led. The two men seem to have differed, for example, on the question of the fate of the righteous heathen, and it is doubtful whether Trevisa would be able to read with equanimity Wyclif's treatise on the Eucharist, completed in 1379. That Wyclif had friends and colleagues who nevertheless differed firmly with him on matters of doctrine is well attested by passages in his treatise on the Church, *De Ecclesia* (1378), and elsewhere. Trevisa may well have been one of these intellectually independent friends. To force Trevisa into the category of enemy or devotee is to subject him to a post-Reformation distortion.

Once we understand the limits of Trevisa's agreement with Wyclif, it is then pertinent to remember that he was indeed influenced by the latter. His severity with monks and friars is well attested in the notes added to his translation of the *Polychronicon,* and the fact that Trevisa translated Fitzralph's sermon against the friars reveals a common ground of agreement with Wyclif. Wyclif's favorite historian was Higden; Trevisa translated Higden's *Polychronicon*. Nicholas of Lyra became a favorite Lollard commentator; Trevisa is acquainted with and uses Lyra.

With all the available facts before us, I now take the liberty of reconstructing the circumstances and chronology of the translation of the first Wycliffite Bible. Some time after the arrival at Queen's of Hereford, Middleworth, Trevisa, and Wyclif, perhaps as early as 1372, work on the translation was begun. I hesitate to say to what extent Wyclif involved himself in the actual task of translation, though there is no doubt that he was the prime mover of this project. The work may have continued to as late as 1378–79, when, as we have seen, legal assaults began to break up the group and force the dispersal of their books "in diverse places in the town" of Oxford. The legal issue in this dispute, of course, was the interpretation of the founder's stipulation regarding the admission of northerners into the college and the consequent contested election of a provost; but I think it would be naïve in the extreme to suppose that this fact rules out the possibility of a deeper motive for the controversy. Academic disputes often display a surface calm, or at least a legal decorum, beneath which may lurk the most profound ideological conflict. Anthony Wood knew this when he indulged in his famous speculation on the cause of the scandal at Queen's: "whether upon account of heresy or election of a Provost I know not." On this point I dare not go further than Wood.

Whether Trevisa, after 1378–79, ever again worked on a translation of the Bible (i.e., the Later Version) is a separate question. I can see no real evidence that he did. Within five years after his expulsion from Queen's, if not earlier, he had become established as chaplain and man of letters for Thomas Lord Berkeley in Gloucestershire, and the new requirements of this position, not to mention his duties as Vicar of Berkeley, must have had a considerable effect on his literary interests and his whole way of life. Trevisa may well have been working on his *Polychronicon* translation during 1383–87, when he was apparently renting rooms at Queen's, and he completed it, as he tells us, in 1387. His *Dialogue between a Lord and a Clerk upon translation* was no doubt written during this period. It is prefixed to his translation of the *Polychronicon* and serves as a kind of preface to that work. To conclude this exploration of the history of the Early Version, I wish to quote a passage from this dialogue, for I believe that it cannot be fully appreciated unless we realize that its author is not only defending English translations in general, but is also carefully defending his own earlier role as a translator of the Wycliffite Bible.

THE CLERK: The Latin is both good and fair, therefore it needeth not to have an English translation.

THE LORD: The reason is worthy to be plunged in a pludde and laid in powder of lewdness and of shame. It might well be that thou makest only in mirth and in game.

THE CLERK: The reason must stand but it be assoiled.

THE LORD: A blear-eyed man, but he were all blind of wit, might see the solution of this reason; and though he were blind he might grope the solution, but if his feeling him failed. For if this reason were aught worth, by such manner arguing men might prove that the three score and ten interpreters, and Aquila, Symachus, Theodocion, and Origines were lewdly occupied when they translated holy writ out of Hebrew into Greek; and also that Saint Jerome was lewdly occupied when he translated holy writ out of Hebrew into Latin, for the Hebrew is both good and fair and y-written by inspiration of the Holy Ghost; and all these for their translations be highly praised of all Holy Church. Then the foresaid lewd reason is worthy to be powdered, laid a-water, and y-soused. . . . Then it needeth to have an English translation, and for to keep it in mind that it be not forgotten, it is better that such a translation be made and written than said and not written. And so this foresaid lewd reason should move no man that hath any wit to leave making of English translation.

THE CLERK: A great deal of these books standeth much by holy writ, by holy doctors, and by philosophy; then these books should not be translated into English.

THE LORD: It is wonder that thou makest so feeble arguments, and hast gone so long to school. Aristotle's books and other books also of logic and of philosophy were translated out of Greek into Latin. Also at praying of King Charles, John Scott translated Deny's books out of Greek into Latin, and then out of Latin into French; then what hath English trespassed that it might not be translated into English? Also King Alfred, that founded the University of Oxford, translated the best laws into English tongue, and a great deal of the Psalter out of Latin into English, and caused Wyrefrith, Bishop of Worcester, to translate Saint Gregory's books, the Dialogues, out of Latin into Saxon. Also Caedmon of Whitby was inspired of the Holy Ghost, and made wonder poesies in English nigh of all the stories of holy writ. Also the holy man Bede translated Saint John's gospel out of Latin into English. Also thou wotest where the Apocalypse is written in the walls and roof of a chapel, both in Latin and in French. Also the gospel, and prophecy, and the right faith of holy church must be taught and preached to English men that can no Latin. Then the gospel, and prophecy, and the right faith of holy church must be told them in English, and that is not done but by English translation, for such English preaching is very translation, and such English preaching is good and needful; then English translation is good and needful.

[159]

The Later Version

Trevisa's argument for English translations is echoed and amplified in later controversy that developed in the wake of the Wyclif Bible. For a sense of the nature of this controversy, we can look briefly at the Prologue to the Later Version, composed in 1395–96 possibly by John Purvey, a disciple of John Wyclif, and the man most likely responsible for the making of the entire Later Version. Purvey seems to have been Wyclif's secretary during the reformer's final three years at Lutterworth, and he held out longer than most Lollards against the Church authorities who sought to force him to renounce his heresies. "John Purvey," wrote the friar Thomas Walden, "was called the glossator and translator of Wyclif, for he was the continual Achates of Wyclif right down till his death, and drank in his most secret teaching." Since the literature of the Lollards is anomymous, it is impossible to connect anyone directly with the individual works, but most modern scholars have followed the lead of Miss Deanesly in assigning the Prologue of the Later Version to Purvey.

The first chapter of the Prologue lists the books of the Bible, and distinguishes between canonical and apocryphal works. No simple man need fear to study the text of holy writ, says the author, and no clerk should be proud of his understanding of it. For understanding without charity damns a man, and pride and covetousness make clerks blind to the true understanding of holy writ, and send them to hell, as Augustine says. The second chapter defines the three divisions of Mosaic law as it applies to Christians. Moral commandments, as in the decalogue, are eternally binding and never change. Judicials include many punishments ordained by God which were in effect in Old Testament times, but since the coming of Christ these judicials are subject to the modifying force of the law of mercy and charity. The third group of laws were the ceremonials, which were observed in the Old Testament period but ceased utterly with the coming of Christ. To observe these now would be to say that Christ did not suffer to redeem mankind, and would deny that the truth and freedom of the gospel is sufficient for salvation. "Therefore," the author concludes, "as it is open heresy to say that the gospel with its truth and freedom sufficeth not to Christian men's salvation without keeping of ceremonies of God's law given to Moses, so it seemeth open heresy to say that the gospel with its truth and freedom sufficeth not to salvation of Christian men without keeping of ceremonies and statutes of sinful men and uncunning, that be made in the time of Satan and Antichrist." This last is a characteristic Lollard charge, drawing an analogy between the ceremonials of the Israelite temple and the sacramental system of the medieval church.

Chapters three through nine of the Prologue contain a summary of the Pentateuch and the historical books down through second chronicles. At the end of each part a moral lesson is drawn from the historical events summarized. In chapter ten, however, the author's restraint deserts him, and he offers his indictment of the Church on the basis of Old Testament examples. The books of Chronicles, he says, show how God punished evil kings and rewarded good kings who governed well the people. And if kings and lords knew only the stories of Jehoshaphat, Hezekiah, and Josiah, they would have sufficient examples for living and governing well.

> But alas, alas, alas! where king Jehoshapat sent his princes and deacons and priests to each city of his realm with the book of God's law, to teach openly God's law to the people, some Christian lords send general letters to all their ministers and liegemen or tenants, that the pardons of the bishops of Rome—that be open lies, for they grant many hundred years of pardon after doomsday—be preached generally in their realms and lordships; and if any wise man againsaith the open errors of Antichrist, and teach men to do their alms to poor needy men, to escape the pains of hell and to win the bliss of heaven, he be prisoned as a man out of Christian belief and traitor to God, and of Christian kings and lords.

Similar use is made of the other two kings. Hezekiah cleansed the sanctuary and ordained deacons; but some so-called Christian lords defile God's sanctuary by bringing in covetous and heretical clerks who suppress God's law and spend their time on secular affairs. Josiah preached God's law openly and did away with idolatry; but now these lords praise friars' letters, which are full of lies and deceit, and cherish those who preach in support of the sinful traditions of men while they suppress the preaching of the gospel. But let these unwise lords remember Elijah, who defended God's truth alone against King Ahab and his priests and prophets. The rest of the chapter is taken up largely with a condemnation of the sins of the clergy, particularly prelates of the established Church.

The summary of the contents of the Old Testament is completed in Chapter eleven, and again some of the lessons drawn from the various books reflect the Lollard sympathies of the author. Judith was praised for slaying Holofernes; how much more praise therefore, shall they have who allow themselves to be martyred for God's cause.

[161]

Many men recite the psalter undevoutly, and they blaspheme God when they sing Psalms loudly in church but do not live in charity. The Song of Solomon teaches love of God and neighbor, and instructs us to bring men to salvation by example, preaching, and voluntary suffering of pain and death, if need be. "This story of Maccabees," he concludes, "should stir men to hold God's law to life and death; and if knights are to use the sword against any condemned men, they should use it principally against lords and priests who would compel men, for dread of prison and death, to forsake the truth and freedom of Christ's gospel; but may God of his great mercy give true repentance to them that thus pursue true men, and grant patience, meekness and charity to them that be thus pursued."

Chapter twelve is quite conventional in what it has to say about exegesis, but the reliance of the Wycliffite translators on Nicholas of Lyra would seem to imply an emphasis on the literal as opposed to allegorical levels, and this is confirmed by the opening statement of this chapter: "Holy scripture," he says, "hath four understandings; literal, allegoric, moral, and anagogic. The literal understanding teacheth the thing done in deed; and literal understanding is ground and foundation of the three ghostly understandings, in so much as Austin, in his epistle to Vincent, and other doctors say, only by the literal understanding may a man argue against an adversary." He goes on to describe and illustrate the four levels in a perfectly orthodox manner, drawing principally on Augustine's *Christian Doctrine*. The discussion then continues through two more chapters with rules for interpreting scripture, recognition of figurative language, and much other practical advice, taken from the Fathers, on methods of studying holy writ.

At one point in his discussion of methods of interpretation, the author pauses to reflect on the state of learning in England, and Oxford in particular. "But alas, alas, alas!" he cries, "the greatest abomination that ever was heard among Christian clerks is now purposed in England, by true men told with great wailing . . . , that no man shall learn divinity, neither holy writ, but he that hath done his form in art; that is, that hath commenced in art, and hath been regent two years after; this would be nine or ten years before that he learn holy writ. . . . This seemeth utterly the devil's purpose, that few men or none shall learn and know God's law." He then goes on to apply the prophecy of Amos concerning Damascus (Amos 1:3–5) to the state of affairs at Oxford: As was true in the case of Damascus, the Lord will not turn away the punishment for three transgressions of Oxford, and for four. The first sin is a widespread worldliness in the university; the second is sodomy; the third is simony; and the fourth sin that will call forth punishment from God is the decision to prevent men from freely studying God's law. But you worldly clerks and pretended religious should know, he warns, that God both can and will, if it pleases Him, bring simple men to as full knowledge of holy writ as masters in the university.

In the Prologue's final chapter, the author explains his method of translation, and offers a defense of translating the Bible into English. "First," he says,

> this simple creature had much travail, with divers fellows and helpers, to gather many old Bibles, and other doctors and common glosses, and to make one Latin Bible somedeal true; and then to study it anew, the text with the gloss, and other doctors, as he might get, and specially Lyra on the Old Testament, that helped full much in this work; the third time to counsel with old grammarians, and old divines, of hard words and hard sentences, how those might best be understood and translated; the fourth time to translate as clearly as he could to the sentence, and to have many good fellows and cunning at the correcting of the translation.

He goes on to say that it is best, when translating, to follow the sense rather than word for word, pointing out, for example, how Latin ablative absolutes should be resolved in English. This of course describes precisely the translation method used in the making of the Later Version. And this inference is confirmed by his subsequent reference to the Early Version in the course of a comment on the unreliability of the Latin text: "the common Latin Bibles have more need to be corrected, as many as I have seen in my life, than hath the English Bible late translated," that is, the Early Version made at Oxford.

The defense of biblical translation seems in part to arise from arguments leveled against it by opponents. Some say it would be acceptable if the translators were as holy as Saint Jerome. Others ask why anyone would dare translate the Bible into English, since the four great Doctors of the church never dared do this? These objections were easily answered.

> Lord God! since at the beginning of faith so many men translated into Latin, and to great profit of Latin men, let one simple creature of God translate into English, for profit of English men. For if worldly clerks look well their chronicles and books, they should find that Bede translated the Bible, and expounded much in Saxon, that was English or common language of this land in his time; and not only Bede but also

[163]

King Alfred, that founded Oxford, translated in his last days the beginning of the psalter into Saxon, and would more, if he had lived longer. Also Frenchmen, Bohemians, and Britons have the Bible and other books of devotion and of exposition translated in their mother language; why Englishmen should not have the same in their mother tongue I can not wit, but for falseness and negligence of clerks, or for our people is not worthy to have so great grace and gift of God, in pain of their old sins. God for his mercy amend these evil causes, and make our people to have and know and keep truly holy writ, to life and death!

On this note the Prologue to the Later Version concludes, and we thus end our review of the making of the Wyclif Bible, a project which, as we have seen, aroused a storm toward the end of the fourteenth century. Let me only add a brief comment on the significance of this controversy. The sharpness of the Church's reaction, and the condemnation of the translation cannot, I think, be adequately accounted for simply as a vigilant response to the heretical views of John Wyclif. Rather it seems to me that two ways of expressing the biblical message, the liturgical and the social, were in conflict. Over the centuries the Church had built up a magnificent liturgy, somewhat at the expense of the social teachings of the gospel. It is therefore not surprising that Wyclif's effort to develop a new and direct social application of the biblical message inevitably seemed to collide with the liturgical and sacramental tradition of the sanctuary, a conflict of values which found its clearest expression in his treatise on the Eucharist. Hence the controversy surrounding the Wyclif Bible reflects a larger crisis of faith in the fourteenth century, a crisis which is also reflected in the literature of the period.

CHAPTER FIVE

The Metrical Bible: Cursor Mundi

H AVING surveyed the Old and Middle English periods, we turn
now to consider major works of the fourteenth century showing biblical influence. One of the most influential of these
was *Cursor Mundi,* composed about A.D. 1300 in nearly thirty thousand lines of rhyming couplets, setting forth the Bible narrative interwoven with legendary additions. "Men shall call it *Courser of the
World,"* says the author, "for almost it overruns all." The prologue
opens with a very interesting revelation of the purpose behind this
huge work (1–28): Men yearn to hear stories and romances of Alexander the Great, Julius Caesar, the Trojan Wars, King Arthur and his
knights, Charlemagne and Roland, Tristram and Iseult, and other
diverse tales in English, French, and Latin. Though he does not say
so, our narrator apparently regards these romances as frivolous, and
hopes that his own poem will be accepted as a superior alternative:

> The wise men will of wisdom hear,
> The fool him draweth to folly near.

Obviously the compiler is anxious that the devil not have all the good
stories, so to speak, and he offers a religious narrative to compete for
public attention against secular literature, notably the famous romance cycles.

"By their fruits ye shall know them," continues the author in his
prologue, pointing out that those who are attracted to worldly stories
reveal that their hearts are inclined to worldly things. Nowadays no

one is accounted worthy unless he has a paramour; fools prefer that vanity to all else, yet it is but a phantom, here today, and tomorrow cast away by chance of death or change of heart. When you think such love is truest, behold, it is over and gone. So let us rather praise that Paramour who helps us in our need, saves us from sin, and leads us to heaven. She is both mother and maiden, and of her Jesus took flesh. He who truly loves this lover, he shall have a love that never fails. In her honor this work is begun.

After summarizing the contents of the Old and New Testaments, the author concludes his prologue with a dedication. Man needs to know, he says, from first to last how he did wax and multiply in the earth, and the history of the world until the establishment of holy Church. This book is translated into the English tongue for the love of English people, so that the common folk of England may better understand it. Seldom do we see the English tongue preached in France; so let each land have its language, and then we do no outrage. I speak to men who understand English, and especially to those who lead sinful lives. Now let us begin our book in Christ's name.

Cursor Mundi is divided into seven parts corresponding to the seven ages of man: the first age extends from the Creation to Noah (lines 271–1,626), the second from the Flood to the Tower of Babel (1,627–2,314), the third from Abraham to Saul (2,315–7,860), the fourth from David to the Babylonian Captivity (7,861–9,228); the fifth corresponds to the remainder of Old Testament history but in the poem is largely occupied with an apocryphal account of the ancestry and childhood of Jesus (9,229–12,712); the sixth is called the age of grace, from the baptism of Jesus to Doomsday (12,713–23,652); and the seventh age marks the establishment of the Kingdom of God, though in the poem this last part contains a miscellany of exhortations, apostrophes, prayers, and moral instruction (23,653–29,555). This is an attractive panorama, but we will have time to examine only a few highlights from each of the seven ages of the world.

The First Age: Creation to Noah

Eternal God in Trinity, creator and governor of the universe, is one God in three persons, as witnessed by the sun; for its form betokens the Father, its light the Son, and its heat the Holy Ghost. At His word the world was created out of nothing, and formed of the four elements, water, earth, air, and fire, which provided the materials for the six days of Creation (as described in Genesis chapter one). Also

[166]

God created nine orders of angels, with Lucifer placed above them all. But Lucifer said, *I will ascend into heaven, I will exalt my throne above the stars of God: I will sit also upon the mount of the congregation, in the sides of the north: I will ascend above the heights of the clouds; I will be like the most High.* (Isaiah 14:13–14). But no filth may dwell in that court, and so Saint Michael cast him out of Heaven, whereupon his name was changed from Lucifer to Satan. He and his followers fell down into Hell, where they shall remain until Doomsday. So great a fall, says Bede, at forty miles a day, would last fully 7,700 years! But God would be worshipped by two kinds of creatures, angels and men. And so Adam was made, to replace the tenth order destroyed by Lucifer's pride. Man is composed of two things—body and soul. His body is formed of the four elements, and may be compared to the universe, a microcosm reflecting the macrocosm. His two eyes correspond to the sun and the moon, his breath is like the wind, and his bones are like the stones of the earth. For these reasons man is called the "lesser world." Likewise man has a soul which consists of spiritual light impressed with the likeness of God, even as wax under the seal. And since God is a Trinity, the soul has three virtues: memory, understanding, and wisdom. But though the soul perceives all things, it remains invisible; no man has the power to see it.

The temptation and Fall of man in *Cursor Mundi* follow the Genesis account very closely, interweaving here and there foretastes of the Redemption along with expanded descriptions of Paradise. All the beasts and other creatures worshipped Adam as if he had been their creator, and they lived together in harmony (685–96):

> Among the wolves lay the sheep,
> Safely might they together sleep;
> The hound harmed not the hare,
> No beast attacked another's lair;
> By the deer that now is wild
> As a lamb lay the lion mild;
> The griffin also beside the bear,
> No beast would harm another there.
> The scorpion forbore his tongue
> From beasts that he lay among:
> All manner thing in diverse wise
> Yielded to Adam their service.

Even the sun and moon shone brighter then, for all things in the world were stronger before Adam sinned. Thus the state of the world before the Fall is seen as a foretaste of the messianic age envisioned by the prophets.

[167]

To the biblical story of the Fall is added a detailed account of its consequences, including God's plan for man's Redemption. Since Adam ate the apple, the children's teeth are set on edge (cp. Jeremiah 31:29), and shall continue so till Doomsday. Strife arose between Adam and Eve, and the stronger beast slew the weaker. For this reason God chose to take on flesh and fill the world with His grace; He became our brother, fought against the fiend, and reconciled us with the Father. But Adam, of course, does not know this; and so when he is driven out of the garden he cries, "Alas, tell me by what means I may be reconciled with Thee?" The Lord replies, "Adam, you shall give me a tenth of all your winning."

After relating the expulsion of Adam and Eve, the author cannot resist giving us another glimpse of Paradise, the *hortus deliciarum* or "garden of delights" which Adam lost because of his sin. It stands in the east, a land of life and peace, where it is always day and never night. The grass is eternally green, and sweet-smelling flowers are everywhere. The various fruits of the trees have wonderful powers: one does away with hunger, another with thirst (Isaiah 49:10), still another with weariness (Isaiah 40:31); and last of all there is another fruit that prevents aging, sickness, and death (Hosea 13:14; 1 Cor. 15:55). From a spring in the midst of that land, four streams run out into the world to form the Tigris, Ganges, Euphrates, and Nile rivers. In these streams are found precious stones brought from Paradise. This land is set so high above the earth that it was undisturbed by the flood that overwhelmed the world in the time of Noah.

The story of Cain and Abel follows Genesis closely, but interesting details are added. Why does God refuse Cain's sacrifice? This point is not clear in the Bible, but in *Cursor Mundi* we are told that it was because Cain offered his tithe grudgingly. In the field, Cain kills Abel with the jawbone of an ass in the manner of Samson (Judges 15:15), but when he tries to bury the body, the earth casts it up. This popular motif recurs in later biblical legends, notably one on the death of Pilate included in the *Golden Legend* and referred to in Chapter I.

Another bit of folklore in the story of Cain and Abel appears in the form of a riddle, posed by the narrator in describing the burial of Abel by Adam and Eve (1187–90):

> This is the man men say was born
> Both his father and mother before;

> He had his grandmother's maidenhead
> And at his burying all manner of people.

This means, I take it, that Abel was born before Adam and Eve in the sense that he was born in the usual way and they were not; he had the virginity of his grandmother (Earth) in that he was the first to be buried in her; and all the people of the world were present at his burial because there were no others in existence yet besides his own family.

Of all the legendary materials in *Cursor Mundi,* none is more significant or pervasive than the legend of Seth. To counterbalance the story of the Fall, the author wishes to proclaim the good news of the Redemption. Seth takes the place of Abel as Adam's good son, and is thus an appropriate spokesman for this theme. The interweaving of this legend into the biblical narrative was an effective means of emphasizing the theme of Redemption from the beginning.

Adam, realizing that he must soon die, instructs Seth to go to Paradise in quest of the oil of mercy. He will be able to find the way by following his parents' footprints, which scorched the grass when they were driven out of the garden. He is to ask the angel who guards the gate two questions: When will my father Adam die? Will he receive the oil of mercy from on high, promised to him when he was driven from Paradise? The old father leans on his shovel and concludes sadly (1,279–82):

> I did against the will of God,
> And now I've paid for it somewhat:
> Since then my sorrow is ever renewed,
> Now let there be time to pity me.

Obediently the son sets out on his mission of mercy.

Arriving at the gates of Paradise, Seth asks his questions, and the angel tells him to go look in at the gates, attending carefully to what he sees. Three times he is sent to look, each time perceiving a little more. First, he sees in the midst of the beautiful garden a great tree, stark and dead, a sharp contrast to the greenness of its surroundings. Second, he sees a great serpent coiled about the tree. The third time he looks carefully at the tree and sees, first, in the topmost branches, a newborn child weeping, wrapped in a swaddling band, and next, down among the roots of the tree, which extended down to hell, he sees his brother Abel.

The angel explains to Seth the meaning of his vision. The child that you have seen (he says) is the Son of God; now he weeps for your father's sin, but when the fullness of time comes he shall cleanse it. This is the oil of mercy promised to Adam and his children. Before dismissing Seth, the angel gives him three seeds from the tree of knowledge, and then carefully instructs him. Your father will die in three days; when this happens, take these three seeds and plant them under his tongue. From them will grow three healing trees, cedar, cypress, and palm, betokening Father, Son, and Holy Ghost. Seth follows these instructions, and buries Adam in the vale of Hebron, where the three trees grow and flourish until the time of Moses.

In later sections of *Cursor Mundi* the motif of the three trees is reintroduced to give us further foretastes of the Redemption. Moses finds them and uses them to sweeten the waters of Marah (Exodus 15:23–26) and to bring forth water from the rock (Exodus 17:1–7; 1 Cor. 10:4). Although he uproots them and carries them with him in the desert, they remain miraculously green and flourishing. Later he puts them in the ark of the covenant for safekeeping, and finally before he dies he plants them in a secret place near Elim (Num. 33:9).

King David, instructed by an angel in a dream, finds the three trees near Moses' grave. The trunks have grown together, but the upper parts retain their separate identities as cedar, cypress, and palm. David approaches the trees to kiss them, creeping upon his knees. Drawing them up gently, without breaking a single bough, he and his men see a beam of light from heaven shining on them. Henceforth the army is victorious wherever it goes, and the sacred tree is used to heal the sick. Then the king meets four black and misshapen Saracens, who ask him to show them the tree. For we know (they say) that the King of bliss shall suffer on that tree, and for that reason it has power against all evils. When they kiss the branches, suddenly they appear before the king with their bodies completely restored to health. Other miracles follow. With these branches the king heals a hermit and parts the waters of the Jordan river. In Jerusalem David puts them in a cistern, where they take root and grow into a mighty tree, under which the king often says his prayers.

In the reign of Solomon the tree withers, and the workmen get permission to take it down for use in building the temple. But no matter how carefully they measure and cut it, the beam will not fit. Because of its miraculous nature, the sacred beam is left in the temple, until one day a lady named Maximilla comes and sits down on it to pray and is set on fire. Immediately she begins to cry out in a

[170]

voice of prophecy that Jesus Christ, born of a virgin, will hang on that tree to save mankind. For this blasphemy she is beheaded, but her soul is taken to heaven by an angel in the sight of all. The tree is then thrown in a nearby pool, known as *piscina probatica,* and henceforth a great miracle has been shown: at certain times angels wondrously bright come down to stir the water; and when they do so, the first man to enter the water is cured of his sickness (John 5:2–4). Subsequently the Jews take the tree from the pool and use it as a bridge over the waters of Shiloah (Isa. 8:6). When the sibyl (i.e., the Queen of Sheba) comes to speak with Solomon (1 Kings 10), as she approaches the tree she bows down to worship it, and wades the stream to avoid walking on it. Then she utters prophecies concerning the day of Doom, and Solomon honors her with many gifts. The tree is preserved in the temple until the time of Christ's Passion, when it is used to make the cross.

From this summary we can see how the legend of Seth and the holy tree ties the Old and New Testament together. The story was extremely popular, and traces of its influence can be seen in medieval art as well. Most early paintings of the Crucifixion show a skull beneath the cross. This reminds us not only that the scene is Golgotha (Mark 15:22), but also that the wood for the cross grew from the seeds planted by Seth under Adam's tongue. Perhaps most fascinating of all is the fact that this entire elaborate story grew from the fertile words of Saint Paul (1 Cor. 15:22): *For as in Adam all die, even so in Christ shall all be made alive.*

The Second Age: The Flood to Babel

Since the story of the flood follows the Bible very closely, we can concentrate on a few changes and expansions which show how the compiler is at times interpreting, at times merely elaborating the narrative. His explanation of the reason for the flood is a case in point. The scriptural author says merely: *God saw that the wickedness of man was great in the earth, and that every imagination of the thoughts of his heart was only evil continually* (Gen. 6:5). In *Cursor Mundi* this idea is considerably elaborated. There was woe enough in Adam's time, but never so much as now, especially among the descendants of Cain, whose will was inclined to evil. Their thoughts were not on their Creator; rather they waxed blind and gave their lives up to lust. Women came together with women, and men with men; they were deceitful and corrupt, and went against the law of nature (1,555–80). This is a rather severe and specific indictment, but undoubtedly what we see here is another instance of the influence of Saint Paul, this time taken from his letter to the Romans (1 Rom.: 18–32).

What was God's reaction to all this wickedness? In the next verse of Genesis we find: *it repented the Lord that he had made man* (Gen. 6:6). The author of *Cursor Mundi* uses the ambiguity of the word "repent" (Vulgate *penitet*) to interpret the statement as another foretaste or prophecy of the Redemption. "Me rueth that ever I made man," said the Lord, but this word was a prophecy spoken out of mercy: He made known his "ruth" (sorrow, pity) when He put Himself on the cross for His chosen ones, saying "Father, forgive them" (Luke 23:34). Even before that, mercy was promised to those who did His will, and destruction to His enemies (Matt. 25:31–46). The flood is simply another illustration of this: Noah is saved, and wicked men are destroyed.

The flood itself is vividly described. Lightning fell, along with thunder and rain, the earth shook, and the sun and moon lost their light. Buildings fell down, water spread over the plains, beasts ran to the mountains, and men and women ran with them. Fowls fluttered on high, and finally fell exhausted; the efforts of man and beast were useless; the waters overtook them all. Side by side swam wolf and man, lion and hart; no beast harmed another. There was no pride in social standing: ladies swam by their servants, no man was jealous of his wife, and all finally drowned together, rich and poor. A real flair for satire appears in this inverted use of the "harmony of creation" theme, which is normally restricted, as we have seen, to the time before the fall or the future messianic age.

After forty days, Noah sent forth first a raven, then a dove, to see if the waters were abated. The raven does not return, though we are not told why. In *Cursor Mundi* we are given a reason: he found the corpse of a drowned beast floating in the water, forgot his errand, and so failed to return to the ark. That is why, says the author, a messenger who delays in his journey is called a "raven"!

When the flood is over, the Lord makes a covenant with Noah, and establishes the rainbow as a token that He will never again destroy the earth with a flood. "If men sin against me," says God, "I will do justice on them at the day of wrath when I come to judge with fire." Here the narrator pauses to inform us that up until the time of Noah there had been no rainbow, and *no rain*. Yet in spite of this men always had enough to eat, for they were vegetarians and the earth was more fruitful then. But now — thanks to man's sin and his pride —

since the flood, the earth is feebler than it was (its strength depleted by the flood waters), and man must now eat flesh.

Nearing the end of the second age of the world, we find that Nimrod is not only a mighty hunter before the Lord (Gen. 10:8–9), he is also the proud builder of the tower of Babel. The foundation was sixty-two fathoms broad, and the tower so high that the workmen could scarcely endure the sun, and had to wear animal hides for protection against the heat. The author concludes the story with an ironical reference to the confusion of tongues (2,255–60):

> But the dear Lord is so gentle
> That He sent a courteous vengeance:
> Those that sought to do him outrage
> He did not deprive of life and limb;
> But He so mingled their mood
> That no man the other understood.

The Third Age: Abraham to Saul

We have seen how the legend of Seth weaves its way through the third age of the world in the life of Moses. Hence there remain only a few features that are needed to fill out our picture of the third age as presented in *Cursor Mundi*. These take the form of folklore, homilies, narrative motifs, figurative interpretations, and the matter of chronology.

As might be expected, the story of Sodom and Gomorrah is embellished with interesting bits of folklore. While Lot and his family were fleeing for their lives, God rained down fire and brimstone, and a great cry arose from the evil cities. Lot's wife heard this cry, and longed to see how the people fared. When she did so, immediately she was turned to a salt stone beside the way, where she shall remain until Doomsday. They say that animals lick her away in the space of a week, but that the next week she is found completely restored.

The Dead Sea is now seen where the wicked cities of the plain used to be. It is a stinking sea, the poet continues, that looks like the lake of hell. Nothing can live in it; lumps of tar may be found on its sandy shores; a cloud stands over it continually, and fire burns on the surface of the water. Nearby are trees on which grow beautiful apples, but these apples crumble in your hand to stinking powder. What a terrible vengeance this was! Clearly the reason for it was the unnatural sins of the people of Sodom. Good Christian men, take

[173]

example from this. If you must sin, limit yourselves to natural sin with women.

This embellishment of the Sodom narrative is a good example of the homiletic passage, a frequent type of addition in *Cursor Mundi*, which points the moral or otherwise meditates on a feature of the Biblical story. In Genesis 27:1, for instance, we are told that *Isaac was old, and his eyes were dim, so that he could not see. . . .* This leads the author to a meditation on old age. However bold a man may have been (he says), his blood waxes dry, his head and hands shake, his bones begin to creak and his hair to fall out, and his sight grows dim. The forehead wrinkles, the nose drops, teeth rot, the breath stinks, and just to live seems like work. He stumbles easily; he praises only things that are in the past; he is quick to anger and slow to reconciliation; he holds himself wise when his wits are gone; he values only wealth; and nothing pleases him at all. What a wonderful thing is age—the young desire it, but when they attain it they are sorry. This is a universal theme which can be traced back to the Bible (Eccles. 12:1–8), but which also appears in the century following *Cursor Mundi*. Chaucer's reeve, Oswald, speaks eloquently on the subject in the *Canterbury Tales* (I, 3,867–98), and the dreamer, in the B-text of *Piers the Plowman* (20:185–97), describes his own decline into age with a wry humor. These few examples suggest that an examination of the literature of geriatrics in the fourteenth century might prove very rewarding.

An even more popular theme, of course, is the power of love, which is the subject of homilies attached to the stories of Joseph and Samson. The first of these is particularly interesting. Potiphar's wife loves Joseph and, according to the Bible, is not hesitant in telling him so (Gen. 39:7): *. . . his master's wife cast her eyes upon Joseph; and she said, Lie with me.* In *Cursor Mundi*, however, she conceals her love for a time, until at last she cannot restrain herself, and reveals her heart. When Joseph refuses her, she longs for him even more, and can find no rest, night or day. What is more painful than to be denied the thing you love best? to be put in a prison that takes away strength and power of reason? For when the heart is not at home, the body is in prison and delights in nothing. No man may control love by force; though his heart were steel and his body brass (Job 6:12), and though he were stronger than Samson, love may humble him, sometimes with a mere glance. His eye can bring a king into slavery. So if you wish to escape when he approaches, flee and do not look

[174]

back, for if you do, no matter how carefully, you will be mortally wounded in the eye by an arrow that burns like wildfire in your heart, a fire that you will seek to quench with sin. Flee, before you stumble and fall!

Certain motifs in the story of Joseph link up with the poem, *Jacob and Joseph,* considered in the preceding chapter. One of these is the mention of the chaff thrown in the Nile, which Napier, in his introduction, considered to have been a feature of the minstrel poem at a point where one leaf was torn from the manuscript. This episode, preserved in *Cursor Mundi,* provides a graphic explanation for the journey of the brothers to Egypt, which in the Bible is simply prompted by Jacob's knowledge that corn was available there (Gen. 42:1–3). When Joseph threshed corn to sell to the people during the famine, he cast the chaff in the Nile, and it floated downstream to Jacob's house (!). Jacob saw the chaff floating by, and summoning his sons he sent them in quest of the corn. One is reminded of *Tristan and Iseult,* in which a meeting between the lovers is signaled when Iseult sees the twigs dropped by Tristan from a point upstream and away from King Mark's castle. We have already noted the possibility of romance influence in the apocryphal life of Moses, and we know from his prologue that the author of *Cursor Mundi* is quite conscious of being in competition with such secular literature. Though he himself probably borrowed these adaptations from earlier compilers, he is nevertheless in effect following the mandate of Saint Augustine to "spoil the Egyptians" (Ex. 12:36), that is, to ornament his own biblical poem with gold and silver taken from the popular romances of the period.

A particularly vivid scene in the earlier poem of *Jacob and Joseph* expresses Jacob's joy when he learns that Joseph is alive. He throws away his crutch, seizes his mantle, and plats his hair with a silken string. Putting on his beaver hat, he rides into Egypt, singing like a little child. This is all the more remarkable in light of the restraint of the biblical narrative (Gen. 45:28): *And Israel said, It is enough; Joseph my son is yet alive: I will go and see him before I die. Cursor Mundi,* though less exuberant than the minstrel poem, nevertheless shows a similiar interest in the rejuvenation of Jacob (5,187–5,201):

> Then Jacob waxed wondrous fain,
> His body began to quicken again.
> "Give me my clothes," then he said,
> "And hastily let us be prepared.

[175]

Children," he said, "let us be gone,
The journey to Egypt seems too long."
Israel then quickly leapt up
Who before could not stride a step;
He asked no help from any of them
Who used to quake in every limb;
And he who for age could scarcely speak
Was now in haste the way to seek.
He cries on them as a young man would:
Then said Reuben, "Dear father good,
I urge you, walk more soberly!"

The life of Moses follows Exodus very closely, except for the apocryphal materials already discussed in connection with the legend of Seth. Here I wish merely to call attention to two passages where the influence of allegorical exegesis can be seen. When Moses approached the burning bush (Ex. 3:1–3), he saw that in spite of the flames it was green with leaf and bloom. This, we are told, is a "fore-showing" of the Virgin, who was to be both mother and pure maiden. The interpretation appears elsewhere, notably in Chaucer, whose ABC prayer to the Virgin includes a similar figurative interpretation. One might expect more such examples of allegorizing in this section of *Cursor Mundi*, but actually there are very few aside from the legend of the holy tree. One other occurs in the story of the Exodus. In telling of the flowering of Aaron's rod (Num. 17:8), the author remarks that the rod betokens our Lady, and the fruit her sweet son Jesus. Thereafter the momentum of the biblical narrative is uninterrupted.

Finally it is worth noting that a decided interest in chronology emerges in the author's account of the third age of the world. After Joshua, Caleb judged Israel (he says), and in his time the fables of classical antiquity were written. These were the stories of Saturn and Jupiter, the siege of Troy, Apollo, Orpheus, Hercules, Priam, and the Amazons. Thus biblical and classical time are synchronized, and then the narrative follows the biblical history very closely down to the death of Saul. At this point we are told that the third age comes to an end, and the passage of time is summarized. The third age, from Abraham to the death of Saul, lasted 942 years; and the total age of the world from the creation until this time was 4,084 years. These calculations have a remarkable precision, and in this they closely resemble the dates that can still be found in modern annotated editions of the King James Bible.

[176]

The Fourth Age: David to the Babylonian Exile

In addition to David's preservation of the sacred tree planted by Seth, the other story given emphasis in *Cursor Mundi* is the affair with Bathsheba, which follows the account in 1 Samuel closely, except that as penance for his sin we are told that David composed the *Miserere* (Ps. 51). More attention is devoted to Solomon his son. The Seth legend is continued in the building of the temple and the visit of the queen of Sheba, as we have observed; and the famous judgment of Solomon (1 Kings 3:16–28) is retold at considerable length (8,583–8,756). Two passages claim our particular attention: one deals with Solomon's childhood, the other with his sin and repentance (8,435–8,508; 8,979–9,114).

When Solomon was young, he often sat under the holy tree that his father David had honored, and there he learned the seven arts, and studied the natural world, especially trees and medicinal herbs. Under that tree he wrote three books: the first, Ecclesiastes, tells of the falseness of this world; the second, Proverbs, shows men how to rule themselves in this wretched world; and the third, Canticles (the Song of Solomon), is called the "Book of Love," for it speaks of the love between man's soul and the Holy Ghost. Since then no scholar has proved his equal in learning. Yet for all his wisdom, Solomon falls victim to his evil nature, and sins by loving non-Israelite women against the commandment of God. What good was all the insight of this king, who ruined himself following a wicked woman's will? Alas, this is an old story, beginning with Adam, and repeated in the lives of Samson and David. And if the wise Solomon was beguiled by women, who can be safe, who? The man she has in her power is taken by her; therefore blessed is he who does not put himself in her power (Eccles. 7:26); for however much he love her, she will lead him into folly. But do not misunderstand:

> Let no man think by this that I
> Will speak of women villainy;
> To do so would be impolite,
> And I mean no woman any spite;
> No man could think so, I am sure,
> For in this world is none so pure
> A creature before God and man,
> None so loving as a good woman.

The ambivalence of this treatment of women is typical, and seems to draw particularly on two of Solomon's books, Ecclesiastes, which gives us the pessimistic view, and Proverbs (31:10–31), which sings the praises of a virtuous woman. A similar ambiguity can be seen in the literature of our period. Sir Gawain was the model of courtesy; but when tricked into accepting a gift from a woman, he excuses his weakness by citing the same precedents beginning with Adam that we have seen listed here. In the *Canterbury Tales*, the Nun's Priest tells of the cock, Chauntecleer, led astray by his wife, Pertelote, and then hastens to deny any intention of casting aspersions against women.

At the last, Solomon repents of his sins, and proposes to do penance. He calls in his counsellors and prophets and confesses to them that he is a sinful wretch, brought down by a heathen woman. Then he offers to resign his crown, but the wise counsellors refuse to allow it. Finally it is decided that he will endure public scourging. His rich crown is removed, and the royal robe torn from his back. Carried through the throng he is beaten until the blood runs; but the king takes it meekly, and hereafter, it seems, he was granted mercy for his misdeeds. This vivid example of penance, as we have seen, eventually came to the attention of William Caxton, who added it to his summary of Old Testament history in *The Golden Legend*.

The Fifth Age: Parentage of the Virgin to John the Baptist

Up to now we have seen how legendary materials are interwoven with the biblical narrative of *Cursor Mundi* to serve as reminders of the coming Redemption. But the fifth age of the world, extending from the Babylonian exile to the baptism of Christ, deals not at all with the history of late Old Testament times. Instead it functions as a bridge between the two testaments, and is occupied mainly with an extended allegory of the Redemption, followed by a mixture of canonical and apocryphal stories of the life of the Virgin Mary and the childhood of Jesus. Significantly, it begins with a genealogy of the holy family taken from Matthew 1:1–17, and ends with a recapitulation of the same family history (9,229–64; 12,733–51).

As a kind of prologue to the Redemption we find certain famous Old Testament prophecies: there shall come forth a rod from the stem of Jesse, and out of it a flower on which shall rest the Holy Ghost, who gives the seven gifts of the spirit (Isa. 11:1–5); in other words, a virgin shall have a son called Immanuel (Isa. 7:14), which means, God with us. Isaiah left his book for later generations to read, but he foresaw that some would not understand his message (Isa. 1:3), and so he said further of this child: the government shall be

[178]

upon his shoulder, and his name shall be called Wonderful, Counsellor, The mighty God, The everlasting Father, The Prince of Peace
(Isa. 9:6). Other prophets also added their testimony. The rod that
bloomed (Num. 17:8) signifies that a virgin shall bear a child, as
Jeremiah realized (Jer. 1:11–12). Moreover, Israel's anointed kings
shall be removed (Hos. 13:9–11, Jer. 22, 23:1–8) until the anointing
of the most Holy (Dan. 9:24–27), that is the baptism of Christ. Are
you so blind that you cannot see the meaning of these things? God
himself, speaking of the Virgin, says, *My beloved is unto me as a
cluster of camphire in the vineyards of Engedi. Behold, thou art fair, my
love; behold, thou art fair; thou hast doves' eyes* (Song of Sol. 1:14–15).

Completing this survey of Old Testament prophecies, the narrator
betrays a decided impatience with the failure of Jews to accept them
as fulfilled. He seizes a nearby text from the Song of Solomon (2:1–2):

> *I am the rose of Sharon,*
> *and the lily of the valleys.*
> *As the lily among thorns,*
> *so is my love among the daughters.*

Just as the rose is ill-suited to the thorn (God says), so is my beloved
(the Virgin) ill-suited to her people! For as the rose springs from
thorns, so was Mary born of the Jews. This is a somewhat unusual
use of the figure, since more often the thorns represent the sins of
mankind after the Fall (Gen. 3:17–19), and the rose the Passion of
Christ that redeems man from sin. The latter significance, as we shall
see, appears in the *Corpus Christi* carol:

> By that bedside there grows a thorn
> That ever has blossomed since Jesus was born.

It also explains why in the morality play known as *The Castle of Perseverance,* the seven virtues drive the deadly sins away from the castle
by pelting them with roses. But when imagery becomes so well
known, we may expect it to be used in many different ways. For
example in *Piers the Plowman,* society itself is likened to a rose
(A X, 117–26): the root represents the common people, the rose is the
episcopate, and the briers are the clergy. Such is the fate of an image
in the hands of a satirist!

The allegory of the Redemption as set forth in *Cursor Mundi* is
taken directly from a thirteenth century work by Robert Grosseteste
(d. 1253), Bishop of Lincoln, entitled *Le Chateau d'Amour.* Although
the original was in French, several English versions survive, of which

the adaptation in *Cursor Mundi* is perhaps the earliest. Grosseteste retells the biblical story, from creation to Redemption, in the form of a chivalric romance. A certain King had a Son, who was his equal, and four daughters named Mercy, Truth, Righteousness, and Peace. He also had a servant, Adam, who disobeyed him and became enslaved to Satan. The King's daughters argued over the fate of Adam. Mercy pleaded that he had fallen through a woman; Truth said that he deserved his punishment; Righteousness agreed, adding that he merited death. The adverse view prevailed, and the world was drowned in its sin, all except Noah and his family. After this calamity Peace spoke up and urged that the outcome of justice should always be peace, and that no final decision should be made unless all four sisters agreed on it. Thereupon a decision was reached to ransom the slave from Satan, by sending the King's Son. Thus the Child from heaven alighted in a fair Castle of Love (Mary), on a lofty rock (her pure heart) protected by four towers (the cardinal virtues), and three baileys (her maidenhead, chastity, and marriage), having seven barbicans (the seven virtues), and painted from foundation to towers in three colors: green (faith), blue (hope), and red (charity). From the midst of the highest tower sprang a well, from which ran streams of grace, and in that tower was a throne whereon sat the Son who became man and redeemed us all from the slavery of sin. The allegory concludes with a resume of the life of Christ, ending with the Resurrection and Ascension.

The notion of a figurative edifice was widespread in medieval allegory. Thus we find a *Temple of Glass, Castle of Labor, Palace of Honor,* and Chaucer's *House of Fame. Piers the Plowman* has two allegorical structures, the Castle of Kynde (A-text) and the Barn of Unity (B-text), while the morality play, *Castle of Perseverance,* bases its entire allegorical action on the concept of the figurative castle, as the title indicates. Moreover, both the poem and the play make effective use of the Four Daughters of God in order to dramatize the reconciliation of Justice and Mercy. Each work uses these motifs in different ways, but both probably derived their basic allegorical materials from the version of Grosseteste's *Castle of Love* in the *Cursor Mundi.*

From the figurative *Castle of Love* the author returns to the biblical and legendary narrative of the life of the Virgin and the childhood of Jesus. The biography of Mary indeed extends beyond this section of the poem in order to treat the entirety of her life corresponding to the five feast days devoted to her memory in the *sanctorale:*

[180]

LIFE OF THE BLESSED VIRGIN

Feast	Date	Passage in *Cursor Mundi*
Conception	December 8	10,123–574
Nativity	September 8	10,575–782
Annunciation	April 7	10,783–934
Purification	February 2	11,287–372
Assumption	August 15	20,011–848

The life of Mary is to some extent spun out of Old Testament materials with the aid of allegorical exegesis. A single incident taken from her childhood will illustrate this. Mary served God in the temple until age fourteen. When the bishop ordered her and all others of her age sent home to be married, Mary announced that she would not marry any man, since she had given herself to God. The bishop was perplexed: he did not want to oppose her vow, but he feared that it might set a bad precedent, since marriage was divinely established for the folk to increase and multiply. So he assembled his wise men, and while they were praying together, a voice spoke to them aloud, reminding them of the prophecy of Isaiah: a rod shall spring out of the stem of Jesse, which shall bring forth a flower on which the Holy Ghost shall rest (Isa. 11:1). After meditating on this prophecy, the council decided to summon all the kin of David (whose father was Jesse), give each of them a rod, and espouse the maiden Mary to the one whose rod blossomed. Among the kin of David was Joseph, an old widower who had no desire to marry, but who perforce came in response to the call of the bishop. When all the rods were drawn, Joseph's was found flourishing with leaf and flower, and a dove from heaven lighted on the branch. Thus Mary was espoused to Joseph. Here we can readily see how the prophecy from Isaiah is combined with the story of Aaron's rod (Num. 17) to produce a fresh incident in the life of the Virgin.

The childhood of Jesus is framed by the Gospel narrative, taken from Luke, beginning with the birth and ending with Jesus in the temple at age twelve. Between these, however, is a host of apocryphal stories. Some of these have no particular merit or significance other than to fill in the gaps of the canonical narrative. What was Jesus' childhood like? Since he worked miracles later, is it not likely that he also did so as a child? The answer of course is yes. He moulded little birds, for example, out of clay, and when he clapped his hands the birds miraculously took to flight.

[181]

As might be expected, the most significant stories are those more closely associated with the biblical narrative. A good example of this can be seen in the flight into Egypt (Matt. 2:13–23). On their way through the desert, Mary and Joseph stopped to rest in a cave (11,606–618):

> Soon they saw an ugly sight:
> As they looked there beside
> Out of this cave they saw glide
> Many dragons suddenly,
> And the servants began to cry.
> When Jesus all their fear did see
> He lighted down from his mother's knee,
> Stood before these beasts so grim
> And they humbly bowed to him.
> Thus came the prophecy to be clear
> As in the book of Psalms we hear:
> "Ye dragons dwelling in your den,
> Praise the Lord and bow to him."

The specific reference here is to Psalm 148:7, though the basic idea undoubtedly comes from Isaiah's description of the messianic age (11:6–9). Lions and leopards also accompanied the holy family on their journey, along with the ox and ass (Isa. 1:3). As a final touch, the baggage is carried on a wagon drawn by two oxen that go their way without having to be guided by anyone. Surely this is an echo of the story concerning the return of the ark of the covenant to Israel (1 Sam. 6:7–14), illustrating once more how apocryphal narrative draws on the Old Testament.

The next resting place in the journey to Egypt is under a palm tree, which miraculously bends down allowing Mary to pluck the fruit. From its roots comes a spring of water to quench their thirst, and an angel carries a branch of this tree to Paradise, in obedience to a command from the child Jesus. As we have seen, this is the story which formed the basis of the cherry tree carol found in oral tradition, and depicted in stained glass in Fairford church. The stream of water and the flourishing of the tree in paradise suggests that this incident may be indirectly a part of the Seth legend already traced in our review of the Old Testament.

When they reached Egypt, Mary visited one of the heathen sanctuaries. When she entered the temple with her son in her arms, all the idols fell to the ground, thus fulfilling the prophecy of Isaiah (19:1): *the idols of Egypt shall be moved at his presence.* Details of this incident may also owe something to the description of the effect of Israel's ark

[182]

on the Philistine god Dagon (1 Sam. 5:1–7). There is, of course, a degree of naïveté in these apocryphal expansions; at the same time it should be noted that they tend as a rule to harmonize with an important New Testament theme: Christ fulfills the Law, and thus becomes a light to the nations.

The Sixth Age: Baptism of Jesus to Doomsday

More than one third of *Cursor Mundi* (nearly eleven thousand lines) is devoted to the sixth age of the world, by far the largest section of the poem; and, as might be expected, over half of this section is taken up with the life of Christ, based on New Testament and apocryphal sources. The sixth age as a whole divides into four parts: the life of Christ (12,713–18,862), the acts of the apostles (18,863–21,346), the history of the holy cross (21,347–846), and an account of Doomsday (21,847–23,652).

The life of Christ in *Cursor Mundi* is essentially an expansion of the Gospel narrative, beginning with John the Baptist and ending with the Crucifixion and burial. Thereafter the account of the Harrowing of Hell and the Resurrection is taken from apocryphal sources, primarily the famous Gospel of Nicodemus. To these stories are added homiletic meditations and discourses on the Passion. It is not difficult to see how this fascinating collage of New Testament themes and narratives became a favorite repository of biblical materials in the fourteenth century, reappearing in a variety of popular forms, in lyrical and narrative poetry, in popular sermons, and on the medieval stage.

John the Baptist, of course, has an important part to play at the beginning of Christ's ministry, and his asceticism is emphasized; he led such a hard life and fasted so strictly it was a wonder that he was able to endure. What an honor it was for him to administer the holy sacrament of baptism to Jesus: a marvel it is to think of this — as if the clerk were to baptize the priest, the son the father, the knight the king! While he was performing this office, the river Jordan stood still as stone in the presence of the Trinity: the voice of the Father saying, "This is my beloved Son," the Son in man's body, and the Holy Ghost in the form of a dove. At this solemn moment the Old Testament ends, and the New Testament begins.

The turning of water into wine at the marriage feast in Cana is related in detail, with one interesting addition. We are told that the bridegroom in this case was Saint John, destined to be the beloved disciple, and that when he witnessed the miracle he forsook the bride and followed Jesus, preferring celibacy to marriage. At the last supper he lay his head on Jesus' breast, drinking of the well of wisdom. Later, in his gospel, he related the story of the miracle in Cana. Of the four Evangelists, John is the most subtle in his sayings.

Although *Cursor Mundi* as a whole is in short rhyming couplets, the author announces that he will employ a longer line to relate the events of Passion week. What follows is essentially an eight-line stanza, with a single rhyme for the even-numbered lines, 14937–44.:

> Jesus went toward Jerusalem
> going upon his feet,
> And he came to a little hill
> that men call Olivet.
> Six days before the Pasch day
> with them he walked the street,
> To his disciples that he led
> These words he spoke so sweet.

No doubt the intention here is to impart a more elevated tone to the passion narrative, but it is worth noting that the metrical form used is very close to that destined to be found in the ballad tradition. The only difference lies in the choice here of an eight-line instead of a four-line stanza.

Speaking of the metrical change at this point in the poem, it may not be entirely coincidental that the Passion narrative contains an apocryphal motif that finds its way later on into the ballad tradition. In *Cursor Mundi* we are told that when Judas betrayed Christ, he went home and told his mother. "Son," she replies, "now you are ruined; for they will put him to death, but he will rise again." "Not so," says Judas, "before he rises again this cock, that was cooked last night, will rise from the dish!" Scarcely had he spoken this word, when the cock stood up, feathered fairer than before, and crowed aloud. This was the very same cock that Peter heard crow when he had forsaken the Lord.

It is interesting to see what happens to our apocryphal story when it is picked up in ballad tradition. We noticed earlier that the "Cherry Tree Carol" takes a similar story and moves it from its original place (the flight into Egypt) to a Christmas setting, connected with the birth of Christ. In the present case a similar shift occurs. A fifteenth century ballad, "St. Stephen and Herod," takes the theme of the cock from its Judas context and again gives it a Christmas setting. No doubt Saint Stephen is chosen to be the spokesman here because his feast day (December 26) immediately follows the Nativity in the

[184]

church calendar. According to the ballad, Stephen was a clerk in King Herod's hall, and served him at table. One time, while serving the king his dinner, he saw the star over Bethlehem. Immediately he came before Herod and announced:

> I forsake thee, King Herod,
> and thy works all;
> There is a child in Bethlehem born
> is better than we all.

What ails you Stephen? asks Herod. Do you lack meat or drink, gold or fee? No, says Stephen, but there is a child born in Bethlehem that shall help us in our need. The king replies that this is no more true than that the capon lying on his dish shall crow. No sooner had he said this than the bird crowed "christus natus est." Whereupon Stephen was taken out and stoned to death; that is why Saint Stephen's eve occurs at Christmas in the calendar.

Our modern sense of chronology is no doubt disturbed by this compression of time which places the stoning of Stephen (Acts 7) at the birth of Christ; but this was no problem to the medieval believer, for whom events in the Bible were re-lived regularly in the course of a calendar year. One other detail in the ballad, the cock crowing *Christus natus est* ("Christ is born"), should remind us of the intimate way the Gospel narrative was woven into the daily lives of the people. Some readers may recall the belief, which has survived into modern times, that the animals worship Christ on his Nativity. Many songs survive from oral tradition that play with this idea, often having each animal utter an appropriate Latin phrase. Thus the cock cries, *christus natus est;* the raven asks, *quando, quando* (when?); the crow replies, *hac nocte* (this night); the ox says, *ubi, ubi* (where?); and the sheep bleats, *Bethlehem.* Most familiar of all is the belief that exactly at midnight on Christmas eve the cattle in the barns get down on their knees. It is this tradition that Thomas Hardy remembers nostalgically in his poem "The Oxen."

Returning now to *Cursor Mundi,* the author concludes the life of Christ with a meditation on the meaning of the Redemption and the intensity of Christ's suffering (16,923–17,110), at which point the special meter comes to an end. The next section consists of a lyrical discourse between Christ and Man, designed to add emotional vividness to the Passion narrative. Lo, how I suffered (says Christ) for the sake of sinful man. Think of my passion, and remember that I did all this for your sake. To which Man replies: Jesus, send us grace and power to love you, and to forsake our sins, so that we may come to eternal bliss.

Such meditations on the Passion were very popular, and their influence can be found in all varieties of medieval literature, notably the lyrics. One of the best known motifs was the exhortation against cursing. Ah, sinful man, says Christ, what ails you that you do not love me? with your great oaths and wicked deeds often you cause my wounds to bleed. This theme is repeated in the sermon of Chaucer's pardoner, where the young rioters are said to "tear the Lord's body" with their great oaths. Themes of this type reflect very clearly the influence of the medieval pulpit, an influence which grows stronger in the later sections of *Cursor Mundi*.

The account of the Resurrection is largely drawn from the apocryphal Gospel of Nicodemus, interwoven with homiletic themes. We first are told of the fortunes of Joseph of Arimathea, who is imprisoned and then miraculously freed. When the word of the Resurrection is reported, the soldiers are bribed to keep silence (prompting a sermon on the evils of cupidity). But other news begins to arrive, particularly from three men who tell of seeing Jesus on the Mount of Olives. At length Joseph is located and brought before the Jews. He explains to them that his miraculous escape from prison was accomplished by the resurrected Christ, who showed him the empty tomb and then took him home, where he had remained until located by the authorities.

Reports of the Resurrection reach their climax in the account of the Harrowing of Hell, given by Carinus and Leucius, the two sons of Simeon who had risen from their graves for this purpose. As we have seen, this is the story of Christ's descent into hell to rescue the patriarchs and prophets. But the *Cursor Mundi* account is much more detailed than that provided in *The Golden Legend*. Extended speeches are provided for Adam, Isaiah, Simeon, and John the Baptist, reminding us of their anticipation of the coming Messiah. Even Seth is brought in, to recapitulate his quest for the oil of mercy in Paradise. Amidst the quarreling of the devils, the voice of the approaching Messiah is heard (Psalm 24:7): *Lift up your heads, O ye gates, and be ye lift up, ye everlasting doors, and the king of glory shall come in.* In reply to this greeting we hear the liturgical responses of the saints in prison. The bars of Hell-gate are broken and Satan is bound and cast in the deepest pit of Hell. In gratitude David cries (Psalm 96:1), *Sing unto the Lord a new song,* and he is followed by the prophets, who again utter their messianic predictions. The story is climaxed by the

[186]

ascent of the saints to Paradise, and their encounter with Enoch, Elijah, and Dismas, similar to that noted earlier in *The Golden Legend.* The Nicodemus narrative concludes with Pilate's letter to the Emperor Claudius, testifying about the miracles performed by Christ and confirming the Resurrection.

The author returns to the canonical text for his account of the appearances of Christ to the disciples just prior to his Ascension, and much of this is taken up with the struggle of doubting Thomas (18,675–706). Along with the biblical narrative, however, there is an interesting emblematic passage in which Christ is likened to a lion (Rev. 5:5). We may truly call him a lion, says the author, for no one is more powerful than he. Moreover, when the lion's whelp is born, it lies apparently lifeless until the third morning; then the father comes and roars, causing it to rise up to life. Just so did Christ arise on the third day at the command of the Father. Also the lion, they say, always sleeps with his eyes open; just as Christ, though he died, never surrendered his Godhead. These strange habits of the lion will not surprise anyone familiar with the medieval bestiaries, which are filled with unnatural natural history and Christian symbolism.

The Ascension narrative in *Cursor Mundi* concludes with a portrait of Christ. I would not presume to describe his appearance as he is now, in heaven, says the author, but only his likeness while he was here on earth. He was of moderate height and very seemly. His countenance was both fearful and loving; his hair was nut-brown, lying on his shoulders, parted in front like a Nazarene. His forehead was spotless and unwrinkled, with a ruddy complexion, fair nose and mouth, and a cleft chin with a full beard parted in the middle like his hair. He had a steady look, and clear, gray eyes. He spoke wisely, and was awesome when he delivered a rebuke; as a teacher he was unmatched in speaking the truth. He wept tears, we find, but never did he laugh. In appearance he resembled his mother, as can be seen by comparing her with the visage of Christ preserved on the handkerchief of Saint Veronica.

Thus the sixth age is occupied largely with the life of Christ from baptism to resurrection. The remainder of this age is concerned with the acts of the Apostles, history of the holy cross, and of course Doomsday. The first section follows the biblical book of Acts very closely until we come to the story of the Assumption of the Virgin, based on apocryphal sources.

Though the Assumption is not related in the New Testament, the story attained near canonical status in the Middle Ages. The earliest versions date from the fourth century, and were ready to hand in numerous Latin versions when Mary's popularity reached its peak in the later medieval period. An English version of the story appeared in the mid thirteenth century, and this seems to have been the text adapted by the compiler of *Cursor Mundi*, and added to the history taken from the book of Acts. The prominence given to the Assumption here reminds us of the window devoted to the subject in the Lady Chapel of Fairford church (Chapter I), as well as the fact that the occasion had long since found its place in the Church calendar as the feast of the Assumption (August 15).

After the Crucifixion John took care of Mary in accordance with Christ's instructions (John 19:25–27), and she dwelt with the virgins of the temple, serving the poor. At last an angel visits her, bringing a palm branch as token from Christ, and promises that in three days she shall be taken up to heaven. Mary prepares herself for death, and prays to Christ for protection against demons. While her friends are mourning, suddenly and miraculously the twelve Apostles are transported from the far corners of the world and are brought into the presence of the Virgin. Each had been preaching the gospel in his own region when suddenly they find themselves brought together and are amazed. Seeing Mary, they kneel and salute her. At the appointed time (noon of the third day), the Virgin lies down in her bed surrounded by the Apostles. They hear a heavenly song, with music so sweet that everyone falls asleep except Mary, who hears the voice of her Son addressing the angels: "Come with me to my beloved." At Mary's command the Apostles awake, and see Jesus enter the bower accompanied by angels and archangels. He blesses her with his right hand, and she yields up her spirit. Jesus gives her soul into the care of Saint Michael, and when she reaches heaven she is crowned queen. Some say the body disappeared from its tomb, and flowers were found growing in its place. But since Saint Jerome says that this cannot be verified, I will say no more. Yet we know well that she is queen of heaven and earth, and is enthroned beside her dear Son, where she never ceases to pray for sinful men.

The ethereal quality of this legend stands in evident contrast to the more substantial biblical narrative which surrounds it, and it is perhaps not easy for the modern reader to recapture the reverent spirit in which it was received. Yet even so worldly a poet as Chaucer was not immune to this spirit, as is evident in his prayer to the Virgin, whom he addresses as "almighty and al merciable queene."

After the Assumption of Our Lady, Acts concludes with an apocryphal account of the life and martyrdom of each of the Apostles and the Evangelists. From these stories medieval artists often derived the emblems for their portraits: the cross of Andrew, the spear of Thomas, the sword of Matthew, for example, represent the instruments used in the execution of these Apostles. To this list is added an allegorical exposition of the four Evangelists and their emblems, the biblical origin of which we have already traced: the man's face (Matthew), the lion (Mark), the ox (Luke), and the eagle (John). These and other emblems can still be seen in the stained-glass portraits of the Apostles and Evangelists in Fairford Church, where they served as a means of identification for a largely illiterate congregation.

To summarize, the author of *Cursor Mundi* gives us a description of Christ's "cart": the four wheels are the four Evangelists, the two axles are the two testaments, the bridle is wisdom, Christ himself is the carter, and His body the yoke. This may well be just a mnemonic device; we smile at its pedantic character. Yet this tendency proved very popular in literature and pulpit in the late Middle Ages. Perhaps the most famous English adaptation of the theme occurs in *Piers the Plowman.* Grace gives Piers a team of four great oxen (Matthew, Mark, Luke, and John) to pull the plow; to harrow the land he gives him also four bullocks (Augustine, Ambrose, Gregory, and Jerome); there are two harrows, an old and a new one (the two testaments), and four kinds of seeds to plant called the Cardinal Virtues (Prudence, Moderation, Fortitude, Justice). Thus Piers is equipped to plow the field of Truth.

The biblical history itself ends with the martyrdom of the Apostles, but the subsequent growth of the Church is perhaps embodied in the story of the finding of the holy cross by Saint Helena. As we have seen, this famous event is commemorated in the church calendar (May 3), and is the subject of the Old English poem, *Elene.* The version in *Cursor Mundi,* however, has been expanded and filled with new motifs and baroque detail. For example, Helena had a goldsmith who owed money to a Jew, and the Jew, named Judas, demands a pound of flesh as payment. The resolution of the problem will be familiar to readers of Shakespeare's *Merchant of Venice:* when the case is taken to court, Judas is awarded the pound of flesh, but warned not to spill a drop of the goldsmith's blood. Unlike Shylock, Judas curses in his disappointment and is threatened with punishment for contempt of court. To avoid this, Judas offers to help Saint Helena find the true cross, and thus we resume the familiar story. When the cross is found, it is divided into four parts which are placed in

[189]

Jerusalem, Rome, Alexandria, and Constantinople. The narrative concludes with a sermon on the virtues of the cross, a summary of its allegorical appearances in the Old Testament, and its symbolic meaning in the life of mankind.

Doomsday

The sixth age (says our author) is called the time of grace, which begins with Christ and ends with the day of doom. Hence the remainder of this section, nearly two thousand lines, is taken up with a description of the close of the sixth age, and the biblical themes associated with apocalypse: tokens of the latter days (21,847–974), the coming of Antichrist (21,975–22,426), the fifteen signs of doom (22,427–710), Doomsday itself with the second coming (22,711–23,194), and, finally, a description of the pains of Hell (23,195–350) and the joys of heaven (23,351–652).

The description of the latter days follows that of the synoptic Gospels (Matt. 24, Mk. 13, Luke 21): nation shall rise against nation, and kingdom against kingdom. But there are some interesting innovations designed, I think, to harmonize the end with the beginning of the world. Why do we not take warning from these tokens of the latter days, and prepare our souls? Every creature of the animal kingdom knows his Maker better than we. Dumb beasts such as lions and bears, heaven and earth, sun and moon, all these serve him in their fashion; but man alone withdraws his service. He would rather hear how Roland and Oliver fought than of the passion of our Lord! The author concludes with an exhortation to man to deny his will in this life so that he can enjoy the hereafter.

Then shall come Antichrist who shall war against the good and exalt the sinful. He shall be from the tribe of Dan (Gen. 49:17), and shall proclaim himself God Almighty. He has had many loyal followers, such as Antiochus and Domitian, and even now he has many supporters among those who disobey their rule, whether secular or religious, whether clerk, monk, or canon! Antichrist will be the incarnation of the devil, and his birth will come as a parody of the birth of Christ. When he has established himself in the temple at Jerusalem, he will send his preachers throughout the world and they will even work miracles. But when all is said and done, our Lord will send judgment on Antichrist and destroy him. Then He will give those who were deceived by Antichrist forty days to repent.

The author lists fifteen signs of the doom. First, a bloody rain shall fall, and children still in the womb shall pray not to be born.

Stars shall fall from the heavens, run on the ground, and disappear into the abyss, their light extinguished. The moon shall become red as blood and fall into the sea. The sun shall be darkened, the beasts shall cry to heaven, valleys shall rise up and hills fall. Trees shall turn top downward and root up; the sea shall overrun the land. All creation shall cry to God for mercy, as Saint Augustine says, including the very devils in hell. A great wind shall rise and lift the earth out of its place, and the rainbow shall fall. Heaven shall be locked, and the angels on their knees shall cry unto Christ for mercy as they see Him preparing for the judgment. Stones shall smite together like thunder, and men shall hide themselves under a hill. Then a great storm of frost, hail, and snow shall occur, and clouds shall hide in the sea. At last, on the fifteenth day, this earth shall burn away, and all things shall return to nought, as before the creation.

At the sound of the trumpet, Christ shall come to judge the quick and the dead, accompanied by those who have been faithful in His service. Those that sleep in the dust of the earth shall awake and appear in the flesh. All who are saved shall be without spot or blemish, with all lameness or other imperfections removed, and they shall be fair and handsome as if at the age of thirty in this life. Do you doubt this? Is anything impossible for the Lord? Gregory cites the case of the man who was eaten by a wolf; the wolf was eaten by a lion; then the lion died and rotted. Where is the man? Gregory assures us that his dust will be parted from the beast's, and he will appear in his flesh at the resurrection; not a hair of his head will be lacking.

The prophet Joel says that the judgment will take place in the vale of Jehoshaphat (Joel 3:2), but this prophecy is misunderstood by many who attend only to the letter and not to the spirit (2 Cor. 3:6). For Jehoshaphat, as Jerome says, means "our Lord's judgment," and Paul tells us that we shall meet the Lord in the clouds (1 Thess. 4:17). Then the sheep shall be separated from the goats; and those who fed the hungry, clothed the naked, and visited those sick and in prison, shall inherit the kingdom (Matt. 25:31–46). But the wicked shall depart into everlasting fire. Ah Lord, he is wise who truly keeps in mind the terrible judgment that will come on this day.

Consider if you will the nine principal pains of hell, that bottomless pit from which no man escapes. One is everlasting fire, another, unspeakable cold. Then there are loathsome dragons and toads that swim in the depths like fishes. Heavy blows rain down like hammers on an anvil, thick darkness covers everything, and a sense of shame

[191]

for sin sweeps over all. A terrible sight it is to see the devils, weeping in their pain. Lastly, all are bound tightly in bands of fire. The nine pains are then related to sins committed in this life, and we are shown how the suffering corresponds to the sins. May the Lord judge us so that we never come in that woe!

After the judgment, Christ shall lead his people into the heavenly city. Eye hath not seen, nor ear heard, nor heart imagined the joys that are prepared for them that love God (1 Cor. 3:9). There shall be seven gifts for the body, and seven more for the soul. You shall be as swift as the speed of light, even as the angels are (Dan. 9:21). Your body shall be beautiful and bright, for the righteous shall shine forth as the sun (Matt. 13:43), and we shall all be changed in the twinkling of an eye (1 Cor. 15:51–52). No bonds shall be able to bind you; you shall be completely free, even as the grave was unable to hold the body of our Lord. Your strength shall be so great that you shall overturn mountains with your foot, and you shall have everlasting pleasure in the love of the Lord and the beauties of heaven.

Your soul shall draw from the well of wisdom, and you shall have knowledge of all things. But memory of past sins will not grieve you, since they are forgiven, any more than a wound suffered in battle which is now healed. The children of God shall enjoy friendship and harmony, and they shall be honored by saints, angels, and all creation. What a joy it will be to see God face to face! (1 Cor. 13:12). What a difference there is between the fate of the saved and the damned: between light and darkness, wisdom and folly, freedom and bondage. May Christ give us grace to come to the bliss of heaven.

The Seventh Age: Kingdom of God

When the doom is completed, and the earth consumed, then there shall be a new heaven and a new earth (Rev. 21:1), and the Kingdom of God shall be established. The universe, that now travails in pain, shall be cleansed and renewed, even as our bodies are at the resurrection. No more shall there be sorrow, nor crying, nor pain (Rev. 21:4). The sun shall be seven times brighter, and water shall gleam like crystal. Where the blood of the saints once flowed, flowers shall spring up that never fade, and the earth shall be blessed forever. In the seventh age, the whole of creation rests from its labors (Heb. 4:1–11).

The remainder of the poem, nearly five thousand lines, is designed to assist the reader in preparing himself spiritually for the judgment. There is an exhortation to repent (23,705–908), a prayer to Our Lady

(23,909–944), and an account of her sorrows (23,945–24,730), followed by a story commemorating her conception (24,731–25,102). Finally the poem ends with a series of prayers (25,103–931) and extensive instructions concerning penance for use in the confessional (25,932–29,555). To the modern reader this conclusion may come as an anticlimax, yet to medieval man preparation for the hereafter was extremely important. Chaucer's *Canterbury Tales* concludes with an extended devotional treatise (the Parson's Tale) very similar in spirit to the ending of *Cursor Mundi.*

Apart from its value as a repository of biblical tradition, *Cursor Mundi* is very useful for its detailed presentation of the medieval world picture. In it we can see the vast panorama of man and society through the eyes of medieval man. In the next chapter, we will observe how this biblical view was utilized by medieval chroniclers in the writing of world history.

CHAPTER SIX

Universal History:
The Polychronicon

O NE of the most popular Latin works of the fourteenth century in England was the *Polychronicon*, a universal history compiled by Ranulph Higden, a monk of Chester. Like *Cursor Mundi*, it divides history into the seven ages of the world, but it omits the seventh in order to concentrate on the sixth age, extending up to the author's own day. Before looking at the *Polychronicon* in detail, however, it will be well to trace the development of medieval historiography from its biblical origins up to the time of Higden's chronicle. For it is only in the light of this background that we can fully appreciate the extent to which the Bible influenced the writing of medieval histories of the world.

Universal Histories

It is customary to stress the differences between the classical and biblical views of history in ancient times: the former is described as cyclical (history repeats itself) and the latter as linear (history has a beginning, a middle, and an end). In a recent study the cyclical view has been aptly likened to the Phoenix, the fabulous bird that is reborn at regular intervals, infinitely repeating its life-cycle; and the linear view is likened to Jacob's ladder, extending from earth to heaven. Like most dichotomies, of course, this one is partly an oversimplification. The four kingdoms of Daniel are to some extent cyclical, and the ages of gold, silver, bronze, and iron in classical tradition imply a (downward) direction to history as well as a principle of repetition. Even so, it is accurate to say that the biblical conception of linear history was the decisive factor in the development of medieval historiography.

The prophetic idea of the Day of the Lord (Isa. 2:2–4) was universalized, after the Babylonian Exile, and expressed, in the Doomsday concept, the apocalyptic conclusion of history. To this the New Testament added the theme of fulfillment in the messianic age (the fullness of time) through taking the light of Israel to the nations. In the early centuries, particularly during the period of persecution, Christian exegetes identified Rome with the fourth kingdom of Daniel, and even more specifically with the beast of Revelation in the New Testament. When Rome became Christian under Constantine, the hostile eschatology of the early Church was gradually replaced by a new vision of empire and church in harmony. An early expression of this vision can be seen in the *Ecclesiastical History* by Eusebius of Caesarea (c. 260–340), where the conversion of Constantine replaces the apocalypse that might otherwise be expected at the conclusion of the history, and Constantine is depicted as a new Moses leading his people to freedom under the banner of Christ.

Less than a century after Eusebius, however, the sacking of Rome by the barbarians in 410 underscored the dangers in too close an identification of church and empire. To meet this crisis, and to separate Christianity from the fate of Rome, Saint Augustine wrote *The City of God.* In it he distinguishes between the earthly and the heavenly cities, the one centered in the self, the other in God. History moves toward its divinely ordained consummation through a continuing series of personal choices which by their nature define each man's citizenship. The Christian, of course, is a citizen of the heavenly city; his concerns for self and the world are contingent, while his commitment to God is absolute. For Augustine this did not imply social irresponsibility, but rather it made possible a social order resting on the free assent of its citizens.

What Augustine accomplished for the early Church may be likened to the achievement of the Old Testament prophets in preparing Israel for the Babylonian Exile. Men like Amos, Hosea, Micah, Isaiah, and Jeremiah realized that if Israel tied itself too securely to the system of temple worship established during the monarchy, its faith would not be able to survive the destruction of the institutions and practices which were a part of that system. Hence they strove to correct imbalances in the Mosaic heritage that had led to overemphasis on ritual at the expense of ethical imperatives. As the Lord said, in the words of Jeremiah (7:22–23): *For I spake not unto your fathers, nor commanded them in the day that I brought them out of the land of Egypt, concerning burnt offerings or sacrifices: but this thing commanded I them, saying, Obey my voice, and I will be your God, and ye shall be my people.* The fact that this kind of teaching was education for survival is brought out clearly in Amos' criticism of the temple worship at Bethel, Gilgal, and Beersheba: *For thus saith the Lord unto the house of Israel, Seek ye me, and ye shall live: But seek not Bethel, nor enter into Gilgal, and pass not to Beersheba: for Gilgal shall surely go into captivity, and Bethel shall come to nought* (Amos 5:4–5). Prophetic teaching such as this enabled the chosen people to keep their faith alive and maintain their cultural identity during the turbulent period of the Babylonian exile.

In a somewhat analogous way, Augustine's *City of God* saved Christianity from too close a cultural identification with Rome. At the same time, the connection between church and empire was never really broken. We can see this, ironically, in the work of one of Augustine's own students, Paulus Orosius. With the support and encouragement of his distinguished master, Orosius wrote a universal history designed to refute pagan charges that Christianity was responsible for the fall of Rome in 410. But his *History against the Pagans,* as it was called, has also a more positive purpose. Augustine believed that the Bible held the key to the meaning of history, and his pupil Orosius therefore attempted to set forth a history of the world designed to bring out that meaning. What resulted was a salvation history beginning with the Bible and extending beyond it to the history of Rome and the early Church. In Orosius' view, church and empire were destined for each other. The *pax romana* was divinely ordained as a preparation for the coming of the Messiah (as Virgil, according to Orosius, perceived in his Fourth Ecologue), and signs and portents from heaven announced the coming of Caesar Augustus. This goes beyond the mandate of Saint Augustine, but it is clear that Orosius believed that Rome would assimilate the barbarian hordes of Europe.

Orosius' *History* was the principal model for universal histories in the Middle Ages. Features such as the seven ages of the world, which Orosius derived from Augustine, became the standard for subsequent chroniclers and historians. Above all, the use of the Bible in the interpretation of subsequent events was of fundamental importance for the future. World history became the history of God's plan for the salvation of mankind.

[196]

National Histories

In addition to universal histories on the model of Orosius, there developed also a series of national histories reflecting the interest of various European peoples in their own national origin and destiny. On the continent appeared the *History of the Franks* by Gregory of Tours (sixth century) and the *History of the Lombards* by Paul the Deacon (eighth century). Of greater interest for our present purpose, however, are the early chroniclers of Britain. The first of these, Gildas, wrote in the sixth century, Bede in the eighth, Nennius in the ninth, and Geoffrey of Monmouth in the twelfth century. All of them wrote in Latin. To a greater or lesser extent, all of these writers show the biblical influence ultimately attributable to Orosius, but in some of them the biblical language is somewhat perfunctory, and the vision of salvation history is replaced by an incipient nationalism. Instead of the creation of the world as described in Genesis, we get a description of the island of Britain, followed by an account of the Roman conquest.

The Destruction and Conquest of Britain was written about the middle of the sixth century by a British monk, Gildas. In it we are given an idealistic description of Britain, the beautiful land being contrasted with its unworthy inhabitants; then follows an account of the fortunes of the Britons under Roman rule. They rebel and are enslaved, they are converted to Christianity and then attacked by their enemies to the north, the Picts and Scots. They rally against their Saxon foes under the leadership of Ambrosius Aurelianus, last of the Romans, and finally achieve an uneasy peace constantly endangered by the sinfulness of the people. The remaining three quarters of the book is taken up with the exhortations of Gildas directed at the untoward generation he is addressing. His moral is similar to that of the book of Judges. When Israel forgot the Lord, the Lord sent enemies against them and they were enslaved; but after a time, in his mercy the Lord sends a deliverer, who frees his people from slavery or oppression. In like manner Gildas views the ups and downs of British history. It is clear that he regarded Britain as the new Israel, and its Celtic inhabitants as the chosen people. Yet he is passionately critical of his nation, and in his fiery attitude he reminds us of Amos (3:2): *You only have I known of all the families of the earth: therefore I will punish you for all your iniquities.*

Nearly two centuries later, the worst fears of Gildas were realized, for the land was now in the possession of Angles and Saxons, while the Britons were driven to hiding places in the west and north, in Wales and Scotland. Moreover, as we have seen, although the influence of Celtic Christianity was significant, particularly in the north, the English ultimately regarded Pope Gregory as their apostle rather than Saint Patrick. It is in the light of these circumstances that we must view the achievement of the Venerable Bede in his *Ecclesiastical History of the English People* (731).

Like Gildas, to whom he was considerably indebted, Bede begins his work with a description of Britain, and then gives the same early history of the Roman occupation and Christianization. In doing so, however, Bede plays down the Old Testament parallels of Gildas that tended to identify the Britons as the new Israel. The reason for these changes is clear: it is the English, not the Britons, who are to be the chosen people of Bede's narrative. With this in mind we can see that his account of the English Church, with its emphasis on the importance of early saints and missionary teachers, links Orosius' salvation history to the destiny of the English nation.

In the century following Bede the cultural aspirations of the English received a severe set-back from the Viking incursions, which began in 787. The effects of this disruption we have already seen in the flight of the monks from Lindisfarne in 793 with the relics of Saint Cuthbert. Not surprisingly, the decline of Anglo-Saxon fortunes at this time was matched by a rise in the national aspirations of the native Celtic population of Britain. Hence it has been reasonably suggested that this Celtic hope was a factor in the production of another British chronicle, Nennius' *History of Britain* (ca. 800). Does the faltering of the English signify that God is about to free his British people from bondage? This question seems to lurk between the lines of Nennius, but it is difficult to be sure, since the work that goes by his name has undergone several revisions made from differing motives. On the one hand, the text is indebted to Gildas for its pro-British perspective, but at the same time it occasionally echoes details from Orosius, for example in its opening summary of the six ages of the world, and its biblical genealogies extending back to the flood.

Nennius' most significant contribution is his legendary history, tracing the nation back to its founder, Brutus, who gave the country its name, Brutain or Britain. The story tells how Brutus, a descendant of Aeneas, flees his Italian homeland and arrives in Britain, where he and his followers live. The settlement took place, says Nennius, in the time of Eli the Prophet. Clearly this legend draws on the prestige of

[198]

Virgil's *Aeneid*, and is designed to make the Britons the inheritors of the grandeur that was Rome. The old order fades, and gives way to the new.

Where he uses Gildas, Nennius softens the criticisms of the British, and emphasizes the villainy of the Saxons. This is brought out most clearly in the central chapters of the *History* (31–49) dealing with the career of that quisling, the wicked British king Guorthigirn (later Vortigern). Here we find what has been aptly called a secular eschatology in the prophecies of the young Ambrosius (later Merlin). The boy expounds the meaning of a battle between two serpents, one red and one white, explaining that they depict the struggle between Britons and Saxons. At last the red one, although apparently the weaker of the two, recovers his strength and drives off the white one. It scarcely needs to be pointed out that the symbolism of biblical apocalypse is here being put to the service of national aspirations. The red dragon of Wales overcomes the white dragon of the Anglo-Saxons.

Other changes in Nennius conform to the patriotic purpose of the Vortigern section. Saint Patrick, for example, replaces Saint Gregory as the missionary hero. Beyond all these things, however, Nennius is famous for his introduction of Arthur as the hero of British resistance to the Anglo-Saxons. Although not here called a king, Arthur is described as a military leader (*dux bellorum*) who achieved twelve victories over the Saxons, climaxed by the battle of Mount Badon. Nennius presents Arthur as a model of piety and heroism, a Christian answer to the evil Vortigern. This is the earliest known reference to the man who was destined to become the greatest of the nine worthies, and a central figure of medieval romance, rivaled only, perhaps, by Alexander the Great.

The climax to the tradition of national histories we have been tracing is found in Geoffrey of Monmouth's *History of the Kings of Britain*, completed about the year 1137, three centuries after Nennius and seventy years after the Norman conquest of England. Geoffrey was a Welshman, but whether Monmouth was his original home is not clear; in any case, in spite of his long residence in Oxford as an Augustinian canon, his Welsh background no doubt explains the pro-British and anti-English attitude reflected in his *History*. The book is dedicated to the famous son of the Norman king Henry I (1100–35), Robert, Earl of Gloucester. Hence it may be that Geoffrey, through his *History of the Kings of Britain*, wished to impress the Norman conquerors with the antiquity and prestige of the British

[199]

people, who were worthy of respect and should be distinguished from the subjugated Anglo-Saxons.

Geoffrey's *History* purports to be a translation into Latin of a book written in the British language, which the author says was given him by a certain Walter, Archdeacon of Oxford. Nothing is known about this British book, however, and scholars now generally assume that it is a purely fictional source. Geoffrey seems to have compiled his text from the earlier histories we have been considering, with some additional materials taken from Celtic oral tradition. But the whole of the narrative is much expanded. It begins with the fall of Troy, and relates the adventures and wanderings of Brutus, the legendary founder of Britain, in much greater detail than Nennius does. Then follows the history of the British kings, which reaches its climax in the glorious reign of Arthur. To some extent the criticisms leveled at the British people by Gildas are preserved in Geoffrey's *History*, but his main purpose, especially in the Arthurian chapters, is to impress the new Norman rulers with the idea that the nation which they now governed was British (rather than Anglo-Saxon), and that the preservation and nurturing of its Celtic heritage was a sacred trust.

One of the most striking ways in which Geoffrey exalts the Celtic tradition in his history can be seen in his use of the Bible. For it is undoubtedly to the Scriptures that Geoffrey owes his depiction of the British as a "chosen people". He takes a biblical narrative, gives it a British setting, and behold, we have a new and exciting incident in the history of the kings of Britain. It is worthwhile, I think, to consider some examples of this, for they offer an interesting glimpse of the pseudo-historian at work.

Geoffrey tells the story of the British king Aurelius (recall Ambrosius Aurelianus in Gildas) in Book VIII, Chapter 7, of the *History*. Aurelius, after a great victory over Hengist and the Saxons, calls together his leaders to decide what to do with the captive Hengist. Whereupon Eldad, Bishop of Gloucester, addresses Aurelius as follows: "Even if all of you were to try to free him, I myself would hew him in pieces. For I would be imitating the prophet Samuel, who, when he had Agag king of Amalek in his power, hewed him in pieces, saying, 'As you have made women childless, so do I make your mother childless among women' [1 Sam. 15:33]. Do thus to him, therefore, for he is another Agag." Unlike Samuel, Bishop Eldad does not actually hew Hengist in pieces before the Lord; instead the Saxon is decapitated by the bishop's brother Eldol (who was not a churchman) and in fact is given a decent burial by Aurelius, who was, says Geoffrey, a "moderate" individual. Yet it is almost beyond question that Geoffrey's whole account of the death of Hengist (for which there is no hint in his sources) is modeled on the biblical story of Samuel and Agag.

That Geoffrey should use the Bible in the construction of his history is of course not at all surprising, considering the precedents we have seen in the work of Augustine and Orosius, as well as Gildas, Bede, and Nennius. The biblical tradition, indeed, provided the only adequate model for him to follow. Geoffrey is therefore following a well-charted course when he speaks (I, 15) of Brutus' voyage to the "promised island," and when, after describing the Saxon conquest and the flight of the Britons to Armorica (Brittany) (XI, 10), he says that later he will tell (though he never does) the story of these Britons by translating the book concerning their "exile."

Geoffrey's incorporation and expansion of the motif of the Britons as God's chosen people might lead one to expect his use of the Bible in the actual compilation of his history to be in harmony with this general concept. And to a certain extent it is. The equation of the British Bishop Eldad with the Israelite prophet Samuel, and the Saxon king Hengist with Agag king of the Amalekites is a good example. The reader's traditional Israelite sympathies are all aligned with the Britons and against the pagan Saxons. Nevertheless, surprising as it may seem, more often than not Geoffrey reverses the roles, making a biblical hero into a Galfredian villain, and *vice versa.* It is of considerable interest, I believe, to observe three examples which I have noted of this latter phenomenon in Geoffrey's history (all of them, curiously, involving the violent death of kings), and which suggest the conclusion that, whatever he may have thought of the role of the British people in the divine plan, Geoffrey seems more interested in the Bible as a storehouse of narrative materials.

After the departure of the Romans, according to Geoffrey, the Britons were defended from the onslaughts of the barbarians by Constantine, brother of the Armorican king Aldroen. Following a great victory over the enemy, Constantine was declared king of Britain, and subsequently became the father of Constans (whom he made a monk), Aurelius Ambrosius, and Uther (father of Arthur). Geoffrey tells us that he reigned ten years. The source for Constantine and his monk-son Constans appears to have been Bede, who mentions both in his *Ecclesiastical History* (I,11), and says that they were put to death on the continent, Constantine at Arles, and Constans at Vienne. Nennius, in his *History of the Britons* (ch. 27), mentions only Constans (or Constantine, according to some manu-scripts), who "reigned sixteen years in Britain, and in the seven-teenth year of his reign died in Britain, at York," although some versions read ". . . died apparently slain by treachery. . . ."

Geoffrey describes the death of Constantine as follows (VI, 5): "Finally, after ten years had passed, there came to him a Pict, who was in his service, and, *pretending to have a secret message for him, all having gone aside*, in a thicket he killed him with a knife."

As we have seen, there is no basis for this in Geoffrey's sources. It has been suggested that Geoffrey is here perhaps economizing invention by recalling known events. But the most striking features of the assassination of Constantine in Geoffrey's history were avail-able to him in the biblical account of the slaying of Eglon, king of Moab, by Ehud of Israel (Judges 3:19–21): "Ehud said to the king: *I have a secret message to thee, O king*. And he commanded silence; *and all being gone out that were about him*, Ehud went in to him; now he was sitting in a summer parlor alone, and he said, I have a word from God to thee. And he forthwith rose up from his throne, and Ehud put forth his left hand, and took the dagger from his right thigh, and thrust it into his belly." A comparison of the italicized words in the two passages quoted reveals that Geoffrey has adopted the outstand-ing features of the biblical story: the pretense of a secret message, and the subsequent removal of the king's attendants, which together make possible the attack. Geoffrey then characteristically alters the other details. The assassin is a Pict, "who was in his service," a feudal touch corresponding to the fact that Ehud, in the biblical account, was responsible for presenting tribute to Eglon (Judges 3:16). Similarly the biblical setting "in a summer parlor" becomes "in a thicket," and whereas Ehud uses a "dagger" (or "sword"), the Pict kills Constantine with a "knife."

Constans the monk became king of Britain after the death of his father, the assassinated king Constantine. This he did, in spite of his religious vows, with the support of Vortigern, the British quis-ling, whose ambitious schemes were directed toward gaining the crown ultimately for himself (VI, 7). Thus Constans became the tool of Vortigern, and before long Vortigern began to consider ways of deposing or otherwise getting rid of the king. Eventually he incited a group of Pictish retainers to kill him. Geoffrey describes the assassination as follows (VI, 8): "Whereupon, breaking into the bed-chamber, the Picts attacked Constans, and, decapitating him, they carried his head to Vortigern. Vortigern, when he saw it, burst into tears as if grief-stricken, although never before had he had such joy. Then he called together the citizens of London (for there all this occurred), ordered all the traitors bound, and then beheaded, because they dared do such a wicked thing."

It is possible that to some extent Geoffrey may have derived the idea for Vortigern's plot from the biblical account of the revolt of Absalom (2 Sam. 13–18). For the details of the slaying of Constans, however, he appears to be indebted to an incident in the life of David. I refer to the assassination of Ishbosheth by the two brothers, Rechab and Baana (2 Sam. 4:5–12). I quote verses 7 and 8 from this passage: *For when they came into the house, he was sleeping upon his bed in a parlor, and they struck him and killed him; and taking away his head they went off by way of the desert all night. And they brought the head of Ishbosheth to David in Hebron; and they said to the king: Behold the head of Ishbosheth, son of Saul, thy enemy, who sought thy life; and the Lord hath revenged my lord the king this day on Saul and on his seed.* David responds to this news by swearing that, just as he had killed the Amalekite who gave Saul his death-wound, so too he would require the blood of Rechab and Baana for the slaying of Ishbosheth. And so he gives the order (verse 12): *And David commanded his servants, and they slew them, and cutting off their hands and feet, hanged them up over the pool in Hebron; but the head of Ishbosheth they took and buried in the sepulchre of Abner in Hebron.*

It will immediately be noted that the biblical story and Geoffrey's account of the death of Constans have several points of congruence: (1) the brothers Rechab and Baana and the Picts both think they are doing something that will be appreciated; (2) both assassinations take place in the victim's bed-chamber; (3) in both cases the victim's head is cut off and taken to the leader; (4) Vortigern feigns grief and David registers genuine remorse at the deed; (5) both groups of assassins are executed; and finally (6) as a direct result of the assassination the leader in each case is made king, Vortigern in VI, 9, and David in 2 Samuel 5:1-3. In addition to these features of the biblical narrative, it is possible that Geoffrey also drew on a passage in the chapter preceding the one just discussed for one other interesting detail. In 2 Samuel 3:32, at the grave of Abner, *king David lifted up his voice, and wept.* This may have been the basis for Geoffrey's description of Vortigern's tears.

Vortigern, impressed by Merlin's prophetic powers, asks him about the ending of his own life. Merlin replies with the following prediction (VIII, 1): "Flee the fire of the sons of Constantine, if flee you can. Even now they prepare ships, even now they depart from the shores of Brittany, even now they sail over the water: they will seek the isle of Britain, invade the Saxon people, subdue the cursed race; but first they will shut you in a tower and burn you." When Aurelius lands in Britain with ten thousand men, he is welcomed by the people and immediately proclaimed king. Instead of marching against the Saxons, however, Aurelius first sets out in pursuit of the usurper Vortigern, who has sought refuge in Cambria at the Fortress of Genoreu. Here is Geoffrey's account of Vortigern's death (VIII, 2): "And without delay they bring various machines, trying to breach the walls. Finally, when all else failed, they brought fire. And when it found fuel, it did not stop until it had burned up the tower and Vortigern in it."

The general idea for Vortigern's death by fire almost certainly came to Geoffrey from Nennius' *History of the Britons* (ch. 47–48). According to Nennius, Saint Germanus and his clergy pursued Vortigern, with prayers rather than weapons, until finally Vortigern fled to a stronghold: "And in the same manner St. Germanus followed him, and going there with all the clergy, remained three days and three nights, and in the fourth night, at about the hour of midnight, suddenly fire fell from the sky, burning up the whole castle; and Vortigern, with all who were with him, including his wives, was killed. This is the end of Vortigern, as it is written in the Book of the Blessed Germanus." Nennius adds (ch. 48) that some say Vortigern wandered from place to place, finally dying of a broken heart, with none to praise him; but that, according to others, the earth opened and swallowed him on the night of the fire.

It is interesting that all three of Nennius' versions of the death of Vortigern appear to be drawn from the Bible. For the fire falling from heaven he is probably indebted to the biblical account of the destruction of Sodom and Gomorrah (Gen. 19:24–25); Vortigern as a wanderer is like Cain (Gen. 4:12); and the way in which the earth opened and swallowed Vortigern is reminiscent of the unhappy fate of Korah (Num. 16:23–33). In general these biblical passages reflect the tenor of Nennius' history at this point. On the other hand, it is possible that in the account of the fire from heaven Nennius is depicting Saint Germanus as "another Elijah." The saint brings down the fire on more than one occasion (as in Nennius, ch. 34), and his use of this divine fire as a kind of personal weapon reminds us of a similar phenomenon in the life of the prophet Elijah (2 Kings 1:9–12).

[204]

Thus we see that, to say the least, the story of Vortigern's death in Geoffrey's source has strong biblical overtones. Why did Geoffrey create still another version? First, of course, there is his well-known tendency to disguise his sources, a practice which is clearly designed to protect his fiction of the "British book." Further, in striving for verisimilitude, Geoffrey very often eliminates the supernatural. But the most striking feature of Geoffrey's version is the description of Vortigern's fiery death in a tower. The story appears to be derived from the biblical account of Abimelech's attack on the people of Shechem. I quote only the most pertinent part of the narrative (Judges 9:47–49):

> *Abimelech also hearing that the men of the tower of Shechem were gathered together, went up into Mt. Selmon, with all his people, and, taking an axe, he cut down the bough of a tree, and laying it on his shoulder and carrying it, he said to his companions: what you see me do, you do quickly. So they cut down boughs from the trees, as fast as possible, and followed the leader. And surrounding the fort, they set it on fire; and so it came to pass that with the smoke and the fire a thousand persons were killed, men and women together, of the inhabitants of the tower of Shechem.*

Three features of the Shechem incident are lodged in Geoffrey's much briefer account. (1) Before Abimelech burned down the tower, *he assaulted the city all that day, and took it, killing the inhabitants of it, and destroyed it, so that he sowed it with salt* (Judges 9:45). In Geoffrey's description we find the medieval equivalent for this kind of assault: "they bring various machines trying to breach the walls." (2) The rather detailed biblical report on the gathering of fuel by Abimelech and his followers undergoes an interesting metamorphosis in the history. Geoffrey says merely "they brought fire," but then he adds, "and when it found fuel. . . ." Abimelech and his men found fuel for the fire; Geoffrey's fire found its own fuel! (3) Finally, of course, the burning of the tower itself constitutes the central feature taken over by Geoffrey. As an added touch, Merlin's prophecy echoes the prophetic parable of Abimelech's brother Jotham (Judges 9:7–20). And it is significant, I think, that whereas in Nennius all three versions of Vortigern's death relate him to biblical villains or sinners, Geoffrey's version by implication aligns Vortigern with the unfortunate victims of the savagery of Abimelech. Thus the biblical villain Abimelech may be equated with Geoffrey's hero, Aurelius, illustrating the curious reversal in roles that often occurs, as we have seen, in Geoffrey's adaptation of biblical material.

This rather strange use of the Bible by Geoffrey may perhaps gain added significance in the light of Robert Hanning's study, *The Vision of History in Early Britain* (1966). After reviewing the work of Gildas, Bede, and Nennius, Hanning suggests that Geoffrey of Monmouth wished to write a history quite different from that of his predecessors. Whereas earlier historians, especially Gildas and Bede, wrote in the tradition of Orosius and his salvation history, Geoffrey preferred to assign a more important role to human causation, free of the traditional Christian emphasis on God's control over human events. The result was to some extent a revival of the pagan conception of cyclical history. In Britain's history this was reflected in the successive rise to power of the Romans, Britons, Saxons, and, finally, the Normans. Hanning therefore plays down the significance of Geoffrey's idea of the Britons as the chosen people.

In effect (says Hanning) we do not find in Geoffrey a pattern of eschatological fulfillment, and "the regulation of history by repetitive patterns of personal behavior and national progress has replaced the Christian system of movement toward a final happiness or reward" (p. 171). Accordingly all peoples, Romans, Britons, and Saxons alike, take their place on the wheel of life, the great mandella, and rise and fall in accordance with the whim of the goddess Fortune. This is a fascinating hypothesis, to which the peculiar use of the Bible by Geoffrey offers some support. For if the theme of the chosen people has lost its meaning, then his free use of biblical narrative without regard for its moral significance is more readily explained. On the other hand, apocalyptic passages in the last book of Geoffrey's history point in a different direction, and suggest that "the Britons should again possess the island by merit of their faith when the appointed time should come" (XII, 17). The biblical language here seems clearly intended to support the idea that the British people are God's chosen ones.

Whatever Geoffrey's belief in these matters, Hanning is certainly right in emphasizing his departure from the earlier histories, and his importance for the future development of romance literature. Particularly interesting is what Hanning calls his concern for the problem of personal fulfillment within the march of history. The life of Vortigern tells us, for example, that the quest for a form of secular salvation, "the pursuit of happiness," leads a society to the brink of chaos. Issues like these assume a position of central importance in the Arthurian romances that were destined to spring from the fertile soil of Geoffrey's *History of the Kings of Britain.*

Higden's Polychronicon

Ranulph Higden was a Benedictine monk who spent most of his life in the abbey of St. Werburgh, Chester, from 1299 until his death in 1363. At the time he decided to write his history, the most popular work of that type was the *Brut* chronicle, derived from Geoffrey of Monmouth. This was, as we have seen, a national history which began with Aeneas and the Troy story rather than Genesis; to this account of Brutus and the settlement of Britain were added continuations extending through the latter half of the fourteenth century. Higden, however, in writing the *Polychronicon,* chose to return to the pattern of universal history represented by Orosius, and hence begins his account with the creation on the biblical model, dividing it into the familiar ages of the world. Within a short time his history had matched and even surpassed the popularity of the *Brut* chronicles. By the end of the fourteenth century, more than a dozen continuations had been added to Higden's *Polychronicon,* and it remained a standard authority down to the seventeenth century, when Sir Walter Raleigh wrote his *History of the World* (1614).

In his study of Higden's work, John Taylor points out that the *Polychronicon* seems to have been written first in the so-called short version which ends with the year 1327. The intermediate version, by far the most popular, extended the history to 1340, and the final, or long version, ended in the year 1352. Moreover, the later versions were much expanded throughout, showing a remarkable interest in ancient history, particularly Rome. Although much of Higden's work was derivative, enough of it was fresh and original to justify the respect accorded to him by his contemporaries.

Higden divides the *Polychronicon* into seven books because, he says, the Lord created the world in six days and rested on the seventh. These books, however, do not correspond to the seven ages of the world: hence they are a valuable index to the emphasis that Higden gives to the different periods of history. The first book is entirely devoted to a geography of the world, accompanied in some manuscripts by a world map of the type that had become popular in Higden's time. In such maps the east is at the top, and the upper half of the globe is occupied by Asia; the lower half shows Europe on the left and Africa on the right. The biblical influence was of course very strong: Paradise is placed at the top, and Jerusalem is set in the center of the world. A very fine example of such a map can be seen on display in Hereford Cathedral in the west of England. The description of the world in Book I of the *Polychronicon* conforms in outlook to this type of map, and is based for the most part on late Roman accounts, becoming more localized and accurate as Higden approaches the lands most familiar or near to himself. The climax of the geographical description, of course, is Great Britain itself.

Book II of the *Polychronicon* covers the first four ages of the world, from the creation to the fall of Jerusalem (586 B.C.). Book III deals entirely with the fifth age, which extends from the Babylonian captivity to the coming of Christ. All the rest of history is of course contained in the sixth age, which will last until Doomsday. In Higden, this is divided as follows: Book IV, from the coming of Christ to the fall of Britain (A.D. 449); Book V, from the Anglo-Saxon settlement to the Danish occupation (A.D. 871); Book VI, from King Alfred to the Norman conquest (A.D. 1066); and finally Book VII, from the Norman conquest to Higden's own time (A.D. 1352). From this brief summary it can be seen that the center of gravity has shifted forward, with the result that major emphasis is placed on Roman times and the early history of Britain. Thus in spite of Higden's famous skepticism about King Arthur, he was undoubtedly influenced in his emphasis by the example of Geoffrey of Monmouth.

Two decades after Higden's death the *Polychronicon* was translated into English by the Oxford scholar, John Trevisa, and a second English translation (anonymous) was made in the fifteenth century. The pioneer English printer, William Caxton, printed a "modernized" form of Trevisa's translation in 1482, and added a continuation of his own extending down to the year 1460. Subsequent reprintings of this translation meant that Higden's *Polychronicon* was available to a growing body of readers in the Renaissance, thus keeping alive the medieval view of universal history as an expression of the divine purpose being worked out in the course of human events.

Before we turn to the *Polychronicon* itself, something should be said about Trevisa's translation, from which I shall be quoting (in modernized form) in the subsequent discussion. John Trevisa was born in Cornwall in 1342, attended Oxford University, served as chaplain to Thomas, Lord Berkeley, in the west of England, and was eventually appointed vicar of Berkeley, where he died in the year 1402. If we may judge by time spent at Oxford, he was better educated than most priests of his day. He was a fellow of Exeter College for three years (1362–65), Queens for nearly ten (1369–78), and later returned to Queens for periods of study in 1383–87, and again for a two year period in 1394–96. As we have seen in an earlier chapter, he was expelled from Queens in 1378, perhaps in connection with his work as a translator of the Bible, in cooperation with Wyclif, Hereford, and Middleworth. The known translations by Trevisa make an impressive list: the apocryphal *Gospel of Nicodemus;* two controversial tracts, *Dialogue between a Knight and a Clerk,* and Archbishop Fitz-Ralph's *Sermon against the Friars (Defensio Curatorum);* the *Polychronicon;* a treatise *On the Rule of Princes;* and a large encyclopedia by Bartholomew Anglicus, *On the Properties of Things.*

Although most of Trevisa's translations are straightforward and sedate, his version of the *Polychronicon* contains numerous notes, signed by Trevisa with comments on the text he is translating. The sharpness of some of Trevisa's observations may be explained by the fact that the translation was made during the most turbulent period of his life, from 1378 to 1387. During this time Trevisa was expelled from Queens, the teachings of his colleague John Wyclif were condemned, and the Peasants' Revolt occurred (1381). At Oxford, the conflict between the secular faculty and the friars reached the boiling point. Even without these incentives, some differences of opinion between author and translator might well be anticipated, since Higden was a monk and Trevisa a secular priest. At one point, for example, Higden mentions that when Odo was made Archbishop of Canterbury, he became a monk in order to conform to tradition and to receive the honor of this high office in a worthy manner. Our priestly translator takes a different view: *"Trevisa.* Odo was ignorantly moved therefore to make him a monk, for Christ nor none of all his apostles was ever monk nor friar." As we look at the *Polychronicon,* therefore, it will be well to take note occasionally of Trevisa's comments, for these often shed light on current controversy, and they show us the reactions of an educated, partisan student of Higden's great chronicle.

Book I: World Geography

After giving the sources, organization, and chronology of his work, Higden begins his geographical survey with a description of the dimensions of the earth and its divisions into continents—Asia, Africa, and Europe—followed by chapters on the Mediterranean Sea and the great ocean which embraces the earth all about like a "garland." According to the view of the world provided on the standard medieval map, Higden begins at the top (east) with a description of Paradise. He identifies the four rivers of Genesis (2:10–14), and locates the garden at the eastern extremity of the earth. Its air is temperate, neither too hot nor too cold, and nothing dies there; the trees are ever green, and flowers never fade. Its location is very high, so that the waters of the flood could not reach it, and it is surrounded by walls to prevent mankind from entering. Only two men, Enoch and Elijah, have been allowed to live there since the Fall.

The provinces of Asia are then described, beginning with India. There is an island of India, for example, called Ophir (1 Kings 9:28), where there is plenty of gold, and the passage to it from the Mediterranean is by the Red Sea. India is not only full of riches, it is a place of great natural wonders. There are black men, pigmies, and dog-headed creatures who live by hunting (baboons?). There are even some men with no mouths, who live by smell, and other strange and wonderful people reminiscent of those described by Othello (I, iii, 143–45): "the Cannibals that each other eat,/The Anthropophagi, and men whose heads/Do grow beneath their shoulders." Not surprisingly, these marvels are found in greatest numbers on Higden's horizon, and tend to diminish as his geographical survey comes closer to home.

In Asia, the fullest description is devoted to biblical lands, and occasional historical information is added. Babylon was built by Nimrod, and enlarged by Semiramis; its dimensions are given in detail, together with an account of its destruction by Cyrus, king of Persia. Arabia is a land filled with incense, and is the home of the Phoenix. There too is Mount Sinai, where Moses received the Commandments. The greatest space is devoted to the land of Israel itself. Judea extends from Dan to Beersheba and has in the middle, as it were in the navel of the earth, the city of Jerusalem. On the top of Mount Zion was a tower, on the side was the temple, and the city was below. Here the great Constantine erected the church of the Holy Sepulchre, whose lamps are lighted every year by fire from heaven. On the north side of the temple is the Mount of Olives. From that mount Christ ascended to heaven, and on that mount He shall judge the world at last. Nearby is the garden of Gethsemane, and other places mentioned in the Gospels. North of Mount Zion is Calvary, where Christ died on the cross.

Higden's tour of the holy land is often anecdotal, and reminds us of the pilgrimage of Etheria referred to in Chapter I. In Idumea (Edom), he says, is Job's well, which changes color four times a year. First it is pale as ashes, second red as blood, third green as grass, and fourth it is clear as water. In Cappadocia are the Amazons, and though Isidore says Alexander the Great destroyed them, Higden relates a story that puts the conqueror in a better light. When Alexander demanded tribute from the Amazons, their queen Thalestris wrote in reply: "We wonder that thou dost desire to fight with women; for if fortune favor us, and thou be overcome, it is great shame and villainy when thou art overcome by women. Also if our gods be wroth with us and thou overcome us, for to win the mastery of women thou gettest but little worship." King Alexander was pleased with this, and granted them freedom, saying: "Women must be overcome with fairness and love, not with sternness and dread."

Africa is described more briefly in two chapters (19–20). The people of Ethiopia are swifter than harts, they eat serpents and adders, and hunt lions and panthers. Some dig caves and dens so as to dwell under the earth, and make sounds with grinding and clicking of teeth rather than with voice in the throat. Some go naked and do no work, some are without heads and have mouth and eyes in the breast. There are elephants, chameleons, basilisks, unicorns, camels, leopards, and dragons, that have in their heads many precious stones. The panther is friendly toward all beasts except the dragon; the basilisk is king of the serpents, and slays beasts and birds merely with a smile and a glance. Once again the marvels grow more numerous as we move toward the perimeter of Higden's world.

Much more attention is devoted to Europe, particularly to Rome as the guardian of civilization. The Greeks were worthy of admiration for their achievements in learning and in deeds of arms, "but that virtue cooled in those that came afterward, and passed from the Greeks to the Latins." The city of Rome is described in detail, and Higden makes no attempt to conceal his admiration of its greatness. Even its ruins bespeak its glory, and Higden quotes the quatrain of Bishop Hildebert, which Trevisa translates as follows:

> Rome, nothing is peer to thee,
> Though thou nigh all fallen be;
> On all thou showest thy bound,
> How great thou were when thou were sound.

Among the great buildings of Rome was the Palace of Peace, where Romulus put his own image of gold, saying: "This shall never fall until a maid bear a child." And that image fell when Christ was born. Thus the description of Rome is provided with signs and wonders indicating, as we have seen, the divine purpose behind the establishment of the *pax romana.*

[211]

Among the many wonders of Rome is a monument depicting two great horses, carved from marble, said to have been erected by the Emperor Tiberius in memory of two philosophers, Praxitellus and Fibia. According to tradition, the two young philosophers came to Rome and walked naked. And when the emperor asked them why they went naked, they replied that it was because they had forsaken all things. Higden's interest in this curious story seems entirely antiquarian, but it reminds his translator, John Trevisa, of his exasperating opponents at Oxford, the friars, who claimed by their vows to have forsaken all things. Here is his comment on Higden's story: "*Trevisa:* The first point of this doing and answer teaches that he who forsaketh all things forsaketh all his clothes: and so it followeth that they that be well clothed, and go about and beg and gather money and corn and goods from other men, do not forsake all things." One is reminded of the similar view of Chaucer, who, in the *Canterbury Tales*, depicts his friar Hubert as a greedy rascal, not at all concerned to uphold his vow of poverty.

From Rome, Higden proceeds through Germany, France, and Spain. The greatest space is devoted to a history of France and a description of her provinces. Brittany, for instance, is said to have its name from the Britons, who twice occupied the land, once in the time of Brennius, and later when they were driven out by the Saxons in Vortigern's time. In Brittany there is a well, and if water from it is taken in an ox horn and poured on a stone that is beside the well, it will rain no matter how fair the weather has been. This Breton well very much resembles one in *Yvain,* a romance by Chrétien de Troyes, and reminds us again of the close connection between history and romance already noted in the work of Geoffrey of Monmouth.

Among the islands of the Mediterranean is Sardinia, which has an herb called "apium" that makes men laugh themselves to death. Outside the pillars of Hercules is the west ocean, and to the north near the frozen sea is Iceland. The men of that island are short-spoken, but true to their word, and clothed in the skin of wild animals. They are fishermen, and have in one man both king and priest. Falcons and hawks are found there, and white bears that break the ice and draw out fish. The island is three days' sailing from Ireland and Britain. Thus as we approach Higden's corner of the globe, we find the descriptions much closer to reality than was the case with India or Africa.

The second half of Higden's geography is devoted entirely to the British isles. Ireland occupies five chapters, Scotland and Wales have

[212]

one each, and the remaining twenty-two chapters describe England. Little of this was original with Higden, but it remained for some time justly popular as the completest account of the subject available to the reading public. In addition to being geographically informative, it is filled with popular lore and legend.

Ireland is richly populated with cattle, fish, and birds. Especially marvelous are the barnacles, birds resembling the wild goose: they grow on trees, and are brought forth in this way as if nature were working against nature. Monks eat these barnacles during fast days, on the theory that they are not meat, since they are not born of fleshy father and mother. But they are wrong to do this, for if a man had eaten of Adam's thigh, he would have eaten flesh, even though Adam had no fleshy mother and father. And as his flesh came miraculously out of the earth, so the flesh of this bird comes miraculously out of the tree.

There are no poisonous beasts in Ireland, which leads some to suppose that this is because Saint Patrick drove them out, whereas it is more likely, the author states, that there were no serpents in the land from the beginning. This is a remarkable instance of the demythologizing effect of scientific historiography, for Higden goes on to point out that poisonous snakes die when men bring them to Ireland from other lands—though we may be skeptical of his statement that their poison leaves them when the ship crosses the mid-point of the Irish sea, or that turf brought from Ireland can be used as a pesticide! On the other hand it is interesting to observe that John Trevisa, in his translation, seems reluctant to accept this debunking of the legend of Saint Patrick and the snakes. Higden says that some men feign (*figunt*) the story, whereas it is more probable (*probabilius est*) that there were no snakes in the first place. Trevisa likewise has "some men feign" in his first clause, but then begins the second clause with *"some men feign that it is* more probable" that there were no snakes. Thus the balance is restored and one is free to think what he likes.

After providing a chapter on the history of Ireland from the time of Noah's flood, and another on the manners and customs of the Irish, Higden speaks of the marvels of the country. To the north is a place called the Isle of the Living, where no man can die, a tradition that reminds us both of the earthly paradise and of the Isle of Avalon in Arthurian legend. Also to the north, in the country of Ossiriens, at the prayer of a holy abbot, every seven years a married couple are turned into wolves and driven out of the land. Then, if they survive, they are restored to human form at the end of seven years, and returned home, at which time another couple are similarly transformed. Here one thinks, naturally, of the werewolf legend, but the abbot's prayer suggests also the notion of expiation through reincarnation in various forms, familiar in modern times in the ballad of "The Cruel Mother."

One of the most famous marvels of Ireland was Saint Patrick's Purgatory, a cavern where men were supposed to be able to witness the pains of the wicked and the joys of the blessed. They say that whoever endures the pains of Patrick's purgatory shall never suffer the pains of hell, unless he die finally without repentance of sin. At this point the translator cannot resist a comment of his own: "*Trevisa*. Though this old saw might be sooth, it is but a jape. For no man that doth deadly sin shall be saved, unless he be truly repentant whatsoever penance he do; And every man that is truly repentant at his life's end of all his misdeeds, he shall be certainly saved and have the bliss of heaven, though he never hear speak of Patrick's purgatory."

It is a curious fact that Higden, who elsewhere uses Latin prose, composes his chapter on Wales in rhyming couplets, and Trevisa does likewise in the English translation, including those passages added by way of commentary. In speaking of Merlin, for example, Higden remarks (following Geoffrey of Monmouth) that he was begotten by a goblin. Trevisa interrupts at this point to make a distinction. While it may be true that a devil (incubus) can make women pregnant, he says, in no case does the child himself have characteristics of the devil. If that were so, the child would be immortal:

> Learned men deny
> That devils ever die;
> But death slew Merlin,
> *Ergo*, Merlin was no goblin!

Not surprisingly, more space is devoted to England than any other country. Care is taken in describing its size, its natural resources, and its wonders. There are the great roads, the rivers, and the famous cities and towns. Included among the latter is the city of Bath, and Higden comments on the medicinal value of its hot springs. To this Trevisa adds a note, comparing the waters of Bath with those of the hot springs in Aachen in Germany and Aix in Savoy. "The baths in Aix," he says, "be as fair and as clear as any cold well stream. I have assayed, and bathed therein."

In his survey of the geography of England Higden draws freely on earlier historians, and occasionally comments on contradictions that he notices in his sources. In these comments, his attitude toward the reliability of Geoffrey of Monmouth seems to fluctuate. Geoffrey has ended his history with a blunt warning to his fellow historians, including William of Malmesbury, ordering them to "be silent as to the Kings of the Britons, seeing that they have not that book in the British speech which Walter, Archdeacon of Oxford, did convey hither, out of Brittany." In one passage, Higden gives two explanations for the name Westmorland, one by William connecting it with the Roman consul Marius, and the other by Geoffrey connecting it with Marius, king of the Britons. But Higden declares the latter explanation to be more "probable", because of the authority of Geoffrey's British book. "William of Malmesbury," he observes, "saw never that book."

Later on, however, in speaking of Caerleon in Wales, Higden mentions that it was here the messengers of Rome came to the great Arthur's court, "if it is permissible to believe it." The immediate source here is Gerald of Wales, and our translator pauses to attack him angrily for this expression of doubt as to the truth of Geoffrey's history. If Gerald was in doubt about the truth of this story (says Trevisa) he should not have included it in his books. For it is a strange sort of dreaming to write a long story, so that it will always be remembered, while remaining ever in doubt as to its authenticity! Trevisa's touchiness about the truth of the Arthurian history may be a reflection of his Celtic origin. We see evidence of this concern for his native heritage when he is critical of the failure of his source to list Cornwall among the counties of England. For Cornwall is in England (he says), is divided into "hundreds", ruled by the law of England, and holds shire days as other shires do. Clearly Trevisa wants Cornwall to move into the mainstream of national life, while at the same time his protective attitude toward the Arthurian tradition suggests that he expected the Celtic peoples to retain their cultural identity.

In the final two chapters of his first book, Higden describes the languages and customs of England. Gaelic is spoken in Scotland, and Welsh in Wales, while Norman French and English are spoken in all the land. English used to be divided into northern, midland, and southern dialects, corresponding to the Germanic tribes of the original settlers, but these have become so mixed, first with the Danes and later with the Normans, that the native language is much impaired. Higden describes the result of this mixture as a strange bellowing and chattering (*boatus et garritus*), but Trevisa calls it a "straunge wlafferynge, chiterynge, harrynge, and garrynge grisbayting."

Two things have had an adverse effect on the English language according to Higden. One is that school children, ever since the Normans first came to England, have had to leave their native language and recite in French. Another is that children of the nobility learn French from the cradle, while others are anxious to learn French for its prestige. Trevisa, writing several decades later, brings Higden up to date in the following comment.

> *Trevisa.* This manner was much used before the first plague [1349], but is since somewhat changed. For John Cornwall, a master of grammar, changed the lore in grammar school and construing from French into English; and Richard Pencrich learned that manner of teaching from him, and other men from Pencrich; so that now, the year of our Lord 1385 [ninth year of Richard II], in all the grammar schools of England, children leave French and construe and learn in English.

Trevisa goes on in his note to point out the advantage and disadvantage of this: children learn their grammar much more quickly than they used to; but now they know no more French "than their left heel," a disadvantage if they should ever go overseas. In this same passage Higden expresses wonder that English is so diverse of sound in its native land, while French, imported from Normandy, has a single correct form wherever it is spoken in England. Once again Trevisa feels compelled to comment in order to correct Higden's provincial view. There are as many different kinds of French in France, he says, as there are forms of English in England. No doubt this comment is based on direct observation by our translator in his continental journeys.

Higden concludes his geographical survey with a bouquet of sayings about Englishmen from various sources. There is a good balance in this assessment of the English character. They are swift afoot and on horse, victorious in fair fight, and they love to seek their fortune abroad. "The men be able to all manner of sleight and wit, but before the deed blundering and hasty, and more wise after the deed, and leave often lightly what they have begun." Pope Eugenius sums up the English in these words: they can do whatever they wish, and could be placed before all others, were they not hindered by a "light wit" (*levitas animi*), by which I take it he means that they couldn't take things seriously.

[216]

Nevertheless there is a hint of doom in Higden's evaluation of his people. When they have destroyed their enemies to the ground, he says, then they fight with themselves, and slay each other, as an empty stomach churns within itself. Borrowing Hannibal's comment on the Romans, he observes that the English are invincible in foreign countries, but in their own land they can be easily overcome. Among them is a great diversity of clothing, concerning which a holy hermit once prophesied: the English, because of their sins, shall be overcome by Danes, then by Normans, and finally by the people they despise most of all, the Scots; then the world shall be so unstable, that this instability of thought shall be signified by the great diversity of clothing worn by the people. With this dark prophecy concerning the latter days, Higden brings his first book to an end.

Book II: Creation to the Fall of Jerusalem

Since in the first book we were concerned with a description of the greater world (macrocosm), says Higden, we must begin the second with the lesser world (microcosm) which is man. He then devotes three chapters to showing how man himself is a little universe, duplicating all the elements, powers, functions, and wonders of the outside world. Much space is given to freaks of nature, and a whole chapter to monsters. Here the translator's interest rivals that of his author, and to Higden's list—Pyrrhus, Strabo, Seneca, and Caesar—Trevisa adds the case of Thomas Hayward of Berkeley, whose skull was so hard that he could break strong doors with his head, in the manner of Chaucer's miller; Roger Bagge of Wotton-under-Edge, who never spat or coughed in his lifetime; and the case of the two-headed French child reported by William Wayte of Berkeley.

Next the ideal state of man before the Fall is described, emphasizing the obedience of the body to the commands of the soul. But alas, ever since the fall the body, corrupted by sin, grieves the soul, and man must die. Animals have shells, wool, feathers, scales, or other covering, but man is born naked and bare, and as soon as he is born begins to weep. Thus he is feebler than any other beast; he cannot help himself, but only weep with all his might: "None hath sickness more grievous, none more liking to do otherwise than he should. None is more cruel. Also, other beasts love every other of the same kind and dwell together, and be not cruel but to beasts of other kind that be contrary to them. But man turneth that manner of doing upside down, and is contrary to himself and cruel to other men; and if he may not reach to grieve others, then he becometh angry and cruel to himself." This indictment of man's sinful nature is a prominent feature of the medieval biblical tradition. Higden has already used it in his denunciation of the perversity of Englishmen, and it occurs also in other literary works of the fourteenth century showing biblical influence. The basic idea, of course, is that man comes off second best in a comparison with the animals, or as the prophet Isaiah said, (1:3), *The ox knoweth his owner and the ass his master's crib: but Israel doth not know, my people doth not consider.*

The first age of the world begins with the creation of Adam and is described mainly in terms of the genealogies of Genesis, with an occasional antiquarian comment like the following, taken by Higden from Isidore of Seville: "Men were first naked and unarmed, not safe against beast or against men, and had no place to betake them, and keep them from cold and heat; then by busying their natural wit they be thought them of dwellings: therefore they built them small cottages and cabins, and wove them and covered them with small twigs and with reeds, that their life might be the more safe."

Another interesting point involves the preservation of knowledge from destruction by the flood. We have already noted, in the Middle English *Genesis and Exodus,* this account of the inscribing of scientific knowledge on duplicate tablets or columns of stone and tile, so as to protect it from the two forms of destruction by water and by fire. Higden repeats this story from Josephus, but Trevisa in his translation gives it a new twist, asserting that the records were not in the form of inscriptions, but rather were in books placed inside the pillars, much in the manner of a modern time capsule: "That time men wist as Adam had said, that they should be destroyed by fire or by water; therefore books that they had made by great travail and study they inclosed in two great pillars made of marble and glazed tile: a pillar of marble for water, and a pillar of tile for fire, so that it should be saved in that way for the help of mankind. Men say that the pillar of stone escaped the flood and is yet in Syria."

This is indeed an unusual form of the story, but not unique. It shows up again later in a Cornish drama, *Creation of the World* (1611), as pointed out by Paula Neuss in an unpublished study of the Cornish play. Here Seth foresees, by reading the stars, that the world is to be destroyed, either by water or by fire. He orders the books enclosed in pillars of brick and marble. The pillars are prepared by Jared (father of Enoch), and Seth places the books in them. Thereafter Noah comes on stage and the story of the flood begins. Perhaps it is not a coincidence that the source used here by the Cornish dramatist

[218]

appears to be the version of the *Polychronicon* produced by the Cornishman, John Trevisa.

Medieval drama will be the subject of a later chapter (in Vol. 2), but we should notice in passing one other point of contact between the *Polychronicon* and the Cornish *Creation*. In his description of Noah's Ark, Higden says that Noah made a window in the ship with a door on the side downward (*in latere deorsum*), and the window was one cubit high (Gen. 6:16). There was considerable interest in the details of the construction of the ark in medieval times, as is evidenced, for example, by frequent sketches and diagrams. In one of the manuscripts of Trevisa's translation (British Museum Additional 24194), reproduced as the frontispiece to Volume 2 of the *Polychronicon*, two careful drawings of the ark show the window amidships, one with its doors swung open, the other with the doors not visible (or perhaps closed).

In the Cornish *Creation*, God tells Noah how to construct the door in the ark. The language of the original is not entirely clear at this point, but I follow the translation of Stokes with one exception:

> GOD: On the side behind, a door
> Thou shalt make, a port it shall be called:
> Joists through it thou shalt place
> That it be not opened (*dyges*) outward.

I take it that the joists prescribed by God are meant to serve as bars to prevent the door from being opened accidentally or irresponsibly from within, as well as braces against the force of waves from without. This would seem to be the Cornish dramatist's means of assuring us that the window was watertight.

Trevisa likewise is concerned about the window in the ark, as can be seen in the note which he adds to Higden's text:

> *Trevisa.* Here men may wonder how the window was made beneath in the side of the ship, for coming in of water. Doctor de Lyra moveth this doubt, and saith that where we have *fenestra*, that is a *fenetre,* a *window* the literal Hebrew hath *lucerna* that is, a *lantern;* and some men say that that lantern was a carbuncle or some other precious stone, that shone and gave light clear enough where it was set. But some others say that that window was a whole crystal stone which took in light and held out water. Many other windows were in the ship, as was needed, for the ship was full great and huge, and had in it full many beasts.

Here we can see not only Trevisa's practical concerns as an experienced traveller, but also his knowledge of biblical commentaries. De Lyra was one of the most influential exegetes of the later Middle

Ages, and, as we have already observed, several of his commentaries were among the books taken by Trevisa and his friends when they were expelled from Queens College.

In addition to detailed exegesis like that on the ark, the *Polychronicon* has many short comments and popular anecdotes tied to the biblical narrative. A few examples will have to suffice here. Why did the waters of the flood cover the highest hills to the depth of fifteen cubits (Gen. 7:19–20)? Because, they say, mankind polluted the air by worshiping fire that smoked and spread up to such a height. Who originated the practice of idolatry? The Assyrian king Ninus did so when he erected an image in memory of his father. Thence the practice spread to other countries as illustrated in Jerome's commentary on Isaiah 18: the Egyptians worshiped Fortune, the god of chance, who holds in his right hand a horn filled with mead. On the last day of November his followers taste of that horn: if they find it full, it bodes a good crop that year, but if it is empty, they go into mourning. If Potiphar was a eunuch (Gen. 37:36, Vulgate *eunucho*), how could Joseph have married his daughter (Gen. 41:45, where the priest Potipherah is equated with Potiphar)? The answer is that Potiphar was not one of those eunuchs that had been castrated in childhood, for he had a wife and children, including the daughter that Joseph wedded. But since Potiphar had admired Joseph's fair appearance, and had bought him in order to misuse him, God made Potiphar so cold that he never again could have sexual relations even with his own wife, any more than if he were a eunuch; therefore, since he was of high rank, he was made a bishop.

The story of Moses in the *Polychronicon* is embellished with the same childhood narratives and romance themes we have noted in the Middle English *Genesis and Exodus*. Occasionally, however, the biblical narrative itself is retouched in an interesting way. Such is the case with Pharaoh's decree that the male children of the Hebrews should die. The usual motive—to hold down the Hebrew population—is given, but then another reason is added. It seems that a prophet, a "writer of holy letters," warned Pharaoh that one should be born of the Hebrews who would bear down the principality of Egypt and raise up the nation of Israel. Therefore it was commanded that the male children of Israel should be slain when they were born. The cross reference here to the slaughter of the innocents in the New Testament is clear enough: sacred history is being retouched to underscore the typological relationship between the birth of Moses

[220]

and the birth of Christ. Modern use of the same technique can be seen in Cecil B. DeMille's production of *The Ten Commandments.*

The lives of the Old Testament prophets offer another opportunity to stress foreshadowing of the New Testament. This is done in the *Polychronicon* by including apocryphal accounts of the martyrdom of Isaiah, Jeremiah, and Ezekiel. The evil king Manasseh ordered Isaiah to be sawed asunder with a wooden saw. While undergoing this torture near the spring of Shiloah, Isaiah asked for water, but no one gave him a drink. Then God from heaven sent water in his mouth, and, afterward he gave up the ghost. He was buried under an oak, fast by the waters of Shiloah, which means "sent." Similarly we are told later that Jeremiah was stoned to death in Egypt, and Ezekiel was drawn and quartered by horses in Chaldea. Thus the cruel execution of the prophets foreshadows the death of Christ on the cross (Matt. 23:29–39), even as the suffering of the early Christians is reminiscent of the hardships of the elders, who *had trial of cruel mockings and scourgings, yea, moreover of bonds and imprisonment; they were stoned, they were sawn asunder, were tempted, were slain with the sword* (Heb. 11:36–37). This theme of martyrdom is shared by prophet and Apostle, a parallelism stressed not only in literature, but also, as we have seen, in the biblical art of the sanctuary, where prophets and Apostles unite in witnessing to the mighty acts of God. In many such ways, too numerous to examine here, the *Polychronicon* reinforces the thesis of all universal histories: the divine purpose is visible in the course of human events to him who has eyes to see.

Book III: Babylonian Exile to the Coming of Christ

In the *Cursor Mundi,* it will be recalled, the fifth age was devoted almost exclusively to allegorical foreshadowing of the Redemption and apocryphal narratives of the life of the Virgin and the childhood of Jesus. The *Polychronicon* sweeps all this aside and presents the fifth age of the world entirely from a historical point of view. The narrative, moreover, is no longer exclusively or even primarily biblical: in the fifth age of the world classical history begins to overshadow the fortunes of the Jews. True, the early part of Book III is taken up with the stories of Jeremiah, Ezekiel, Nebuchadnezzar, Daniel, Cyrus and the Persian dynasty, Zerubbabbel, Ezra, and Nehemiah; but toward the middle of the book these are gradually replaced by such names as Pythagoras, Socrates, Diogenes, Plato, Phillip of Macedon, Aristotle, Alexander, Hannibal, Cicero, Mithridates, Pompey, Caesar, and Augustus. Finally, at the end of the last chapter, biblical events resume with an account of the family of the Virgin Mary and the birth of John the Baptist.

In the biblical portion of book III an interesting distinction is made between canonical and apocryphal sources in reference to the story of Susannah and the Elders. This story happened in the time of Evilmerodach (says Higden), but is called a "fable," not for any feigning that is in it, but because it says the elders were stoned to death, whereas Jerome says they were burned in fire. Also it is a fable in the sense that we say it was written by Daniel whereas actually it was written by a Greek, as can be seen from the fact that there is no Hebrew original for that portion of Daniel containing the story of Susannah. Thus the historicity of the story is not questioned, but the precedent of Jerome is used to show that the received text may be inaccurate in details, and the question of authorship is legitimately raised.

Extra-biblical sources are used to compile the biography of Cyrus the Great, the Persian conqueror who captured Babylon and freed the Jews. Higden gives the traditional foundling story, complete with a prediction that Cyrus will rule over all of Asia. At the same time the biblical connection is also stressed: "Cyrus, when he had heard Isaiah's prophecy which was written of him a hundred and twenty years beforehand in this manner, *To my Christ, Cyrus, whose right hand I have taken* [Isaiah 45:1], and so forth, he delivered the Jews the first year of his kingdom, and made free nigh fifty thousand men. . . ." Here the prophecy of Isaiah is seen to have a direct impact on Cyrus, the instrument prepared by God for the deliverance of his chosen people. The king hears the prophecy and consequently fulfills it, thus illustrating the prophetic concept of "the power of the word."

Many of the classical stories have a biblical flavor despite their secular subject. Socrates, for example, is presented as a kind of pagan saint. Although the point is not made explicit, we are given the impression that Socrates was guided constantly by the Holy Spirit, and that he died a martyr to the cause of monotheism. At the same time, the homely side of the great philosopher is not overlooked. In his old age Socrates took up harping with the remark, "better late than never!" Also included is the story of his two shrewish wives, made famous by Chaucer in the prologue to the Wife of Bath's tale, particularly Xantippa, who "caste pisse upon his heed." The wife describes Socrates' reaction:

[222]

This sely man sat stille as he were deed;
He wiped his heed, namoore dorste he seyn,
But "Er that thonder stynte, cometh a reyn!"

Biblical influence in classical history is not confined to details of style or technique. The historian is sometimes required to make sense out of events that seem to have no rationale in the divine plan, or else he must deal with issues that involve gentile religious beliefs. A good instance of the latter occurs in the chapter describing the conquest of Greece and Rome by the Gauls. At one point Brennius enters Macedonia and despoils the temples of the gods, saying merrily, "Rich gods must give men some of their riches." When the jesting conqueror approaches the temple of Apollo on Mount Parnassus, the Greeks pray and a great part of the hill falls on the Gauls, together with hail stones, so that great numbers are killed. Brennius himself is wounded, and slays himself with a sword. The vengeance here by Apollo is very similar to that taken by Jehovah in a number of Old Testament stories. Perhaps for this reason the historian feels called upon to give the reader a note of explanation: "No man should wonder though Apollo took vengeance on them that spoiled the gods and the temples. For God suffered Apollo to destroy many nations because of their trespass and evil living and deeds. For it is certain that the spirits of the air may use their shrewdness against them that be miscreant and evil of deeds, for grace is withdrawn from such manner of men, and evil spirits are given leave to annoy them and to grieve them." Thus God's control over human history is maintained by delegating it to the spirits of the air, and biblical monotheism is not compromised by the efficacy of pagan prayers.

The Greek philosophers are for the most part highly regarded by Higden. He expresses skepticism about the opinion that Plato knew any of the prophets, or read any of their books, since these had not yet been translated into Greek. But he goes on to point out that "many things be found in Plato's books that accord with the sayings of the prophets." Aristotle is also praised, and called *the* philosopher, but falls short of the glory of Plato. In keeping with his reservations about the reliability of Aristotle, Higden tells a somewhat unflattering story of his death. It seems that Aristotle spent a long time studying the behavior of the tide at Black Bridge, in an effort to understand the reason behind the strange ebbing and flowing of the waters there. At last, unable to solve the problem, he spoke to the water in great indignation, saying, "Since I cannot comprehend and

[223]

take thee, thou shalt take me!" And so he fell into the water and drowned himself. It is clear that this story was designed to illustrate the futility of human wisdom. Gregory Nazianzenus had used it in his treatise on the words of Saint Paul (1 Cor. 3:19): *For the wisdom of this world is foolishness with God.*

Higden's translator, however, flatly disagrees with this attitude toward Aristotle:

> *Trevisa.* It is wonder that Gregory Nazianzenus telleth so mad a magel tale of so worthy a prince of philosophers as Aristotle was. Why telleth he not how Aristotle declareth the matter of ebbing and flowing of the sea in book II of the *Metaphysics?* Why telleth he not how it is written in the book of the apple? How Aristotle died and held an apple in his hand and had comfort of the smell, and taught his scholars how they should live and come to God, and be with God without end. And at the last his hand began to quake, and the apple fell down from his hand, and his face waxed all wan, and so Aristotle yielded up the ghost and died.

Obviously Trevisa prefers the version of Aristotle's death that places him, by implication, among the saints, a holy philosopher who had mastered the art of dying.

By far the greatest space in the history of the fifth age is devoted to Alexander the Great, a magnetic personality who both attracted and repelled medieval man. As a conqueror, he was honestly admired, and his career provided the model for other biographies, such as that of King Arthur. When Alexander goes to Darius' camp disguised as a messenger, one thinks of Harold of England's similar tactic at the battle of Stamford Bridge. When Darius scornfully sends Alexander a scourge, a ball, and expense money, we are reminded of the tennis balls that the Dauphin sent to Henry V. Even when read for the first time, the legend of Alexander seems hauntingly familiar, because of its tremendous influence in medieval and renaissance literature.

If Alexander was widely admired, however, he was also held in contempt. Despite all his great victories and pretentious claims, in the end everything he won turned to ashes. Inevitably Christian commentators conclude by saying to Alexander: thou fool! For the ascetic Christian historian, the wars and victories of the Greek conquerors are essentially a meaningless activity. Nowhere is this point of view brought out more clearly than in the confrontation of Alexander and Dindimus, king of the Brahmans. There is some evidence that the original author of the correspondence of Alexander and Dindimus meant to allow Alexander to win the argument, but in the Middle Ages Christian interpreters made it a critique of the conqueror, and had nothing but praise for the Brahman. This latter view is reflected in Higden's version, which is based on the *Speculum Historiale* of Vincent of Beauvais.

When Alexander had conquered all the lands, he prepared to assault the Brahmans, who lived in an island off the coast. The Brahmans meanwhile sent him a letter, asking why he wished to conquer them. We have no riches (they write), no fine clothing, and our women desire no more fairness than they have by nature. Our homes are but dens which serve a double purpose: they are our harbor while we live, and our grave when we are dead. We have a king, as is natural, but no wrangling or litigation, because our desires are held in check by nature. A common poverty makes us all rich. It is unlawful among us to wound (*vulnerare*) the hills with colter and with plowshare. Having no gluttony, we are never sick; we wage no war, and we make peace with good living, not with force. We seek no plays and entertainments, for we are fully satisfied to behold the welkin and the stars. We are men of simple speech, and do not lie. Our God is the God of all, who is not pleased with worldly riches, but with holy works and deeds.

To this letter Alexander responds by accusing the Brahmans of being overly pleased with themselves and critical of others. If what you say is true (he writes), only you are without sin, and you consider the benefits and crafts ordained by God to be evil. Either you claim to be gods, or you have envy toward God, which leads you to be critical of man, the noblest of His creatures.

In response to this charge, Dindimus, king of the Brahmans, replies with a statement of ascetic faith reminiscent of the Desert Fathers. We are not at home in this world (he says), but we are strangers and guests; we came not to dwell here, but to go hence. "We say not that we be gods, nor do we have envy to God; but we say that we will not misuse the goodness of God almighty. Not all things are seemly that are lawful. God hath put the use of things in man's freedom; then he that leaveth the worse and followeth the better is not God, but he is made God's friend." Your pride makes you forget that you are men; you build temples to yourself in which you shed blood, and so I call you mad, for you know not what you do.

Alexander replies to this by charging that the Brahmans live as they do out of ignorance rather than virtue, and hence resemble the animals rather than man. Or, he says, if you knowingly refuse the benefits bestowed by God, you shall be guilty of pride for refusing

[225]

gifts, or else of envy, that the gifts come from someone better than you. To which Dindimus responds: you war against men, because you have not overcome the enemy within; but we have won the inner battle of our own members, and hence rest secure and have no outward battle. We are satisfied with simple things, and take heed of the life to come. You say what should be done, but you do not do it. You hunger and thirst after gold, servants, and honor. Water quenches our natural thirst; gold increases yours, which proves how unnatural is the thirst for gold.

Then Alexander, perhaps out of exasperation, sends a messenger to Dindimus, who lay in the forest on a bed of leaves: "Alexander, the great God Jupiter's Son, and Lord of the World, commandeth thee that thou come to him; and if thou comest he will give thee many great gifts; and if thou comest not thou shalt forego thy head and thy life." Dindimus of course refuses, lying unperturbed on his woodland couch. Alexander is no God (he replies), and I have no need of his gifts; neither can he slay my soul. Tell Alexander that I do not dread death; if he will have anything of mine, let him come to me.

This cool response to the imperial command impresses Alexander, who then puts off all pomp and pride, and pays Dindimus a visit. Teach me (he says) the wit and wisdom that you have received from God. Though you desire all the world, replies the Brahman, at the last you will need no more earth than the little amount you see me lying on. If you learn this wisdom from me, you will have all you desire. I have heaven for a roof, and the earth instead of a bed; the river provides my drink, and the wood my food. The flesh of beasts does not rot within my guts; I am not a sepulchre for dead bodies. I live as I am made. Say now, is it more just to mistreat men, or to defend them and do them right? to kill and to scatter, or to keep and to save? If you slay me, I go to God, and you cannot escape his hand; so do not destroy what God has fashioned and made.

At this point Alexander's opposition crumbles, and the victory of Dindimus is complete. Alexander confesses to the Brahman as if to his priest. I live in constant fear, he says; I am more in dread of my friends than my enemies. If I kill those that I fear, I am full of woe; and if I am lenient, then I am despised. Yet if I were to dwell with you in valleys and dens, I could not endure. As a last, desperate gesture, Alexander offers Dindimus gold, silver, clothes, bread, and oil. Will all this make the birds sing better? the Brahman asks. But lest Alexander be grieved by a complete refusal, he accepts the oil, and, throwing it on a fire, he sings a hymn of praise to God. The reader is left in no doubt as to the outcome of this contest of philosophies.

The way of life advocated by the Brahmans in this story was by no means rare in medieval literature. Its origin, as I have suggested, can be traced to the Desert Fathers, and it was given classical expression in Boethius' *Consolation of Philosophy.* In one sense it expressed the Greek notion of a Golden Age; in another it depicted by implication the biblical concept of the ideal life of man before the fall. Geoffrey Chaucer skillfully combined these traditions in his short poem, *The Former Age.* He describes a pre-agricultural way of life very similar to that of the Brahmans. The ground was not yet "wounded" by the plow, vines were not cultivated, and no one ground spices in the mortar. There were no merchant ships, no money, no art of war. And why should they fight, since no man stored up wealth? Tyrants do not launch an assault against the wilderness; no, they search out wealth and riches, and when they find them they assail the city with all their host. But in the former age there were no palaces and halls, for the people slept in caves or in the woods, and had no compulsion to fight:

> Yit was not Jupiter the likerous,
> That first was fader of delicacye,
> Come in this world; ne Nembrot, desirous
> To regne, had nat maad his toures hye.
> Allas, allas! now may men wepe and crye!
> For in oure dayes nis but covetyse,
> Doublenesse, and tresoun, and envye,
> Poyson, manslauhtre, and mordre in sondry wyse.

Already in Chaucer, as well as Higden, we can see the concept of the Golden Age being used as an instrument of moral and social criticism. Less than two centuries later, in the Renaissance, the theme was destined to be given classical expression in Saint Thomas More's *Utopia,* the model for a succession of utopian satires that have remained popular down to the present day. It is therefore interesting, though perhaps not suprising, to find one of the seeds of this literary development embedded in Higden's universal history.

Book IV: Birth of Christ to the Fall of Britain (449)

In the 42nd year of Octavian, in the 31st year of Herod, in the 3rd year of the 190th Olympiad, 705 years after the building of Rome, 6 months after the conception of John the Baptist, on Friday the 25th of March, the 10th day of the moon, the 12th indiction, at Nazareth in Galilee, Christ was conceived of the Virgin Mary, Joseph's spouse. And so ends the fifth age of the world, as it were the old age, often grieved with care and woe, from the exile of the Jews to Christ, that is from March before the burning of the temple, that was done in harvest, to March in the 42nd year of Augustus, under 14 generations, containing 541 years, according to Bede; Isidore says 545; Elpericus 589; but the fairest accounts of all say 591.

The sixth age of the world begins with Christ, but is not fixed in generations nor years, but shall be ended as it were by death, the last age of all the world. Some say this sixth age began at the Incarnation of Christ; some say at the birth of Christ, on the authority of the apostle Paul, who said, *But when the fulness of the time was come, God sent forth his Son born of a woman* (Galatians 4:4); some count from the baptism of Christ, when water was given the power to bring forth spiritual children and circumcision ceased; some count from Christ's passion, when the gate of Paradise was opened. Then the years from the beginning of the world, which was the 18th of March in which the world began, down to the incarnation of Christ, were 5,200 — so says Orosius. But the more common calculation is 5,196, and Marcius says 5,189.

Such is the precision with which Higden introduces his account of the sixth age of the world. He then goes on to elaborate the parallels between Adam and Christ suggested by Saint Paul. Adam sinned on Friday and later died on a Friday; and on such a Friday Christ, the second Adam, took on flesh, ended his fasting, and suffered death for mankind. In the very hour on Friday that Adam was put out of Paradise (the ninth hour as reported in *Cursor Mundi*, 981–88), in exactly that same hour the penitent thief was brought into Paradise (Luke 23:42–46). Finally, we are told, Christ suffered death when he was thirty three years old.

Returning once more to Roman history, Higden describes the signs and wonders given to the gentiles. When our Lord was born, a well of oil sprang beyond the Tiber out of the tavern Emeritoria and ran all day; and a circle was seen about the sun. A whole chapter is devoted to the Emperor Augustus, whose magnificent reign was ordained by God to coincide with the birth of Christ. Augustus was very popular, a man of peace and a steadfast friend. He was a writer (who invented the letter x, a figure of the cross) and a builder. Concerning Rome he said: "I found a city of glazed tile, and now I leave a city of marble." He was a handsome man, but he had vices, especially wrath and greed. He gambled, drank, and was lecherous. Yet certain incidents in his life remind us of the divine purpose of his reign. When the Romans wanted to make him a god, he refused, but nevertheless consulted the sibyl Tiburtina, and she prophesied to him the coming of Christ. Augustus himself saw a vision of the Virgin and Christ-child, at the place in Rome where there is now a church of Our Lady called the Altar of Heaven.

Apart from the emperor's religious importance, Higden seems fascinated by the man himself, and gives several anecdotes illustrating his tolerance and humor. On one occasion a man came to Rome who looked exactly like Augustus, and was brought before him. "Tell me, young man," said the emperor, "was thy mother ever in Rome?" "Nay," he replied, "but my father was very often." Far from being angry, Augustus sent him away with a rich present. Another story tells of a Greek writer who used to compose ditties in praise of Caesar Augustus and give them to him. When he had done this often without any reward, Caesar composed some praises in reply and gave them to the poor writer. The Greek promptly read the emperor's ditty aloud with solemnity, and then offered him money. Whereupon everyone laughed, and Caesar ordered his treasurer to give the Greek his money back, and a great deal more. With these and other endearing anecdotes Higden paints the picture of a ruler who was widely admired in his lifetime, and universally mourned when he died.

The history continues with a chronicle of Roman emperors, interwoven with biblical and legendary materials. Canonical and apocryphal stories go side by side in the march of New Testament narrative. Thus an apocryphal account of the birth and death of Pilate is immediately followed by a very knowledgeable explanation of the beliefs of the three major Jewish sects — the Sadducees, the Pharisees, and the Essenes — with considerable information on the last taken from the Jewish historian Josephus. A very brief life of Christ, taken from the Gospels, is followed by a section on John the Baptist, most of which is devoted to a history of the loss and recovery of his bones, particularly the bone of the finger used to point out Christ in the desert (John 1:29). The reigns of Claudius and Nero provide the background for an apocryphal history of the Apostles and early martyrs of the church, very similar to what we have noted in *Cursor Mundi*, but with additional material drawn from the legendary life of Judas, and the correspondence of Paul and Seneca. The climax of the biblical section of Book IV is a lengthy account, based on Josephus, of the siege of Jerusalem by the Roman emperors Titus and Vespasian, a story popularized in two Middle English romances, *Titus and Vespasian* and the alliterative *Siege of Jerusalem*. With this famous and horrible story, the New Testament portion of this book draws to a close, ending with the death of the emperor Domitian and the return of Saint John from the isle of Patmos.

The remainder of Book IV of the *Polychronicon* is concerned with the history of empire and church, while increasing attention is also devoted to events in Britain up to the time of Vortigern. Higden maintains a balanced view of Rome during this period, not ignoring the persecutions of Christianity but at the same time praising the good emperors. As might be expected, one of his favorites is Trajan, and he gives several anecdotes illustrating the emperor's justice and generosity. "For such great righteousness," he concludes, "it seemth that St. Gregory won his soul out of hell." In this comment Higden alludes to the fame of Trajan as an example of a righteous heathen who was nevertheless saved by the prayers of a pope. The theological basis, however, of Trajan's salvation was a matter often in dispute, as can be seen by the reaction of the translator to Higden's remark: "Trevisa. So it might seem to a man that were worse than wood (=mad), and out of right belief." This criticism calls for an alternative explanation of Trajan's status, but Trevisa does not give us his opinion.

The conversion of Rome to Christianity under Constantine receives its due, but again Higden avoids a one-sided presentation of events. The momentous conversion of the emperor is related, but this is balanced against the adverse effects of the famous "donation" of Constantine, which so enriched the Church that it was turned from spiritual devotion to secular business. In this connection Higden tells a story that was very popular in the later Middle Ages, when the wealth of the monasteries had become a serious problem. "Therefore it is written," he says, "that when Constantine had made that gift to churches then the old enemy (*hostis antiquus*) cried openly in the air, 'This day is venom poured and shed into holy church.'" Since Higden was himself a monk we should perhaps admire his willingness to include this statement at all, and not be too critical of the fact that it is put in the mouth of the devil (the "old enemy"). Nevertheless it is interesting that in at least one manuscript of Trevisa's translation, the phrase "old enemy" is changed to read "angel of heaven," thus giving divine sanction to criticism of the wealth of the monasteries.

With Roman history itself Higden has interwoven several strands of ecclesiastical history, developments that have been touched on in earlier chapters of this study. Thus he mentions the various translations of the Bible, notably the projects of Aquila, Symmachus, Theodotion, Origen, and Jerome. In like manner various early leaders of the Church are singled out for their contributions to the development of the Mass and the clarification of church doctrine. Above all, Higden includes an extended roll call of the early saints and martyrs, many of whom we have met already in the pages of *The Golden Legend.* Among these are the seven sleepers of Ephesus, Saint Maurice, Saint Sebastian, and Saint Agnes. We are told also of the heroism of Saint Alban, serving as a reminder of the beginnings of Christianity in Britain, a nation which gains in prominence as the fortunes of Rome decline.

Book V: Anglo-Saxon Settlement (449) to the Danish Occupation (871)

The struggle between the Britons and the Saxons begins with the reign of the British King Vortigern, and Higden, following the lead of Gildas and Bede, stresses that the people of Britain at this time were corrupted and ripe for overthrow. In the time of Vortigern (he says), there were full harvests and great prosperity, but instead of giving thanks the people turned to lechery and evil-doing. This infection spread not only in society at large, but also among the members of the flock of our Lord. Such was the curse of affluence that the true man was treated as a traitor, and men gave themselves to drunkenness, strife, and envy. Suddenly a great mortal pestilence fell on men of evil life, so that the living were scarcely able to bury the dead. This led to an even more terrible vengeance later, for it was just after this that Vortigern and his counsellors invited the Saxons from beyond the sea to come and help them against their enemies. Thus God chose to punish the people for their sins.

The basis for this passage is Bede's *Ecclesiastical History* (I, 14), but it is also a good illustration of salvation history that remained popular throughout the Middle Ages. In Higden's own lifetime the cycle of prosperity, sin, and punishment was graphically re-enacted in the glorious victories of the Hundred Years' War, the economic oppression of the reign of Edward III, and the sudden onslaught of the Black Death in England in 1349. Would the people recognize the hand of God and repent of their sins? Or would the survivors merely say, *Let us eat and drink; for tomorrow we shall die* (Isa. 22:12–14)? In his apocalyptic view of British history, Higden seems to have set forth a warning to his contemporaries.

Since the influence of the *Polychronicon* on other literature of the period is quite extensive, we will pause here only long enough to notice a single instance where Higden's historical view is reflected in the apocalyptic ending to the B-text of *Piers the Plowman*. In the final section of this poem the army of Antichrist attacks Holy Church, and society is punished for its sins by wave after wave of the plague, which kills great numbers of the population. Then Conscience, who is leader of the defenders of Holy Church, prays for the plague to cease, in hope that the people will repent of their sins:

> Fortune then flattered the few that were alive,
> And promised them long life, and lechery he sent
> Among all manner of men, wedded and unwedded,
> And gathered a great host all against Conscience.

There follows an allegorical action showing how various of the deadly sins are indulged in by the populace at large. Good Faith is forced to flee, and Falsehood abides. In this poetry we hear echoes of Higden, Bede, and ultimately of biblical apocalypse itself (Rev. 9:20–21): *And the rest of the men which were not killed by these plagues yet repented not of the works of their hands. . . . : neither repented they of their murders, nor of their sorceries, nor of their fornication, nor of their thefts.*

After the death of Vortigern, the Saxon settlement continues at a rapid pace, slowed only by the heroic resistance of Arthur, leader of the Britons. Here Higden necessarily follows Geoffrey of Monmouth for the story of Arthur, and yet at the same time, interestingly, he expresses skepticism as to its authenticity. In this connection he quotes the famous dictum of William of Malmesbury that Arthur, of whom the Britons tell idle tales, is worthy to be praised in true histories, and recounts also the "discovery" of his body at Glastonbury in the time of Henry II. But if Arthur had conquered thirty kingdoms as Geoffrey says (wonders Higden), why is this not related in other histories? And why are not other men also mentioned? Who is Frollo, and what about the emperor Lucius, overcome by Arthur? It is a wonder that Geoffrey of Monmouth praises so many people who are not even mentioned elsewhere. Higden's solution to this problem is significant. But perhaps (he says) it is the custom of each nation to overpraise its own heroes, as the Greeks do Alexander, the Romans Octavian, the English their Richard Lion-heart, Frenchmen their Charlemagne, and Britons their Arthur. As Josephus says, it is done to embellish the story, to please the reader, or to praise the historian's own race. When we consider that the question of Geoffrey's authenticity has been argued even in modern times, Higden displays here a remarkable sophistication.

On the other hand, Higden was not a Celt, and so his ox was not gored by the denial of Arthurian tradition. Our translator John Trevisa, however, born in the Celtic hinterlands of Cornwall, might be expected to have a different attitude, and indeed he does. Following the critique of Geoffrey, Trevisa appends one of his longest commentaries. William of Malmesbury (he says) tells an idle tale of his own without evidence; and Ranulph Higden's arguments against Geoffrey and Arthur cannot stand scrutiny. Saint John in his gospel tells many things that Matthew, Mark, and Luke speak not of in their gospels: *ergo*, John's gospel is not to be believed? So Geoffrey's history is not disproved if others speak darkly, or make no mention of Arthur, especially when some of these writers were Arthur's enemies. Also Higden himself remarks (III, 9) it is no wonder that William of Malmesbury was deceived, since he had not read Geoffrey's British book. And still, even if Geoffrey had never spoken of Arthur, many noble nations speak of Arthur and his deeds. It may well be that Arthur, like others, is often overpraised; but true statements are never the worse, though mad men tell idle tales. Thus some mad men say that Arthur shall come again, and be king of Britain; but that is an idle tale, and so are many others told about him as well as other men.

Trevisa's impassioned defense of Arthur may not be due entirely to Celtic bias, for in other passages unrelated to Arthurian tradition we see him reacting sharply to Higden's skepticism. The latter reports the discovery, for example, of our Lord's seamless robe in the Vale of Jehoshaphat; it was found by Gregory, Bishop of Antioch, and brought to Jerusalem. But Higden goes on to observe that this disagrees with the story of the death of Pilate, who is said to have been immune to condemnation as long as he was wearing the seamless robe of Christ. If Pilate had this robe with him at Rome, he says, it seems that it was not afterward taken hence and brought again into the Vale of Jehoshaphat; or if it *was* found in the Vale of Jehoshaphat, then Pilate did not have it with him at Rome. To which Trevisa replies: It was no more mastery to bring that robe out of

[233]

Rome into the Vale of Jehoshaphat, than it was to bring the robe out of Jerusalem into Rome; and so it may well stand that Pilate had on that robe at Rome, and that it was afterward found in the Vale of Jehoshaphat. It is interesting to find Trevisa here defending the veracity of legend in something of a fundamentalist spirit. In this sense his view of history seems even more conservative than Higden's.

On the other hand there is evidence that Trevisa read the *Polychronicon* with a lively sense of its relevance to the turbulent events of his own time. His translation was made in the mid 1380s, shortly after the violence of the Peasants' Revolt (1381), a time of riots, burnings, and assassinations. One is conscious of this in reading Higden's account of the assassination of the Anglian king Siegebert by a certain earl and his brother, who had been excommunicated by Saint Chad. When asked why they had done the deed, the assassins replied that the king was too easy toward his enemies, and would lightly forgive wrongs and trespasses. At this point in the narrative Trevisa adds a comment of his own: "It is sooth that cursed men hate good men and their good deeds: and so the cursed earl slew the king, because he was gracious and good." Could Trevisa be thinking here of Simon Sudbury, Archbishop of Canterbury, by whom he was ordained priest on June 8, 1370? Sudbury was beheaded by a London mob in June 1381, and Trevisa's patron, Thomas IV Lord Berkeley, for whom the *Polychronicon* translation was being made, was one of those commissioned to investigate the murder.

Of course Higden himself wrote his history with a strong sense of the connection between past and present. Though a loyal monk, he was concerned about the decline of the monastic ideal, and no doubt viewed with alarm, rather than amusement, the worldliness of his brothers, as Chaucer describes it in his prologue to the Canterbury Tales. This problem was no doubt very much in Higden's mind as he read Bede's praise (III, 26) of the spirituality of Bishop Colman and his brothers. In that time (he says), doctors were busy to serve God and not the world, the heart and not the belly. Therefore the religious habit was then in great honor, so that a monk or a clerk would be gladly received; and men that went by the way prayed his blessing; and they went about the ways and streets for no other cause than to preach and teach and baptize, and for the salvation of a man's soul. And they would take no possessions to build abbeys, unless it were proffered them, and they were driven to accept it by force from the lords. The tone of this passage is partly one of nostalgia, a yearning for the lost prestige of the monastic orders, and partly one of sober rebuke, and exhortation to return to the spirituality of the older tradition.

But Higden and Trevisa do not always agree on what constitutes authentic spirituality. In a passage on the life of St. Aldhelm, for instance, Higden tells how the good man, when he was tempted by the flesh, would respond to this challenge by holding a fair maid with him in his bed while he recited the psalter from beginning to end. This feat of ascetic derring-do seems to have appealed to the imagination of medieval man, for it re-appears in the lives of other saints, notably Saint Bernard, and, indeed, it is found in secular Arthurian literature among the adventures of none other than Sir Lancelot. But John Trevisa will have none of it: "Save reverence of St. Aldhelm, this seemeth none holiness nor wisdom, but pure folly, both for himself and for peril and dread of temptation of the woman, as it may be proved both by authority and by reason."

Though the history of Britain has begun to overshadow all else in book V of the *Polychronicon*, Higden does devote an interesting chapter to Charlemagne. In it we find the story of Aygolandus, pagan prince of Spain, who came to Charles to be christened. The prince noticed that all at the royal table were finely clothed and pleasingly fed, while nearby there were thirteen poor men on the ground being given poor and simple food without any table; so he asked who these were. "These thirteen be God's messengers," was the reply, "who pray for us and remind us of the number of Christ's disciples." "Your law is not right," quoth the prince, "that suffereth God's messengers to be thus poorly treated; he serveth badly his Lord that thus receiveth his servants." And so, taking offense at this, he despised baptism and went home again. But Charles afterward honored poor men the more. Something about the story displeased Trevisa, who adds this comment: "Aygolandus was a lewd ghost [stupid fellow], and lewdly moved as the devil taught, and blinded him, so that he did not know that men should be served as their estate asketh [according to social rank]."

One is reminded by this story, and Trevisa's comment on it, of the ceremonial nature of medieval feasts, and the emphasis placed on respect for the social hierarchy in the seating of guests, a concern that is reflected in the poetry of the period, notably the alliterative *Cleanness* and *Piers the Plowman*. In the latter poem, the Dreamer is assured that there is a hierarchical seating arrangement at the heavenly feast, and that the penitent thief, for instance, will be set lower than St. John and other saints (B-text, XII, 198–202). Later on the Dreamer is invited to an allegorical dinner by Conscience, and is seated with Patience at a side table, while the place of honor goes to a learned friar (B-text, XIII, 21ff.).

Higden goes on to tell how Charlemagne founded as many abbeys as there are letters in the alphabet. In each of these abbeys, in the order of their foundation, he set a letter in gold, each weighing a hundred pounds turonian (of Tours). This reference leads Trevisa to add an interesting footnote on weights and measures: "God wot what weight that should be! But, by a statute of the University of Oxford, when any man is sent there to commence in any faculty, he must swear that he will not spend at his commencement more than three thousand groats turonian. The turonian groat is worth something less than an English groat; for at Breisach-upon-the-Rhine I have received in change eleven turonian groats for a ducat, which is worth half an English noble." He goes on to distinguish two turonian weights, and to speculate further about the value of the pounds referred to in Charlemagne's bequest. The true value of the turonian pound need not concern us, but we may be grateful for the additional evidence of Trevisa's travels on the continent, and his knowledge of Oxford statutes. The need for a limit on expenditures at Oxford, incidentally, is well illustrated in the history of the Berkeley family. Eudo de Berkeley, an ancestor of Trevisa's patron, began his studies at the university in 1327, as we are informed by the seventeenth century family historian, John Smyth, in his *Lives of the Berkeleys* (I, 27): "At whose inception there, (soe is the word,) the twentieth of Edward the second, the parson of Slimbridge, (which I conceive to bee his Vncle James,) presented him with a boare, which in the feedinge had eaten one Quarter and two Bushells of beanes."

The flavor of the chapter on Charlemagne is well conveyed in the story Higden tells in connection with his death. The day that Charles died in Vienna, Archbishop Turpin was saying his prayers, when he saw a company of black knights going to take Charles's soul. The churchman conjured the last of them to come back when they had finished, and tell him how they sped. Later, when the fiend returned, Turpin asked him, "What have you done?" to which the fiend replied: "We have weighed Charles' soul; but that James of Spain, who was beheaded, laid so many stones and trees in the balance that Charles' good deeds had the mastery, weighing more than his evil deeds; and so we have brought back nothing with us." Then, lest the point be missed: "Charles," quoth the fiend, "used to build many churches in honor of St. James." In such stories as this we find a curious blend of hagiography and romance.

One more example of Higden as social historian occurs near the end of book V (chap. 32). After the death of Saint Edmund, king and martyr, at the hands of the Danes in 870, the king's brother retired to the monastery of Cerne in Dorset, an institution later to be famous as the home of the biblical scholar Ælfric. Mention of this famous place leads Higden once more to reflect on the subsequent decline of the monasteries. The Abbey of Cerne flourished as long as its members were truly God's servants, he says; but in our time covetousness and pride have so changed everything in England, that bequests to abbeys in old times are now more wasted in gluttony and outrage of the owners than in sustinence and help of needy men and guests. In Higden's time this deplorable situation raised in some men's minds the issue of responsibility: were those who gave their wealth to monasteries responsible for its misuse by the monks? Not at all, says Higden: "But certainly the givers shall not lose their meed [reward] for their will and their intent is weighed in God's balance."

Trevisa offers no comment here, but the issue was an important one for him and for his patron, since the Berkeley family had for many years given generously to monastic foundations, particularly to Saint Augustine's in Bristol. John Smyth, in his *Lives of the Berkeleys* (I, 338) praises the "doctrine" of John Trevisa, and refers to the passage from the *Polychronicon* quoted above. It is possible that Trevisa had some influence through his translation of Higden, since we learn from Smyth (II, 19) that Thomas IV Lord Berkeley (Trevisa's patron) withheld the generous bequests to the monasteries which had been so frequently bestowed on them by his ancestors.

As might be expected, the issue of monastic wealth raised by Higden shows up also in the literature of the period. *Piers the Plowman* again provides a good example, in a sermon by Anima (Soul) delivered to the Dreamer (B-text, XV, 304–36). The religious orders should live austerely, says Anima, and set an example for laymen, instead of living off the fat of the land. As it is written: *Doth the wild ass bray when he hath grass? or loweth the ox over his fodder?* (Job 6:5). If laymen knew the commentary on this verse they would be more reluctant to sign away their property to monks or canons.

From these few examples of social history in Book V of the *Polychronicon* a pattern begins to emerge. As the narrative approaches "modern" times, Higden shows an increasing consciousness of the ways in which social and religious issues impinge on his interpretation of events and his description of institutions and doctrine. And where Higden himself is silent, we can expect to hear occasionally from John Trevisa, opinionated translator and unrestrained critic of Higden and anyone else with whom he happens to disagree.

Book VI: King Alfred to the Norman Conquest

Higden's biography of King Alfred, which opens Book VI of the *Polychronicon*, contains much that is traditional, but also occasional details that are new. We are told how he learned to read at the age of twelve, and how he memorized Saxon poetry; of his devotion to study and his translation of the psalms into English; and of his encouragement of scholarship and education, particularly his role in persuading his friend Wærferth, Bishop of Worcester, to translate Gregory's *Dialogues*. Higden is the first to claim Alfred as the founder of the University of Oxford: "Therefore by counsel of Neot the abbot, whom he visited full oft, he was the first that ordained common school at Oxford of diverse arts and sciences, and procured freedom and privileges in many articles to that city." St. Neot figures importantly in Alfred's biography, and his legendary life is intriguingly depicted in the stained glass windows of Saint Neot's church near Liskeard in Cornwall. Did the Cornishman John Trevisa have any special knowledge of the role of Alfred or St. Neot in the establishment of the university? If so, he does not tell us what it is. But in his *Dialogue on Translation,* prefixed to the *Polychronicon,* he refers confidently to King Alfred as founder of the University of Oxford. This dubious assertion went unquestioned until the sixteenth century, when it was challenged by the Cambridge scholar, John Caius.

A prominent feature of Book VI is Higden's concern with the supernatural, particularly life after death. This first appears in the account of Alfred's death, derived from William of Malmesbury. When the king died, he was buried in the cathedral church at Winchester; but when the canons complained that the body walked about at night from house to house, the next king, Edward, removed his father's body and placed it in the new abbey. How could such things be? The explanation is interesting: this is an old superstition of Englishmen, that after a man's death the body walks about by moving of the fiend, an idea borrowed from Virgil, who speaks in the *Aeneid* of shapes that seem to flit about when death comes (X, 641).

Another tradition relating to life after death is attached to the wicked king Edwin (Eadwig) who died in 960 and was buried at Winchester. According to Higden, his soul was delivered out of hell by the prayer of Saint Dunstan, and translated to the lot of souls that do penance on the way to salvation, that is, to purgatory. This idea had become theologically precarious in the fourteenth century, when debates were raging over such issues as the fate of the righteous heathen, and the relative merits of the ethical and sacramental means of personal salvation. Not surprisingly, John Trevisa interrupts his translation with the following comment:

> Here take heed, Christian men, of the meaning, for the words be perilously set. Therefore have mind now of two manner hells: in the one was Adam, Abraham, Isaac, and Jacob, and other holy forefathers that died before Christ. Into that hell Christ alighted after his passion, and brought with him thence the holy fathers that were there. The other hell is a place for them that shall be damned forevermore: he that cometh in that hell shall never after be saved, neither come out of pain. But as men say in common speech that a thief is delivered from hanging and from the gallows though he come not there, if he is delivered out of the power of those that would lead him to the gallows and hang him thereupon, so in a manner of speaking he that is delivered out of the fiend's power, that would bring him in hell, is delivered out of hell, though he come not there. So meaneth the prophet in the psalter, who saith: *Thou hast delivered my soul out of the lower hell* [Ps. 86:13].

Trevisa's simile of the thief delivered from the gallows is interestingly paralleled in the Harrowing of Hell episode in *Piers the Plowman*, where Christ addresses Satan, announcing that He has come to rescue mankind, and likening Himself to a king who looks upon a condemned criminal, thereby granting him a reprieve from the gallows (B-text, XVIII, 377–91).

The specter of ecclesiastical corruption is raised once more by Higden when he describes the reforms brought about during the reign of King Edgar (960–75) through the leadership of Archbishop Dunstan. The king punished the wicked and cherished the good, repaired churches, and in many places he put away clerks that lived in outrage, and put monks in their place. This last point is too much for that clerk John Trevisa, who comments: "In that, saving the reverence of Edgar, he was lewdly [ignorantly] moved, while there were other clerks who lived well enough."

Higden goes on to list the numerous monasteries founded by King Edgar, among which was the new abbey at Winchester. Here we are told that the clerks lived in luxury, neglecting divine services, spending the Church's money on themselves, and hiring vicars for a mere pittance to discharge their responsibilities for them. After repeated warnings, the king threw out these clerks and assigned their income to the starving vicars. When the vicars became even more corrupt than their predecessors, the king finally had to throw them out and put monks in their place. No doubt for Higden, this seemed a fitting and final solution to the problem.

But our translator, Trevisa, is scarcely able to finish the story without intruding his own angry comment on the status of the monasteries in his own time:

And now for the most part monks be worst of all, for they be too rich, and that maketh them to take more heed about secular business than ghostly devotion. Therefore, as it is said before [IV, 26] by Jerome, since Holy Church increased in possessions it has decreased in virtues. Therefore secular lords should take away the superfluity of their possessions and give it to them that have need, or else when they know that, they be cause and maintainers of their evil deeds, since they help not to amend it when it is in their power, whatever covetous priests say. For it were more alms to take away the superfluity of their possessions now, than it was at the first foundation to give them what they needed.

Here Trevisa failed to sign his name, but there can be little doubt that these words express his passionate conviction. As we have seen, there is some evidence that he may have influenced his patron, Thomas IV, to withhold the bequests to monasteries traditionally made by the Berkeley family.

Once again when we turn to *Piers the Plowman*, Trevisa's words are echoed in the thoughts of the poet. The relevant passage occurs immediately following Anima's reference to the poisonous donation of Constantine. When Constantine endowed Holy Church with lands and income, he says, an angel cried on high, "This day hath the Church drunk venom, and those that have the power of Peter are poisoned!" Anima then proposes a remedy: since possessions are a hindrance, the best medicine would be for lords to take them away, and let them live by tithes (B-text, XV, 524–29):

> A medecyne mote ther-to, that may amende prelates,
> That sholde preye for the pees; possessioun hem letteth,
> Take her landes, ye lordes, and let hem lyve by dymes.
> If possessioun be poysoun and imparfit hem make,
> Good were to dischargen hem for holicherche sake,
> And purgen hem of poysoun or more perile falle.

This revolutionary proposal, espoused in Trevisa's day by John Wyclif, was adopted some 150 years later by Henry VIII as a major policy of the Reformation. In the fourteenth century, however, it was an idea whose time had not yet come.

At the same time, though Trevisa's antagonism toward the monasteries is obvious, it would be wrong to suppose that Higden was insensitive to the defects that called forth these criticisms. His awareness simply takes a different form. One can see this, for instance, in his description of the "golden age" of St. Dunstan (VI, 10):

> The order of monks was thrifty in that time, for it had religious rulers, clear of science and of knowledge; and so between the accord of the good living of the king and of the archbishop, clerks had choice whether they would amend their life or bid their benefice farewell, and leave dwelling places to better men than they were. And thus should there be no discord between the fairness of the house and the lives of them that dwell therein. Then the fields answered the tillers with plenty of corn and of fruit; every grove shone with trees full of fruit [cf. Amos 9:13–15; Hosea 2:21–23]. The elements were clear and pleasing; scarcely was there any distempering of the weather; and in that time both war and pestilence were far away.

Here one sees the philosophy of history expressed in the biblical book of Judges: the land has peace as long as the people call upon the name of the Lord.

Apart from its biblical philosophy of history, the *Polychronicon* owed its great popularity in large part to a simple narrative appeal. The chapter on Hardeknute and the emperor Henry III (VI, 21) is a good illustration of this. Here we are told (from William of Malmesbury) about the marriage of Hardeknute's beautiful sister, Gunhild, to Henry, and the charge of adultery that was later brought against her. She was dramatically cleared of the charge by a child she had brought from England, who fought as her champion against a giant and overcame him. The boy's victory was regarded as a manifest case of divine intervention to vindicate the queen in judicial combat, and had all the popular appeal of David's victory over Goliath. The story was widespread in Europe in the Middle Ages, especially in England and Scandinavia. It survives to modern times in the ballad of "Sir Aldingar" (Child no. 59), the name given to the false accuser. Before the battle, the little boy speaks out boldly:

> Hee sayd, Come hither, Sir Aldingar,
> Thou seemest as bigge as a ffooder [barrel];

> I trust to God, ere I have done with thee,
> God will send to us an auger.

The auger is reminiscent of David's sling, though it is, of course, merely a figure of speech here. The child wins by cutting off Sir Aldingar's legs at the knee, and the dying man confesses publicly that his accusation was false. "Falsing never doth well," he says.

Higden takes several other stories from William of Malmesbury about the emperor Henry III. One involves a sister of the emperor who was a nun, but who had fallen in love with a cleric of the court. Henry loved his sister, and kept close watch over her, but despite his precautions one night the lovers slept together undetected. During the night snow fell, and in the early morning the emperor arose to relieve himself. Happening by chance to look out the window, he saw his sister carrying the cleric on her back across the courtyard. He said nothing, however, until a bishopric was vacant, and then he said to the cleric: "Take this bishopric, and look that henceforth thou ride not on a woman's back." Later, when an abbey of nuns was vacant, he said to his sister, "Take this abbey, and look that thou bear never any cleric a-riding." Having been thus found out, we are told, the lovers abstained forever after.

On another occasion the emperor stopped at a small chapel beside the forest to hear Mass. While listening to the divine service, he noticed that the priest was very foul and unattractive, and he wondered to himself why God, who was so fair, would allow so foul a creature to handle His sacraments. When they reached the part of the Mass which begins, "Know ye that the Lord, He is God," the priest, as if rebuking the dullness and sloth of his altar boy, looking straight at the emperor, continued and said, *It is he that hath made us and not we ourselves* (Ps. 100:3). Smitten by the aptness of this verse, the emperor soon made the priest a bishop.

In a subsequent chapter (VI, 25) Higden inserts the legend of the witch of Berkeley, which must have interested Trevisa because of its locale if for no other reason. The earliest known version comes from William of Malmesbury, who reports it as an eyewitness account dated about 1065. A woman at Berkeley who had practiced evil crafts was feasting one day when her pet chough (*corvicula*) croaked louder than usual. When she heard that, the knife fell from her hand and her face turned pale. Sighing and groaning she said, "This day my plow has come to the last furrow." While she was

[242]

speaking a messenger came and said that the house had fallen on her son, and that he and all his family were dead (cf. Job 1:18–19). Calling her surviving children, a son and a daughter who had entered religious orders, to her bedside, the dying woman confessed that she had dabbled in witchcraft, and gave detailed instructions for her funeral in the hope that she might escape damnation. They are to sew her body in a hart's skin, place it in a stone coffin, seal it with lead and iron, and bind it with three chains. Masses are to be sung continually, night and day, and if the body lies undisturbed for three nights, then the fourth day they are to bury it in the earth. When the woman died these instructions were carried out to the letter, but to no purpose. While the psalms were being sung, fiends smashed through the doors and broke two of the chains. The third night, about cock-crow, a huge devil commanded the body to rise, broke the last of the bonds, and carried her out of the church. He set her on a black horse that neighed before the doors, and carried her off, while her cries were heard for four miles around. Though this be wonderful (says Higden), he who hath read Gregory's *Dialogues* will not deem that it might not be true. Nor does Trevisa express any skepticism here. Indeed, the legend has survived to modern times, and can be seen at present depicted episodically on several prayer cushions in Berkeley Church. Belief in such manifestations has of course dimmed through the years, but I suspect that the motifs survive, secularized, in ballads such as "The Wife Wrapt in Wether's Skin" (Child no. 277), where the idea of exorcism seems to be adapted for use in the taming of a shrew.

Book VII: Norman Conquest to Higden's Time (1352)

In the seventh and last book of the *Polychronicon*, as Higden approaches his own century, the history tends increasingly to become a chronical of events. Like most other historians, Higden found it difficult to see his own time in perspective. Yet in some indefinable way the context of universal history, in which current events are placed, tends to impart an apocalyptic tone to the narrative. This is particularly true of accounts of natural disasters like the plague, storms, famine, and floods, which stand in mute contrast to the beautiful days (for example) of Archbishop Dunstan, when the plowman overtook the reaper and the mountains dropped sweet wine. But our journey with Ranulph Higden has been a long one, and there is space here for only a few examples from this seventh book, most of which I have chosen because they relate importantly to literary tradition.

The undertone of Apocalypse can be detected quite early in Higden's account of the Norman conquest. King William's making of the Doomsday Book is likened to David's ruinous effort to take a census of Israel (2 Sam. 24): "the land was grieved," says Higden, "with many mischiefs and mishaps that befell because of that deed." And he concludes that the miseries of the Conqueror's reign were brought about by the will of God. When William was king, he observed, there was scarcely a lord in England who was English. For they were made slaves, so that it was a shame to be called an Englishman. To bear down and destroy the English, God had ordained cruel men and stern (the Normans), who are of such a nature that when they have borne down their enemies, then they bear down themselves. We have seen this philosophy expressed before. Conquerors tend to self-destruct, and their conquests are essentially meaningless unless viewed in the light of divine purpose.

It may be worth noting that the monastic viewpoint of Higden persists to the end of his work, and that it continues to be challenged by his translator, John Trevisa. In Book VI Higden incurred Trevisa's wrath when he suggested that Paternus, who chose to die rather than leave his burning monastery, was motivated by love of martyrdom. Trevisa: "In that doing Paternus the monk seemeth a lewd ghost [stupid fellow], who knew not the cause and circumstance of true martyrdom; for there is no true martyrdom but it be by maintaining of truth and withstanding of wrong and of sin. But God grant if it be His will, that Paternus be not damned for his blind devotion."

A second clash between historian and translator occurs in Book VII (chap. 7), where Higden tells how Roger, Earl of Shrewbury, when he was ill and on the point of dying, had himself made a monk, presumably to improve his chances of salvation. Trevisa: "A wise man would ween that Earl Roger had as much meed [reward] that he was a monk, as Malkyn of her maidenhood, whom no man would have, and not a deal more." This trenchant use of the proverbial Malkyn is unusual. She is normally a wanton, similar to the modern "farmer's daughter," as Chaucer's Harry Bailly obviously regards her in the *Canterbury Tales* (II, 30–31). But Trevisa depicts her as an unattractive girl, whose virginity is not necessarily the consequence of her virtue. A similar use may be seen in *Piers the Plowman*, where the poet is being critical of rich men who are loyal church-goers, but who fail to share their wealth with the poor (A-text, I, 155–158):

> But-yif ye love lelly and lene the pore,
> Of such good as God sent goodlyche parten,
> Ye have no more meryt in masse ne in oures
> Thanne Malkyn of hire maidenhood, that no man desireth.

Thus both the earl who becomes a monk, and the rich man who goes regularly to Mass, are awarded the merit of Malkyn, when their religious profession is not matched by deeds of charity.

Much space is devoted to the martyrdom of Thomas à Becket (VII, 22) and the subsequent decline of the fortunes of Henry II. One of the sins of the king was the imprisonment of Queen Eleanor, and his affair with the beautiful Rosamond. For this fair wench, says Higden, the king made at Woodstock a chamber wondrously devised in the manner of Daedalus (i.e., a labyrinth), lest the queen find a way to take Rosamond. But the wench dies soon, and is buried in the chapter house at Godstow beside Oxford, with this inscription on her tomb:

Hic jacet in tumba rosa mundi, non rosa munda.
Non redolet, sed olet, quae redolere solet,

which Trevisa translates:

Here lieth in tomb the rose of the world, not a clean rose.
It smelleth not sweet, but it stinketh, that was wont to smell full sweet.

Higden concludes with a description of her tomb which is wondrously carved. In a later chapter (VII, 25) the anonymous fifteenth century translator adds a further passage relating to Rosamond. In the year 1192 Saint Hugh, Bishop of Lincoln, came on a visitation to the monastery of Godstow and saw a marvelous tomb there, before the high altar, covered with cloths of silk, with lamps and tapers burning about it. Informed that this was the tomb of Rosamond, friend of King Henry II, the bishop ordered her tomb removed, and commanded that she be buried outside with the other people, as an example for women to avoid adultery and lechery. This unsentimental view of Rosamond tended to prevail in the medieval period. In *Piers the Plowman*, for example, the poet concludes (B-text, XII, 49): "The beauty of her body in badness she dispended."

A final passage from the *Polychronicon* (VII, 23) is of interest because it touches on Arthurian legend. From Gerald of Wales Higden takes an account of the discovery of Arthur's grave during the reign of Henry II. At Glastonbury (he reports) between two pillars, Arthur's body was found buried deep in the earth. And so he was taken up and translated honorably into the church, and laid in a tomb of marble stone. With him was found a cross of lead, on which was carved an inscription: "Hic jacet sepultus inclitus rex Arthurus cum Wennerva uxore sua secunda in insula Avalona," which Trevisa translates: "Here lieth buried the noble king Arthur with his second wife Guinevere in the island of Avalon." The bones were laid in the grave so that the two parts of the grave toward the head contained the man's bones, and the third part toward the feet contained the woman's bones, where also the yellow hair of the woman's tresses was found whole and sound, with all its original freshness of color and hue. But a monk touched it covetously with his hand, and it fell all to dust.

Higden goes on to explain that King Henry had heard from a Breton singer that Arthur's body would be found in a hollow oak about fifteen feet deep in the earth. The skeleton is described in detail, including the evidence of head-wounds, and the unusual length of his shin bone. Henry ordered an inscription placed over the grave, recording the circumstances of the discovery. It is not difficult to see in this incident echoes of the lives of the saints, including the "invention" and veneration of their remains. In this case the saint, King Arthur, was secular, and his invention in the reign of Henry II was no doubt a political event. At the same time it was a vindication of that great creative historian, Geoffrey of Monmouth, and a promise of things to come in the evolution of Arthurian romance in England.

Bibliographical Essay

CHAPTER ONE. *The Bible in the Middle Ages*

Of fundamental importance for this entire subject is *The Cambridge History of the Bible*, vol. 2: *The West from the Fathers to the Reformation*, ed. G. W. H. Lampe (Cambridge: Cambridge University Press, 1969). The first five chapters are concerned with the ancient versions, text, and transmission of the Bible, and subsection 4 of chapter VI deals with the Bible in liturgical use. For the discovery of Codex Sinaiticus, see Ludwig Schneller, *Search on Sinai: The Story of Tischendorf's Life and the Search for a Lost Manuscript*, trans. Dorothee Schröder (London: Epworth Press, 1939).

Two excellent articles, with photographs in color, tell the story of the monastery of Saint Catherine on Mount Sinai: George H. Forsyth, "Island of Faith in the Sinai Wilderness," *National Geographic*, 125 (Jan. 1964): 80–106; and Kurt Weitzmann, "Mount Sinai's Holy Treasures," *ibid.*, pp. 107–27. More recently appeared a study by Weitzmann (and others), *Icons from Southeastern Europe and Sinai*, trans. R. E. Wolf from *Ikone sa Balkana* (London: Thames & Hudson, 1968).

There is no better introduction to the history of the text and transmission of the Bible than Stanley Rypins, *The Book of Thirty Centuries* (New York: Macmillan, 1951). Also useful are the relevant entries in *The Interpreter's Dictionary of the Bible*, ed. George A. Buttrick, 4 vols. (New York: Abingdon Press, 1962). Among the innumerable books on the Dead Sea scrolls, I recommend Theodore H. Gaster, *The Dead Sea Scriptures* (New York: Doubleday, 1956), both for its concise but informative introduction, and for its inclusion of translations of the most important texts. Other books I have found useful are: M. R. James, *The Apocryphal New Testament* (Oxford: Clarendon Press, 1924); *The Pilgrimage of Etheria*, trans. M. L. McClure and

C. L. Feltoe (London: Macmillan, 1919), and there has recently appeared another translation by George E. Gingras, *Egeria: Diary of a Pilgrimage* (New York: Newman Press, 1970 [Ancient Christian Writers, no. 38]); Helen Waddell, *The Desert Fathers* (London: Constable, 1936); Herbert Musurillo, *Symbolism and the Christian Imagination* (Dublin: Helicon Press, 1962); *Butler's Lives of the Saints*, revised by Herbert Thurston and Donald Attwater, 4 vols. (New York: Kenedy, 1956–59); Beverly Boyd, *Chaucer and the Liturgy* (Philadelphia: Dorrance, 1967); *The Golden Legend, or Lives of the Saints, as Englished by William Caxton*, ed. F. S. Ellis (London: J. M. Dent, 1900 [Temple Classics, 7 vols.]); Oscar G. Farmer, *Fairford Church and Its Stained Glass Windows*, 8th ed. ([Fairford], 1968); D. E. Nineham (ed.), *The Church's Use of the Bible, Past and Present* (London: S.P.C.K., 1963); and N. F. Blake, "The Biblical Additions in Caxton's 'Golden Legend,'" *Traditio*, 25 (1969): 231–47. I am particularly indebted to Mr. Richard Hamer of Christ Church, Oxford, for freely putting at my disposal his extensive knowledge of the texts and versions of the *Golden Legend*.

CHAPTER TWO. *Medieval Exegesis*

This is a vast subject, and this chapter only scratches the surface. For an excellent bibliography, of much larger scope than the present study, consult *Typology and Early American Literature*, ed. Sacvan Bercovitch (Amherst: University of Massachusetts Press, 1972), pp. 245–337. *The Cambridge History of the Bible*, vol. 2, already cited, is very useful, in particular the sixth chapter, "The Exposition and Exegesis of Scripture." My treatment of this subject may seem biased in that I tend to imply the superiority of the historical approach to Scripture, although I believe my admiration for "moral Gregory" will be evident. There can be no doubt that modern historical interpretation emerged triumphant in the sixteenth century, though some perceptive commentators foresaw the dangers of exclusive concern for literal interpretation. In this connection note particularly Erasmus, *Enchiridion*, trans. Raymond Himelick (Bloomington: Indiana University Press, 1963), esp. ch. 3, pp. 46–58. Today, in the midst of the flourishing of the historical method, it is interesting to observe signs of dissatisfaction and a desire to return to an emphasis on moral interpretation. For a summons to what might be called neo-tropology, see Walter Wink, *The Bible in Human Transformation: Toward a New Paradigm for Biblical Study* (Philadelphia: Fortress Press, 1973).

Medieval scholarship likewise evinces a growing appreciation of early Biblical exegesis. Of fundamental importance here is Henri de Lubac, *Exégèse Médiévale: Les Quatre Sens de L'Écriture*, 4 vols. (Paris: Aubier, 1959–64). For a sympathetic and expert use of exegesis in the study of literature, see D. W. Robertson, Jr., *A Preface to Chaucer: Studies in Medieval Perspectives* (Princeton, N.J.: Princeton University Press, 1962). An excellent book stressing the emergence of an historical approach to Scripture in the later Middle Ages is Beryl Smalley, *The Study of the Bible in the Middle Ages*

(Oxford: Basil Blackwell, 1952). Erich Auerbach's essay, "Figura," is conveniently available in English in a paperback with the title *Scenes from the Drama of European Literature* (New York: Meridian Books, 1959). A good survey is available in Jean Daniélou, *From Shadows to Reality: Studies in the Biblical Typology of the Fathers*, trans. Dom Wulstan Hibberd (London: Burns and Oates, 1961). For the influence of Rashi of Troyes on Nicholas of Lyra, consult Herman Hailperin, *Rashi and the Christian Scholars* (Pittsburgh, Pa.: University of Pittsburgh Press, 1963); also *Rashi, Commentaries on the Pentateuch*, trans. Chaim Pearl (New York: Viking Press, 1970). The English translation of Gregory's commentary on *Job*, which I have used with only occasional changes, is *Morals on the Book of Job by S. Gregory the Great*, trans. J. Bliss, 3 vols. in 4 (London: J. H. Parker, 1844–50 [A Library of the Fathers of the Holy Catholic Church, vols. 18, 21, 23, 31]). A very readable life of Gregory is Pierre Batiffol, *Saint Gregory the Great*, trans. John L. Stoddard (London: Burns, Oates, and Washbourne, 1929). See also Dom Paul Meyvaert, "Bede and Gregory the Great," *Jarrow Lecture*, 1964.

CHAPTER THREE. *Old English Translations and Paraphrases*

The Cambridge History of the Bible, Chapter 9, "The Vernacular Scriptures," contains good background reading, in particular the first two sections: (1) The Gothic Bible, and (2) English Versions of the Scriptures before Wyclif. A very reliable survey of the early literature as a whole is Stanley B. Greenfield, *A Critical History of Old English Literature* (New York: New York University Press, 1965); also T. A. Shippey, *Old English Verse* (London: Hutchinson, 1973). For the historical background consult R. H. Hodgkin, *A History of the Anglo-Saxons*, 2 vols. (2d ed.; Oxford: Clarendon Press, 1939). A good source book, containing the relevant portions of Bede's *Ecclesiastical History* as well as other valuable materials, is Dorothy Whitelock (ed.), *English Historical Documents c. 500–1042* (London: Eyre and Spottiswoode, 1955). See also *Bede's Ecclesiastical History of the English People*, ed. Bertram Colgrave and R. B. Y. Mynors (Oxford: Clarendon Press, 1969). For the Bible itself in this period the indispensible guide is Minnie C. Morrell, *A Manual of Old English Biblical Materials* (Knoxville: University of Tennessee Press, 1965). In addition to being an accurate guide to the manuscripts and editions of texts referred to or quoted in this chapter, the manual contains an interesting and readable account of the scholarship on the subject.

The Latin text and Old English gloss of Ælfric's *Colloquy* is available in a modern edition by G. N. Garmondsway (London: Methuen, 1939). Recent useful studies of Ælfric have been made by Peter Clemoes and Ann E. Nichols. See E. G. Stanley (ed.), *Continuations and Beginnings: Studies in Old English Literature* (London: Nelson, 1966), chapter on Ælfric by Peter Clemoes, pp. 176–209; and the following articles by Ann E. Nichols, "Awendan: A Note on Ælfric's Vocabulary," *Journal of English and Germanic Philology*, 63 (1964): 7–13; "Ælfric's Prefaces: Rhetoric and Genre," *English*

Studies, 49 (1968): 215–23; "Ælfric and the Brief Style," *Journal of English and Germanic Philology,* 70 (1971): 1–12.

The complete corpus of Old English poetry is available in *The Anglo-Saxon Poetic Records,* 6 vols., ed. G. P. Krapp and E. V. K. Dobie (New York: Columbia University Press, 1931–53). An excellent and readable study of these poems is Charles W. Kennedy, *The Earliest English Poetry* (New York: Oxford University Press, 1943). Kennedy also published verse translations of the best poems which are now available in paperback: *An Anthology of Old English Poetry* (New York: Oxford University Press, 1960), and *Early English Christian Poetry* (New York: Oxford University Press, 1963). For an especially perceptive analysis of the *Phoenix,* see Daniel G. Calder, "The Vision of Paradise: A Symbolic Reading of the Old English *Phoenix,*" in *Anglo-Saxon England,* 1 (1972): 167–81. The best edition of *Beowulf* is still that of Friedrich Klaeber (3d ed.; Boston: D. C. Heath, 1950). A prose translation is easily available in *Anglo-Saxon Poetry,* trans. R. K. Gordon (London: J. M. Dent, 1926 Everyman's Library, 794), which also has prose translations of most of the other poetry discussed in this chapter. For a panorama of Beowulf studies see Lewis E. Nicholson, *An Anthology of Beowulf Criticism* (South Bend, Ind.: University of Notre Dame Press, 1963), particulary the articles by J. R. R. Tolkien, R. E. Kaske, and D. W. Robertson, Jr. A more conservative approach is represented by Kenneth Sisam, *The Structure of Beowulf* (Oxford: Clarendon Press, 1965). The tendency of mid–twentieth century scholarship has been to move away from a pagan reading, and to regard *Beowulf* and other Old English poetry as thoroughly Christian. See, for example, Margaret E. Goldsmith, *The Mode and Meaning of Beowulf* (London: Athlone Press, 1970); Bernard F. Huppé, *Doctrine and Poetry: Augustine's Influence on Old English Poetry* (Albany: State University of New York Press, 1959), and, more recently, *The Web of Words: Structural Analyses of the Old English Poems Vainglory, The Wonder of Creation, The Dream of the Rood, and Judith* (Albany: State University of New York Press, 1970); also Alvin A. Lee, *The Guest-Hall of Eden: Four Essays on the Design of Old English Poetry* (New Haven, Conn.: Yale University Press, 1972). More conservative, but very illuminating, is Edward B. Irving, Jr., *A Reading of Beowulf* (New Haven, Conn.: Yale University Press, 1968).

In the last decade, however, a reaction against excessive Christianization has developed, beginning with the article by Robert D. Stevick, "Christian Elements and the Genesis of *Beowulf,*" *Modern Philology,* 61 (1963): 79–89. Wisdom literature has been neglected, but an impressive manifesto for future study has now been provided by Morton W. Bloomfield in a seminal essay, "Understanding Old English Poetry," *Annuale mediaevale,* 9 (1968): 5–25, and reprinted in his *Essays and Explorations* (Cambridge, Mass.: Harvard University Press, 1970), pp. 59–80. This essay stresses the public and functional character of Old English poetry, and argues effectively for grouping the so-called "elegies" with Old English wisdom literature. Anyone who would like to try his hand at reading Old English poetry in the original will find several readers available with apparatus to assist the beginner. An example is *Seven Old English Poems*, ed. John C. Pope (New York: Bobbs-Merrill, 1966); the seven poems are "Caedmon's Hymn," "The Battle of Brunanburh," "The Dream of the Rood," "The Battle of Maldon," "The Wanderer," "The Seafarer," and "Deor." Another type is the recent anthology by Richard Hamer, *A Choice of Anglo-Saxon Verse* (London: Faber, 1970), which has an excellent selection of some two dozen Old English poems, with text and translation on opposite pages.

CHAPTER FOUR. *Middle English Translations: The Wyclif Bible*

The Cambridge History of the Bible, Chapter 9, "The Vernacular Scriptures," has a section on "The Wycliffite Versions," pp. 387–415, which includes brief comments on other translations. A thorough, up-to-date bibiliography for this period, covering Wyclif, Bible translations, saints' legends, and other religious literature, is J. B. Severs (ed.), *A Manual of the Writings in Middle English, 1050–1500*, vol. 2 (Connecticut Academy of Arts and Sciences: Archon Books, 1970). A standard literary history of the period can be found in Book 1, Part 2, of A. C. Baugh (ed.), *A Literary History of England* (rev. ed.; New York: Appleton-Century-Crofts, 1967). Among the many books on historical background that might be mentioned, I particularly recommend W. A. Pantin, *The English Church in the Fourteenth Century* (Cambridge: Cambridge University Press, 1955).

Editions of individual works may be found in *A Manual of the Writings in Middle English* (see above), but ones that I have found especially valuable are the following: Olof Arngart (ed.), *The Middle English Genesis and Exodus* (Lund: Gleerup, 1968 [Lund Studies in English, 36]). Arthur S. Napier (ed.), *Iacob and Iosep: A Middle English Poem of the Thirteenth Century* (Oxford: Clarendon Press, 1916). Herbert Kalen (ed.), *A Middle English Metrical Paraphrase of the Old Testament*, vol. 1 (1923); completed by Urban Ohlander (ed.), vols. 2 (1955), 3 (1960), 4 (1963) (Stockholm: Almqvist & Wiksell, 1923–63). Alice Miskimin (ed.), *Susannah, An Alliterative Poem of the Fourteenth Century* (New Haven, Conn.: Yale University Press, 1969 [Yale Studies in English, 170]). Hope Emily Allen (ed.), *English Writings of Richard Rolle, Hermit of Hampole* (Oxford: Clarendon Press, 1931). G. C. Heseltine (ed.), *Selected Works of Richard Rolle, Hermit* (London: Longmans, Green and Co., 1930). H. R. Bramley (ed.), *The Psalter or Psalms of David and Certain Canticles with a Translation and Exposition in English by Richard Rolle of Hampole* (Oxford: Clarendon Press, 1884). Margery Goates (ed.), *The Pepysian Gospel Harmony* (London: Oxford University Press, 1922 [Early English Text Society, Original Series, 157]). Frances A. Foster (ed.), *A Stanzaic Life of Christ* (London: Oxford University Press, 1926 [Early English Text Society, Original Series, 166]). Anna C. Paues (ed.), *A Fourteenth Century English Biblical Version* (Cambridge: Cambridge University Press, 1902). Margaret J. Powell (ed.), *The Pauline Epistles contained in MS Parker 32 . . .* (London:

Oxford University Press, 1916 [Early English Text Society, Extra Series, 116]). W. H. Hulme (ed.), *The Middle English Harrowing of Hell and Gospel of Nicodemus* (London: Oxford University Press, 1907 [Early English Text Society, Extra Series, 100]).

The only complete printed edition of the Wyclif Bible is: Josiah Forshall and Frederic Madden (eds.), *The Holy Bible containing the Old and New Testaments with the Apocryphal Books, in the Earliest English Versions made from the Latin Vulgate by John Wycliffe and his Followers*, 4 vols. (Oxford: Clarendon Press, 1850). An important text of the Early Version is being edited by Conrad Lindberg, *The Earlier Version of the Wycliffite Bible* (Stockholm: Almqvist & Wiksell, 1959— [Stockholm Studies in English, 6, 8, 10, 13, 20, 29, etc.]). Lindberg has also taken a census of manuscripts in his article, "The Manuscripts and Versions of the Wycliffite Bible," *Studia Neophilologica*, 42 (1970): 333–47. The two most valuable modern studies are Margaret Deanesley, *The Lollard Bible* (Cambridge: Cambridge University Press, 1920); and Sven L. Fristedt, *The Wycliffe Bible*, Part 1 (1953), Part 2 (1969), and Part 3 (1973) (Stockholm: Almqvist & Wiksells, 1953–73 [Stockholm Studies in English, 4, 21, 28]).

Additional articles by Fristedt are: "New Light on John Wycliffe and the First Full English Bible," *Stockholm Studies in Modern Philology*, n.s. 3 (1968): 61–86, and "A Note on Some Obscurities in the History of the Lollard Bible: Amplification of *The Wycliffe Bible. Part II*," *Stockholm Studies in Modern Philology*, n.s. 4 (1972): 38–45. A concise and lucid summary of Fristedt's contributions can be found in a review of *The Wycliffe Bible, Part II* by Bror Danielsson in *Studia Neophilologica*, 44 (1972): 188–95.

For Wyclif himself there are likewise two principal books: H. B. Workman, *John Wyclif*, 2 vols. (Oxford: Clarendon Press, 1926); and K. B. McFarlane, *John Wycliffe and the Beginnings of English Non-Conformity* (London: English Universities Press, 1952). For information on scholars at Oxford in the Middle Ages, by far the most reliable reference work is A. B. Emden, *A Biographical Register of the University of Oxford to A.D. 1500*, 3 vols, (Oxford: Clarendon Press, 1957–59). My account in this chapter of the controversy at Queen's College, Oxford, in 1376–80 first appeared as part of an article entitled "John Trevisa and the English Bible," *Modern Philology*, 58 (1960): 81–98.

CHAPTER FIVE. *The Metrical Bible:* Cursor Mundi

Four versions of the *Cursor Mundi* were edited by Richard Morris for the Early English Text Society, Original Series, vols. 57, 59, 62, 66, 68, 99, 101 (London: 1874–93, and reprinted London: Oxford University Press, 1961–66). No critical edition has appeared, although portions were prepared for Morris' introduction by H. Hupe (vol. 99, pp. 201–43). Recently a recension of the flood narrative has been made by J. J. Lamberts, "The Noah Story in *Cursor Mundi* (vv. 1625–1916)," *Mediaeval Studies*, 24 (1962): 217–32.

Until recently, studies of *Cursor Mundi* have been largely confined to the matter of sources: Lois Borland, "Herman's *Bible* and the *Cursor Mundi*," *Studies in Philology*, 30 (1933): 427–44; Philip Buehler, "The *Cursor Mundi* and Herman's *Bible*: Some Additional Parallels," *Studies in Philology*, 61 (1964): 485–99; Kari Sajavaara, "The Use of Robert Grosseteste's *Chateau d'Amour* as a Source of the *Cursor Mundi*: Additional Evidence," *Neuphilologische Mitteilungen*, 68 (1967): 184–93. This last is a supplement to the unpublished study by Sister Mary Creek (PhD. diss., Yale University, 1941). Renewed interest in the *Cursor Mundi* as a literary work is represented by a recent study: Ernest G. Mardon, *The Narrative Unity of the Cursor Mundi* (Glasgow: William MacLellan, 1970).

The following are book-length studies of motifs that appear in *Cursor Mundi*: Hope Traver, *The Four Daughters of God* (Bryn Mawr College, 1907); Roberta D. Cornelius, *The Figurative Castle* (Bryn Mawr College, 1930); William W. Heist, *The Fifteen Signs before Doomsday* (Michigan State College Press, 1952).

CHAPTER SIX. *Universal History:* The Polychronicon

The *Polychronicon* is edited by Churchill Babington and J. R. Lumby in the Rolls Series, 9 vols. (London: Great Britain Public Record Office, 1865–86); the Latin text appears with the English translations of John Trevisa and the anonymous fifteenth century translator given on the opposite page. A new edition of the Trevisa translation has been prepared by Richard Seeger (University of Washington dissertation, 1974). Translations of the Latin chronicles discussed in this chapter are as follows:

Hugh Williams (ed. & trans.), *The Works of Gildas*, 2 vols. (London: Cymmrodorion Society Record Series, 1899–1901).
Leo Sherley-Price (trans.), *Bede: A History of the English Church and People* (London: Hammondsworth, 1955 [Penguin Books L42]).
A. W. Wade-Evans (trans.), *Nennius: History of the Britons* . . . (London: Church Historical Society, 1938 [n.s. 34]).
Sebastian Evans (trans.), *Geoffrey of Monmouth: History of the Kings of Britain* (London: J. M. Dent, 1912 [Everyman's Library, 577]).
John Sharpe (trans.), *William of Malmesbury: Chronicle of the Kings of England*, rev. J. A. Giles (London: Bohn's Antiquarian Library, 1904).

Several studies of universal histories with differing emphases are relevant to the present chapter. J. P. S. Tatlock, *The Legendary History of Britain* (Berkeley: University of California Press, 1950), is a thorough study, with emphasis on Geoffrey of Monmouth. C. A. Patrides, *The Phoenix and the Ladder: The Rise and Decline of the Christian View of History* (Berkeley: University of California Press, 1964), is much larger in scope, and hence necessarily briefer in its details, but provides valuable perspective on the whole subject. Robert W. Hanning, *The Vision of History in Early Britain* (New York:

Columbia University Press, 1966), surveys the early Latin chronicles, but also develops an interesting thesis on the significance of Geoffrey of Monmouth's achievement. John Taylor, *The Universal Chronicle of Ranulph Higden* (Oxford: Clarendon Press, 1966) is the authoritative work on the *Polychronicon* and its continuations.

Some special developments touched on in this chapter are treated in important book-length studies: George Cary, *The Medieval Alexander,* ed. D. J. A. Ross (Cambridge: Cambridge University Press, 1956); Shane Leslie, *St. Patrick's Purgatory: A Record from History and Literature* (London: Burns, Oates & Washbourne, 1932); Virgil B. Heltzel, *Fair Rosamond: A Study of the Development of a Literary Theme* (Evanston, Ill.: Northwestern University Press, 1947). John Smyth, *The Lives of the Berkeleys,* ed. Sir John Maclean, 3 vols. (Gloucester: J. Bellows, 1883–85). Part of the discussion of Geoffrey of Monmouth originally appeared in my essay, "Some Biblical Influences on Geoffrey of Monmouth's Historiography," *Traditio,* 14 (1958): 378–85. See also John E. Housman, "Higden, Trevisa, Caxton, and the Beginnings of Arthurian Criticism," *Review of English Studies,* 23 (1947): 209–17.

For background information on John Trevisa, see the introduction to Aaron J. Perry (ed.), *Dialogus inter militem et clericum, Richard Fitz Ralph's Sermon: "Defensio curatorum" and Methodius: 'þe Beginning of þe World and þe Ende of Worldes' By John Trevisa . . .* (London: Oxford University Press, 1925 [Early English Text Society, Original Series, 167]). As a supplement to Perry's research, I have published the following articles: "John Trevisa and the English Bible," *Modern Philology,* 58 (1960): 81–98; "New Light on John Trevisa," *Traditio,* 18 (1962): 289–317; "John Trevisa: Scholar and Translator," *Transactions of the Bristol and Gloucester Archaeological Society,* 89 (1970): 99–108; and "More about John Trevisa," *Modern Language Quarterly,* 32 (1971): 253–54. An edition of Trevisa's largest work of translation has just recently appeared: M. C. Seymour et al. (eds.), *On the Properties of Things: John Trevisa's Translation of Bartholomaeus Anglicus De Proprietatibus Rerum* (2 vols.; London: Oxford University Press, 1975).

Standard editions of literary works dealt with in this chapter are listed below:

Whitley Stokes (ed.), *Gwreans an Bys: The Creation of the World, A Cornish Mystery* (London: Williams & Norgate, 1864).

W. W. Skeat (ed.), *Alexander and Dindimus* (London: Oxford University Press, 1878 [Early English Text Society, Extra Series, 31]).

W. W. Skeat (ed.), *Piers the Plowman: Parallel Texts,* 2 vols. (Oxford: Clarendon Press, 1886).

T. A. Knott & D. C. Fowler (eds.), *Piers the Plowman: A Critical Edition of the A-Version* (Baltimore, Md.: The Johns Hopkins Press, 1952).

Francis J. Child (ed.), *The English and Scottish Popular Ballads,* 5 vols. (Boston, Mass.: Houghton Mifflin, 1882–98).

Index

Index

New Testament, 7, 30, 42, 195; apocryphal accounts in, 15, 24, 31, 220, 229; relationship to Old Testament, 41, 50; literary influence of, 48, 64, 69; translation of, 146, 147–48, 152; Epistles in, 148, 152. *See also Treatise on the Old and New Testaments*

Nicholas, Saint, 16, 17

Nicodemus, Gospel of, 33, 146

Noah, 50; and the Flood, 135, 172–73, 213; and the Ark, 218, 219, 220

Norman Conquest, 125, 244

Normandy, loss of, 126, 127

The Northern Passion, 127

Northumbria: culture of, 84, 85, 86; religion of, 85, 86; mentioned, 83

Numbers (book of), 6, 7, 131

Office. *See* Canonical hours

Old English, 125, 142; influences on literature of, 84, 87, 104, 116, 126; biblical translations, 95–96, 103, 106; poetry, 104, 106, 110, 118–21, 122–24

Old Testament, 43, 48, 125, 133, 195; apocryphal accounts in, 22–24, 221; relationship to New Testament, 41, 50; literary influence of, 64, 132, 133; translation of, 96, 132, 134, 161; mentioned, 29, 34, 127, 160, 163, 221. *See also Treatise on the Old and New Testaments*

On Christian Doctrine (Augustine), 105

"On the Day of Judgment" (Ælfric), 99

Opus Imperfectum (Chrysostom), 156

Ordinary Gloss, 44

Origen, 42, 43

Origo Mundi, 132

Orosius, Paulus, 196, 197, 198, 201, 206, 207, 228

Oswald (king), 86, 87

Oxford, University of: Wyclif scholars at, 148–49, 153–54, 162–63; mentioned, 44, 143, 158, 159, 164, 208, 209, 212, 238

Palace of Honor, 180

Paradise, 167–69 *passim,* 192–93

Paris Psalter, 94, 95, 96, 100

Passion narratives, 6, 7, 125, 146, 184, 185

Pastoral Care, treatise on (Gregory), 4, 8, 78

Patrick, Saint, 81, 198, 199, 213, 214

Paues, Anna C., 147, 148

Paul, Saint, 18, 171, 224, 228, 229; correspondence of, 41, 64, 147

Pauline Epistles, 146, 147

Paulinus, Bishop, 85

Pax romana, 196, 211

Pearl, 127

Pelagius II (pope), 45, 46

Pentateuch, 7, 8, 56, 127, 161

"The People of Israel" (Ælfric), 99

Peter, Saint, 26, 39

Pharoah, 127, 129, 133, 137

The Phoenix (Lactantius), 113–15

Physiologus (Bestiary), 115–16

Piers the Plowman: mentioned, 95, 127, 174, 175, 180, 189, 232, 235, 237, 239, 240, 244–45

Pilate, 19, 229, 233–34

Piran, Saint, 82

Plato, 223

Polychronicon (Higden): Christ in, 147, 221, 227–29; translation of, 157, 207, 208, 209, 233; Higden as author of, 194, 211, 217, 220, 233, 243, 244; historical point of view in, 194, 207, 208, 211–12, 221, 223, 227, 228–31, 238, 239; biblical influence in, 207, 210–11, 217–22 *passim,* 227–29; contents of, 207, 208, 209, 217, 221–22, 227–28, 231–32, 238–43; geography of the world in, 207–8, 209–17; Britain in, 208, 212–17, 227, 231–38, 239, 243–44; Romans in, 208, 211–12, 223, 228–31; King Arthur in, 213, 215, 233; influence of the Church in, 214, 230, 231, 239, 244; literary technique in, 214, 221, 241; supernatural in, 214, 238–39, 242–43; Creation in, 217, 218–19, 220; Noah in, 218, 219, 220; apocryphal sources in, 221, 222, 229; Babylonian exile in, 221, 222; apocalyptic view in, 232, 243, 244. *See also* Higden, Ranulph; Trevisa, John

Pope Gregory. *See* Gregory, Saint

Potiphar, 133, 136, 220

Prophecies, 41–42, 113, 222. *See also* Christ: prophecies regarding

Prophets (books of), 7

Proverbs (book of), 6, 143

Psalm Twenty-Three. *See* Twenty-third Psalm

Psalms (book of), 141–42, 162

Psalters, 141, 159, 162; glossed, 93–96; translations of, 125, 142–43

Ptolemy II Philadelphus, 8

Purvey, John, 160